Behavioral Corporate Finance

Decisions that Create Value

The McGraw-Hill/Irwin Series in Finance, Insurance and Real Estate

Stephen A. Ross
Franco Modigliani Professor of Finance and Economics
Sloan School of Management
Massachusetts Institute of Technology
Consulting Editor

FINANCIAL MANAGEMENT

Adair
Excel Applications for Corporate Finance
First Edition

Benninga and Sarig
Corporate Finance: A Valuation Approach

Block and Hirt
Foundations of Financial Management
Eleventh Edition

Brealey, Myers, and Allen
Principles of Corporate Finance
Eighth Edition

Brealey, Myers, and Marcus
Fundamentals of Corporate Finance
Fifth Edition

Brooks
FinGame Online 4.0

Bruner
Case Studies in Finance: Managing for Corporate Value Creation
Fifth Edition

Chew
The New Corporate Finance: Where Theory Meets Practice
Third Edition

Chew and Gillan
Corporate Governance at the Crossroads: A Book of Readings
First Edition

DeMello
Cases in Finance
Second Edition

Grinblatt and Titman
Financial Markets and Corporate Strategy
Second Edition

Helfert
Techniques of Financial Analysis: A Guide to Value Creation
Eleventh Edition

Higgins
Analysis for Financial Management
Eighth Edition

Kester, Ruback, and Tufano
Case Problems in Finance
Twelfth Edition

Ross, Westerfield, and Jaffe
Corporate Finance
Seventh Edition

Ross, Westerfield, Jaffe, and Jordan
Corporate Finance: Core Principles and Applications
First Edition

Ross, Westerfield, and Jordan
Essentials of Corporate Finance
Fifth Edition

Ross, Westerfield, and Jordan
Fundamentals of Corporate Finance
Seventh Edition

Shefrin
Behavioral Corporate Finance: Decisions that Create Value
First Edition

Smith
The Modern Theory of Corporate Finance
Second Edition

White
Financial Analysis with an Electronic Calculator
Sixth Edition

INVESTMENTS

Bodie, Kane, and Marcus
Essentials of Investments
Sixth Edition

Bodie, Kane, and Marcus
Investments
Sixth Edition

Cohen, Zinbarg, and Zeikel
Investment Analysis and Portfolio Management
Fifth Edition

Corrado and Jordan
Fundamentals of Investments: Valuation and Management
Third Edition

Hirt and Block
Fundamentals of Investment Management
Eighth Edition

FINANCIAL INSTITUTIONS AND MARKETS

Cornett and Saunders
Fundamentals of Financial Institutions Management

Rose and Hudgins
Bank Management and Financial Services
Sixth Edition

Rose and Marquis
Money and Capital Markets: Financial Institutions and Instruments in a Global Marketplace
Ninth Edition

Santomero and Babbel
Financial Markets, Instruments, and Institutions
Second Edition

Saunders and Cornett
Financial Institutions Management: A Risk Management Approach
Fifth Edition

Saunders and Cornett
Financial Markets and Institutions: An Introduction to the Risk Management Approach
Third Edition

INTERNATIONAL FINANCE

Beim and Calomiris
Emerging Financial Markets

Eun and Resnick
International Financial Management
Fourth Edition

Kuemmerle
Case Studies in International Entrepreneurship: Managing and Financing Ventures in the Global Economy
First Edition

Levich
International Financial Markets: Prices and Policies
Second Edition

REAL ESTATE

Brueggeman and Fisher
Real Estate Finance and Investments
Twelfth Edition

Corgel, Ling, and Smith
Real Estate Perspectives: An Introduction to Real Estate
Fourth Edition

Ling and Archer
Real Estate Principles: A Value Approach
First Edition

FINANCIAL PLANNING AND INSURANCE

Allen, Melone, Rosenbloom, and Mahoney
Pension Planning: Pension, Profit-Sharing, and Other Deferred Compensation Plans
Ninth Edition

Altfest
Personal Financial Planning
First Edition

Crawford
Life and Health Insurance Law
Eighth Edition (LOMA)

Harrington and Niehaus
Risk Management and Insurance
Second Edition

Hirsch
Casualty Claim Practice
Sixth Edition

Kapoor, Dlabay, and Hughes
Focus on Personal Finance: An Active Approach to Help You Develop Successful Financial Skills
First Edition

Kapoor, Dlabay, and Hughes
Personal Finance
Eighth Edition

Behavioral Corporate Finance

Decisions that Create Value

Hersh Shefrin

Department of Finance
Santa Clara University

Boston   Burr Ridge, IL   Dubuque, IA   Madison, WI   New York   San Francisco   St. Louis
Bangkok   Bogotá   Caracas   Kuala Lumpur   Lisbon   London   Madrid   Mexico City
Milan   Montreal   New Delhi   Santiago   Seoul   Singapore   Sydney   Taipei   Toronto

McGraw-Hill Irwin

BEHAVIORAL CORPORATE FINANCE: DECISIONS THAT CREATE VALUE

ISBN-13: 978-0-07-284865-6

ISBN-10: 0-07-284865-0

Publisher: *Stephen M. Patterson*
Developmental editor II: *Christina Kouvelis*
Marketing manager: *Julie Phifer*
Lead producer, Media technology: *Kai Chiang*
Lead project manager: *Mary Conzachi*
Senior production supervisor: *Rose Hepburn*
Lead designer: *Matthew Baldwin*
Media project manager: *Lynn Bluhm*
Cover Designer: *Jillian Lindner*
Cover Image: *© Getty Images*
Typeface: *10/12 Times Roman*
Compositor: *Interactive Composition Corporation*
Printer: *R. R. Donnelley*

Library of Congress Cataloging-in-Publication Data

Shefrin, Hersh, 1948-
   Behavioral corporate finance : decisions that create value / Hersh Shefrin.
      p. cm. -- (The McGraw-Hill/Irwin series in finance, insurance, and real estate)
   Includes index
   ISBN-13: 978-0-07-284865-6
   ISBN-10: 0-07-284865-0 (alk. paper)
    1. Corporations--Finance. 2. Decision making--Psychological aspects. I. Title. II. Series.
HG4515.15.S5215 2007
658.15--dc22

                                                                    2005053417

www.mhhe.com

To my Executive MBA students
for their many hours beta testing
the approach in this book;

and to my wife Arna
for her unfailing support
and gracious forbearance
for the many hours I spent developing the
manuscript.

About the Author

Hersh Shefrin *Santa Clara University*

Hersh Shefrin, who holds the Mario L. Belotti Chair in the Department of Finance at the Leavey School of Business, is one of the pioneers of behavioral finance. He has published widely in the area and writes for both academics and practitioners. Professor Shefrin regularly teaches a graduate course in behavioral finance and often speaks on the subject to portfolio managers, security analysts, and financial planners both in the U.S. and abroad.

In 1999, his book, *Beyond Greed and Fear: Understanding Behavioral Finance and the Psychology of Investing,* was published by Harvard Business School Press. This is the first comprehensive treatment of behavioral finance written specifically for practitioners. In 2002, Oxford University Press, who assumed publication of the book, released an edition with a revised preface to reflect recent events and developments.

In 2001, Professor Shefrin edited a three-volume collection, entitled *Behavioral Finance,* published by Edward Elgar. In addition to seminal papers in this rapidly developing field, these volumes contain some of the pioneering works in psychology, upon which behavioral finance is based.

In 2005, his book, *A Behavioral Approach to Asset Pricing,* was published by Elsevier. This is the first book providing a unified, comprehensive behavioral approach to the main elements of asset pricing theory: stochastic discount factor, mean-variance portfolios, beta, option pricing, and the term structure of interest rates.

Professor Shefrin's scholarly articles have appeared in the Journal of Finance, the Journal of Financial Economics, the Review of Financial Studies, the Journal of Financial and Quantitative Analysis, Financial Management, the Financial Analysts Journal, and the Journal of Portfolio Management.

Professor Shefrin completed his PhD at the London School of Economics in the economics of uncertainty; he earned a Master of Mathematics from the University of Waterloo and a BS (Honors) in economics and mathematics from the University of Manitoba.

Brief Contents

Preface   xiv

Acknowledgments   xvii

1   Behavioral Foundations   1

2   Valuation   20

3   Capital Budgeting   38

4   Perceptions about Risk and Return   56

5   Inefficient Markets and Corporate Decisions   74

6   Capital Structure   92

7   Dividend Policy   110

8   Agency Conflicts and Corporate Governance   127

9   Group Process   145

10   Mergers and Acquisitions   161

11   Application of Real-Option Techniques to Capital Budgeting and Capital Structure (**only available at www.mhhe.com/shefrin**)   181

GLOSSARY   183

ENDNOTES   186

INDEX   195

Table of Contents

Preface   xiv

Acknowledgments   xvii

Chapter 1
Behavioral Foundations   1

1.1   Traditional Treatment of Corporate Financial Decisions   1
1.2   Behavioral Treatment of Corporate Financial Decisions   2
1.3   Illustrative Example   3
1.4   Biases   3
    Excessive Optimism   3
    Overconfidence   6
    Confirmation Bias   7
    Illusion of Control   8
1.5   Heuristics   8
    Representativeness   8
    Availability   9
    Anchoring and Adjustment   9
    Affect Heuristic   10
1.6   Framing Effects   10
    Loss Aversion   11
    Aversion to a Sure Loss   13
1.7   Debiasing   15
    Summary   16
    Additional Behavioral Readings   16
    Key Terms   16
    Explore the Web   17
    Chapter Questions   17
Additional Resources and Materials for Chapter 1 are available at www.mhhe.com/shefrin   18
    Minicase: Wall Street of the Southwest   18
    Case Analysis Questions   18
How Psychologists Identify Behavioral Phenomena   A1-1

A1.1   Biases   A1-1
    Excessive Optimism   A1-1
    Overconfidence   A1-3
    Confirmation Bias   A1-5
    Illusion of Control   A1-6
A1.2   Heuristics   A1-7
    Representativeness   A1-7
    Availability   A1-9
    Anchoring and Adjustment   A1-10
    Interacting Phenomena   A1-11
A1.3   Framing Effects   A1-12
    Attitudes toward Risk and Loss   A1-12
    Aversion to a Sure Loss   A1-13
    Narrow Framing Bias   A1-15

Chapter 2
Valuation   20

2.1   Traditional Approach to Valuation   20
2.2   Valuation Heuristics   21
    P/E Heuristic   21
    PEG Heuristic   21
    Price-to-Sales Heuristic   22
2.3   A CFO's Reliance on Valuation Heuristics   22
2.4   How Analysts Value Firms: An Illustrative Example   23
    Analyst Mary Meeker   23
    Mary Meeker's Target Prices for eBay   24
2.5   Biases   27
    Biases and Heuristics   27
    Biases and Framing Effects   27
2.6   Other Sources of Bias   31
    Growth Opportunities   31
    PEG and DCF   32
    The 1/n Heuristic   33
    Excessive Optimism   33
2.7   Agency Conflicts   34
    Summary   35

Additional Behavioral Readings   35
Key Terms   35
Explore the Web   35
Chapter Questions   36
**Additional Resources and Materials for Chapter 2
are available at www.mhhe.com/shefrin   37**
Minicase: Palm Inc.   37
Case Analysis Questions   37
**Computing Free Cash Flows and Growth
Opportunities   A2-1**
A2.1 eBay's Financial Statements   A2-1
A2.2 Free Cash Flows   A2-2
Deriving Free Cash Flows   A2-3
Interpreting Sources of Free Cash Flow   A2-4
Interpreting Uses of Free Cash Flow   A2-4
Cash Earnings   A2-4
A2.3 Confusing Growth Opportunities
and Earnings Growth   A2-5
PEG   A2-5
*The Market's Judgment
about eBay's (N)PVGO   A2-6*
*Book-to-Market Equity: What Makes eBay a
Growth Stock?   A2-7*
EVA and Value   A2-7
The Growth Opportunities Formula   A2-8

Chapter 3
Capital Budgeting   38

3.1 Traditional Treatment
of Capital Budgeting   38
3.2 Survey Evidence   39
Project Adoption Criteria   39
The Importance of Intuition   40
3.3 The Affect Heuristic   40
Choice, Value, and the Affect Heuristic   41
3.4 Overconfidence   42
*Psychological Determinants
of Overconfidence   42*
*Illustrative Example of Overconfident Capital
Budgeting   43*
3.5 Excessive Optimism in Capital Budgeting   44
Excessive Optimism in Public-Sector Projects   44
*Excessive Optimism in Private-Sector
Projects   44*

*Psychological Determinants
of Excessive Optimism   45*
*Agency Conflict Determinants of Excessive
Optimism   46*
3.6 Reluctance to Terminate Losing Projects   48
Aversion to a Sure Loss   48
Escalation of Commitment   49
3.7 Confirmation Bias: Illustrative Example   50
*Behavioral Bias and Agency Conflicts
at Syntex   50*
Summary   52
Additional Behavioral Readings   53
Key Terms   53
Explore the Web   53
Chapter Questions   53
**Additional Resources and Materials for Chapter 3
are available at www.mhhe.com/shefrin   54**
Minicase: CompuSys   54
Case Analysis Questions   55
**Excessive Optimism, Framing Effects, and Cost
Accounting   A3-1**
A3.1 Using Forecasts Prepared by Others   A3-1
Implications   A3-3
A3.2 Cost Accounting   A3-3
The Framing of Costs   A3-3
Heuristics   A3-4

Chapter 4
Perceptions about Risk and Return   56

4.1 Traditional Treatment of Risk and Return   56
4.2 Risk and Return for Individual Stocks   57
Example   57
Risk, Representativeness, and Bias   58
*Evidence That Executives Rely on
Representativeness   59*
Sign of Relationship between Risk and Return   59
The Affect Heuristic   60
Heuristics, Biases, and Factors   61
Analysts' Return Expectations   62
4.3 Financial Executives and the Market Risk
Premium   64
Die-Rolling   64
Extrapolation Bias: The Hot-Hand Fallacy   65
Biased Financial Executives' Estimates   66

4.4   Investor Biases in Estimating the Market Risk
        Premium   66
          Individual Investors and the Hot-Hand Fallacy   66
          Professional Investors and Gambler's Fallacy   66
4.5   Executives, Insider Trading, and Gambler's
        Fallacy   68
4.6   Survey Evidence on Project Discount Rates   70
        Summary   70
        Additional Behavioral Readings   71
        Key Terms   71
        Explore the Web   71
        Chapter Questions   72
        Minicase: Intel and eBay   72
          Case Analysis Questions   73

Chapter 5
Inefficient Markets and Corporate Decisions   74

5.1   Traditional Approach to Market Efficiency   74
5.2   The Market Efficiency Debate: Anomalies   75
          Long-Term Reversals: Winner–Loser Effect   76
          Momentum: Short-Term Continuation   76
          Post-Earnings-Announcement Drift   77
5.3   Limits of Arbitrage   78
          Pick-a-Number Game   78
5.4   Market Efficiency, Earnings Guidance,
        and NPV   80
5.5   Stock Splits   81
          Example: Tandy's Stock Split   81
5.6   To IPO or Not to IPO?   82
          Three Phenomena   82
          IPO Decisions   83
        Summary   88
        Additional Behavioral Readings   89
        Key Terms   89
        Explore the Web   89
        Chapter Questions   89
        Minicase: The IPO of Palm   90
          Case Analysis Questions   91

Chapter 6
Capital Structure   92

6.1   Traditional Approach to Capital Structure   92

6.2   How Do Managers Choose Capital Structure in
        Practice?   93
          New Equity: Market Timing   93
          New Debt: Financial Flexibility   94
          Target Debt-to-Equity Ratio   95
          Traditional Pecking Order   96
6.3   Behavioral APV   96
          Perception of Overvalued Equity: New Issues   96
          *Perception of Undervalued Equity:
          Repurchases*   96
6.4   Financial Flexibility and Project
        Hurdle Rates   98
          *Undervalued Equity: Cash-Poor Firms Reject
          Some Positive NPV Projects*   98
          *Undervalued Equity for Cash-Limited Firms:
          Invest or Repurchase?*   98
6.5   Sensitivity of Investment to Cash Flow   99
6.6   Excessive Optimism, Overconfidence,
        and Cash   101
          *Identifying Excessively Optimistic, Overconfident
          Executives*   102
          Assessing Value   104
6.7   Conflict Between Short-Term and Long-Term
        Horizons   105
        Summary   106
        Additional Behavioral Readings   107
        Key Terms   107
        Explore the Web   107
        Chapter Questions   107
        Minicase: PSINet   109
          Case Analysis Questions   109

Chapter 7
Dividend Policy   110

7.1   Traditional Approach to Payouts   110
7.2   Changes in Tax Policy   111
          *Changing Attitudes and Perceptions
          about Risk*   111
7.3   Dividends and Individual Investors:
        Psychology   112
          *Self-Control and Behavioral
          Life Cycle Hypothesis*   114
          Dividends and Risk   115
          Insights from Financial Columnists   116

7.4   Empirical Evidence   116
   Contrast with Institutional Investors   117
7.5   How Managers Think about Dividends   118
   Changing Payout Policies: Some History   118
   Survey Evidence   119
7.6   Catering to Investors' Tastes
   for Dividends   122
   Citizens Utilities Company   123
   Catering and Price Effects   123
   Summary   124
   Additional Behavioral Readings   124
   Key Terms   125
   Explore the Web   125
   Chapter Questions   125
   Minicase: Nipsco   126
   Case Analysis Questions   126

Chapter 8
Agency Conflicts and
Corporate Governance   127

8.1   Traditional Approach
   to Agency Conflicts   127
8.2   Paying for Performance in Practice   128
   Low Variability   128
   Dismissal   129
   Stock Options   129
   Shareholder Rights   129
   Behavioral Phenomena   130
8.3   Overconfidence among Directors
   and Executives   130
   Overconfident Directors   130
   Insufficient Variability in
   Pay for Performance   130
   Better-Than-Average Effect in the Boardroom:
   Overpayment   131
8.4   Stock Option–Based Compensation   132
   Overvaluing Options   132
   Casino Effect   132
8.5   Auditing: Agency Conflicts
   and Prospect Theory   133
   Traditional Perspective   134
8.6   Sarbanes-Oxley   135
8.7   Fraud and Stock Options:
   Illustrative Example   136

   Signs of Disease?   139
   Summary   141
   Additional Behavioral Readings   141
   Key Terms   141
   Explore the Web   141
   Chapter Questions   142
Additional Resources and Materials for Chapter 8
are available at www.mhhe.com/shefrin   143
   Minicase: Tyco   143
   Case Analysis Question   144
Ethics and Fairness in Finance   A8-1
A8.1 Unethical Behavior Starts Early   A8-1
   Why Students Cheat   A8-2
   Ethics and Psychology   A8-2
A8.2 Ethics, Fairness, and Financial Market
   Regulation   A8-3
   Behavioral Aspects of Fairness   A8-4
   Fairness and Confidence   A8-6

Chapter 9
Group Process   145

9.1   Traditional Approach
   to Group Process   145
9.2   Process Loss   145
9.3   General Reasons for Group Errors   146
   Groupthink   146
   Poor Information Sharing   146
   Inadequate Motivation   147
9.4   Groupthink and Poor Information Sharing:
   Illustrative Examples   147
   Enron   148
   Imagine Yourself in the Boardroom   151
   WorldCom   152
   PSINet   153
9.5   Polarization and the Reluctance to Terminate
   Losing Projects   154
9.6   Debiasing: Illustrative Example   155
   Standards   155
   Planning   156
   Compensation   156
   Information Sharing   157
   Stock Ownership   157
   Summary   158
   Additional Behavioral Readings   158

Key Terms   158
Explore the Web   158
Chapter Questions   159

**Additional Resources and Materials for Chapter 9
are available at www.mhhe.com/shefrin   160**
Minicase: Shugart   160
Case Analysis Questions   160

Examples of Poor Group Process   A9-1
A9.1 The Packard Foundation   A9-1
Governance and Groups   A9-1
A9.2 The Hewlett Foundation   A9-4
A9.3 General Findings
about Investment Committees   A9-4
A9.4 The Endowment Effect   A9-5
A9.5 Motivation and Incentives:
Residual Income   A9-6
Illustrative Example: AT&T   A9-7
Questions   A9-8

Chapter 10
Mergers and Acquisitions   161

10.1 Traditional Approach to M&A   161
10.2 The Winner's Curse   162
10.3 Optimistic, Overconfident Executives   162
10.4 Theory   165
*Symmetric Information, Rational Managers, and
Efficient Prices   165*
*Excessive Optimism and Overconfidence When
Prices Are Efficient   166*
*Inefficient Prices and Acquisition
Premium   167*
Asymmetric Information   168
10.5 AOL Time Warner:
The Danger of Trusting Market Prices   169
Strategy and Synergy   169
Valuation   169
Asset Writedown   171
Hubris   172
10.6 Hewlett-Packard and Compaq Computer:
Board Decisions   173
The Merger Alternative   174
*Psychological Basis for the Decision to Acquire
Compaq   174*

Valuation   175
H-P's Board Accepts Reality   176
Summary   177
Additional Behavioral Readings   177
Key Terms   178
Explore the Web   178
Chapter Questions   178

**Additional Resources and Materials for Chapter 10
are available at www.mhhe.com/shefrin   179**
Minicase: PSA Peugeot Citroen SA and
DaimlerChrysler AG   179
Case Analysis Question   180

Avoiding the Winner's Curse in M&A   A10-1
A10.1 Avoiding the Winner's Curse   A10-1
Analytical Solution   A10-1
A10.2 Two Monty Hall Problems   A10-6
A10.3 Illustrative Example:
Cisco Systems   A10-8
Cerent Corporation   A10-9
A10.4 Illustrative Example: AT&T   A10-12
A10.5 Illustrative Example:
3COM and U.S. Robotics   A10-13
Risks and Benefits   A10-14
Outcome   A10-14
Additional Questions   A10-15

Chapter 11
Application of Real-Option Techniques
to Capital Budgeting and Capital
Structure   181

*The remaining contents of this chapter are
available at* **www.mhhe.com/shefrin**   *181*

Chapter 11
Application of Real-Option Techniques
to Capital Budgeting
and Capital Structure   A11-1

11.1 Traditional Approach to Option
Theory   A11-1
11.2 Do Managers Use Real-Option
Techniques?   A11-2
Opaque Framing?   A11-2

11.3 Valuing Levered Equity   A11-5
    Example   A11-6
11.4 Conflicts of Interest   A11-9
    Example: Small-Scale Project   A11-9
    Asset Substitution   A11-10
    Debt Overhang   A11-11
    Capital Structure   A11-12
11.5 Overconfidence and Excessive Optimism   A11-12
    Overconfidence   A11-12
    Excessive Optimism   A11-13
    Capital Structure   A11-17

Summary   A11-18
Additional Behavioral Readings   A11-18
Key Terms   A11-18
Explore the Web   A11-19
Chapter Questions   A11-19
Minicase: The Savings and Loan Crisis of the 1980s   A11-20
    Case Analysis Question   A11-21

Glossary   183
Endnotes   186
Index   195

Preface

GOALS AND STRUCTURE

Behavioral Corporate Finance identifies the key psychological obstacles to value maximizing behavior, along with steps that managers can take to mitigate the effects of these obstacles. In this respect, instructors should view this book as a complement to traditional texts in corporate finance, not as a substitute. The main goal of the book is to help students learn how to put the traditional tools of corporate finance to their best use, and mitigate the effects of psychological obstacles that reduce value.

Neither students nor instructors require a background in psychology to understand the key psychological concepts. All the key concepts can be grasped intuitively, and are easily related to financial decisions.

ORGANIZATIONAL DESIGN

This book identifies the key behavioral concepts associated with every major topic in corporate finance: capital budgeting, capital structure, valuation, dividend policy, corporate governance, and mergers and acquisitions. However, the book provides only a brief summary of the traditional approach to each topic, whose purpose is to provide context. Instructors are assumed to teach the traditional approach from the traditional textbook of their choice.

I have written *Behavioral Corporate Finance* with the idea that instructors will cover corporate finance topics in the traditional manner, and then will follow up the discussion by introducing the behavioral dimension. Some instructors may choose to lecture on the behavioral material, using PowerPoint slides provided for this purpose. Others might simply assign the chapters as additional reading. In any case, the main learning objectives for students pertain to an appreciation of the obstacles that stand in the way of implementing traditional techniques. Questions and mini-cases appearing at the end of the chapters are designed to help students recognize the strength, magnitude, and persistence of behavioral phenomena in corporate financial decision making.

With one exception, each chapter is devoted to a traditional topic. The exception is Chapter 1, which presents the key psychological concepts used throughout the book. Chapter 1 is a prerequisite for every other chapter. Every other chapter explains how concepts developed in Chapter 1 apply to traditional topics in corporate finance.

For example, Chapter 1 introduces students to the concept of excessive optimism. Chapter 2 then describes how excessive optimism affects valuation. Chapter 3 describes how excessive optimism affects capital budgeting. Chapter 6 describes how excessive optimism affects capital structure. The main issue is not to be repetitive about the fact that corporate managers tend to be excessively optimistic. The main issue is to explain how excessive optimism impacts the different decisions that managers are called upon to make.

Chapter 9 is entitled Group Process, and is the only chapter topic that does not have an obvious counterpart in traditional textbooks on corporate finance. However, much of that chapter deals with process issues in corporate boards, and so can be viewed as an extension of Chapter 8 that covers corporate governance.

Chapters follow a set format. Behavioral objectives for learning introduce each chapter. Most chapters have a section that provides a brief overview of the traditional approach to the topic at hand. The remainder of the chapter then focuses on developing the behavioral concepts and applications.

In order to help students focus on the underlying psychological issues, "Concept Preview Questions" are used. These are intended to help students reflect on how their own minds approach information and decision tasks. Thematic boxes, labeled "Behavioral Pitfalls" provide brief illustrations of business situations that feature the psychological phenomena being discussed. Hints for mitigating bias and error are provided in thematic boxes labeled "Debiasing for Better Decisions."

Chapter summaries review the main points of the chapter in relation to the behavioral objectives. Chapter questions provide focused exercises to help students learn the key points in the chapter. Every chapter concludes with a minicase, allowing students the opportunity to develop the skills of recognizing psychological phenomena within the context of real world events.

The behavioral objectives, concept preview questions, thematic boxes and chapter summaries contain the major points in the book. Illustrative examples, anecdotes and cases serve as the most effective way of communicating general findings and ideas. Most students relate easily to stories. However, the stories are only intended to communicate the main points. The general evidence is based on the academic studies described in the book.

As was mentioned above, Chapter 1 is a prerequisite to all the remaining chapters. However, all remaining chapters essentially stand alone, so that instructors have the flexibility to choose whichever chapters they deem appropriate, and in whatever order they find most useful.

INTENDED MARKET: CORPORATE FINANCE COURSES

I have written *Behavioral Corporate Finance* for use in any MBA level course devoted to teaching corporate finance. For traditional courses in corporate finance, I see the book being used as a supplement to any traditional textbook that serves as the primary course text. This pairing of a traditional primary corporate finance text and *Behavioral Corporate Finance* provides a powerful way to augment the teaching of traditional skills with an understanding of the psychological factors that influence the application of these skills in practice. In this respect, *Behavioral Corporate Finance* contains many real world examples and case studies, designed to bring the behavioral concepts to life.

Behavioral traps represent one of the most important obstacles to the successful implementation of the skills taught in traditional corporate finance courses. When it comes to improving the financial decision process, understanding these traps is absolutely essential. Therefore, a crucial challenge is to teach students how to avoid falling into the behavioral traps identified in the behavioral decision literature, as well as how to deal with others that do fall into these traps.

In recent years, the authors of traditional textbooks have begun to incorporate topics from behavioral finance into revised editions. That is a welcome advance, in so far as the addition of real world phenomena is concerned. At the same time, the coverage of behavioral issues in traditional texts has tended to be at best surface level, providing students with a behavioral flavor but not in-depth skills required to understand, to identify, and to deal with behavioral phenomena.

TEACHING PACKAGE AND ADDITIONAL RESOURCES

An **Instructor's Resource CD, ISBN: 0072848677,** is available to accompany this text. This comprehensive CD contains all the following instructor supplements. We put them in one place for easier access and convenience. Print copies are available through your McGraw-Hill/Irwin representative.

- The ***Instructor's Manual*** includes a chapter overview, learning objectives, key terms, and presentation of the material which organizes the material around the PowerPoint Presentation. Solutions to the end of chapter questions and mini-cases are also provided.
- ***PowerPoint Presentation Slides*** contain key points and summaries to help instructors give lectures on the main ideas in the chapter.
- ***Test Bank,*** prepared by David Distad of the University of California, Berkeley, contains a variety of true/false questions, multiple choice, and essay questions. Complete answers are provided for all test questions and problems.

For those interested in using *Behavioral Corporate Finance* as a text in a course dedicated to behavioral finance, additional teaching resources are provided on the book website at **www.mhhe.com/shefrin.** These resources expand the material presented in most chapters and have been referenced in the text. In addition, a separate chapter dealing with real options is also available on the web.

Acknowledgments

In the course of writing this book I benefited from discussions with managers, academics, consultants, and students. I learned a great deal from my fellow members of the Santa Clara Valley chapter of Financial Executives International. I especially thank those who gave guest lectures to my classes about how they practice corporate finance in their firms. Their insights were invaluable. My biggest debt is to the students I taught in Santa Clara University's executive MBA program, and to my wife Arna. My executive MBA students all had at least ten years of management experience. By teaching them both traditional and behavioral corporate finance, I learned how to structure the approach in the book. Among the individuals to whom I would like to express appreciation are: Martha Amram, Herzel Ashkenazi, Eric Benhamou, Brigida Bergkamp, Ray Bingham, Bill Black, David Bostwick, Alon Brav, Judy Bruner, Marshall Burak, Larry Carter, Kris Chellam, Jeff Clarke, Tom Cupples, George Davis, Rajiv Dutta, Denise Esguerra-Aguilar, Rami Fernandez, Jennifer Fromm, Diane Gale, Ken Goldman, John Graham, Sal Gutierrez, Campbell Harvey, Dirk Hackbarth, Mike Hope, Mark Keil, Fred Kurland, Bruce Lange, Eddie Le, Sonia Li, Tim Loughran, Ulrike Malmendier, Greg Matz, Webb McKinney, Laura McLeod, Manoj Mittal, Chris Paisley, Bill Palmer, John Payne, Betsy Raphael, George Reyes, Brian Reynolds, Jay Ritter, Chris Robell, Mark Rubash, Christine Russell, Joanne Shapiro, Gurkirpal Singh, Paul Slovic, Scott Smart, Meir Statman, Don Taylor, Ed Teach, Paul Tufano, George Vera, Kip Witter, Arnold Wood, Jeffrey Wurgler, and David Young.

I am indebted to the following people for their insightful reviews of the proposal and various drafts of *Behavioral Corporate Finance* and their suggestions in the preparation of this 1st edition.

Paul Adams,
University of Cincinnati

Malcolm Baker,
Harvard Business School

Candy Bianco,
Bentley College

Kirt Butler,
Michigan State University

Joseph Chen,
University of Southern California

Werner DeBondt,
DePaul University

David Distad,
University of California, Berkeley

Robert Duvic,
University of Texas at Austin

Christophe Faugere,
State University of New York, Albany

Manu Gupta
University of Missouri

Gordon Hanka
Vanderbilt University

Hugh Hunter,
San Diego State University

Nancy Jay,
Mercer University

D. Scott Lee,
Texas A&M University

David Lins,
University of Illinois, Urbana-Champaign

Tim Manuel,
University of Montana

Joe Messina,
San Francisco State University

Roni Michaely,
Cornell University

Terrance Odean,
University of California, Berkeley

Dilip Patro,
Rutgers University

Raghavendra Rau,
Purdue University

Thomas Rietz,
University of Iowa

Robert Ritchey,
Texas Tech University

Scott Smart,
Indiana University

Richard Taffler,
Cranfield University, UK

Bijesh Tolia,
Chicago State University

P.V. Viswanath,
Pace University

John Wald,
Rutgers University

I appreciate the exceptional direction and tremendous coaching by Steve Patterson, Publisher; Christina Kouvelis, Developmental Editor II; Julie Phifer, Marketing Manager; Mary Conzachi, Lead Project Manager; Rose Hepburn, Senior Production Supervisor; Kai Chiang, Lead Media Producer; Lynn Bluhm, Media Project Manager; and Matt Baldwin, Lead Designer on the development, design, editing, and the production of this book.

Finally, I would like to acknowledge financial support provided by the Dean Witter Foundation and the Leavey School of Business at Santa Clara University. Lastly, my wife Arna contributed many behavioral examples from her own work experience. She was especially gracious about my having devoted untold hours developing the manuscript.

Hersh Shefrin
Santa Clara University

Chapter One

Behavioral Foundations

The main objective of this chapter is for students to demonstrate that they can identify 10 psychological phenomena that cause corporate managers to commit expensive mistakes when making decisions. These phenomena are divided into two groups. The first group is called *heuristics and biases,* and the second group is called *framing effects.*

After completing this chapter students will be able to:

1. Identify the key biases that lead managers to make faulty financial decisions about risky alternatives.
2. Explain why reliance on heuristics and susceptibility to framing effects render managers vulnerable to making faulty decisions that reduce firm value.
3. Recognize that investors are susceptible to the same biases as managers and that mispricing stemming from investor errors can cause managers to make faulty decisions that reduce firm value.

1.1 TRADITIONAL TREATMENT OF CORPORATE FINANCIAL DECISIONS

Firms raise funds by borrowing on lines of credit, issuing commercial paper, selling corporate bonds, issuing new equity, and generating operating cash flows. Firms use funds when they undertake projects, acquire fixed assets, build inventory, pay dividends, engage in mergers and acquisitions, and deal with legal and regulatory issues.

The traditional value-maximizing approach is based on discounted cash flow (DCF) analysis. Virtually all the decisions just mentioned involve risk. Because the cash flows are uncertain, expected or mean values are used to assess value. Risk enters into the analysis through the discount rate that is applied to the expected cash flows. According to DCF analysis, projects should be undertaken if the present value of the expected future cash flows exceeds the initial investment required. In the same vein, funding decisions should be made in order to maximize the value of the firm, based on DCF analysis. For example, the use of debt provides a tax shield, which managers should balance off against potential bankruptcy costs.

In theory, managers serve the interests of investors, the owners of the firm. In practice, the interests of managers and investors might not be perfectly aligned. Conflicts of interest are known as agency conflicts, in that investors are principals whose interests are being served by managers acting as their agents. In general, agency conflicts may prevent the firm's managers from making decisions that result in full value maximization. In these situations, the attendant costs are known as agency costs.

1.2 BEHAVIORAL TREATMENT OF CORPORATE FINANCIAL DECISIONS

The traditional material taught in corporate finance courses offers powerful techniques that in theory help managers to make value-maximizing decisions for their firms. Yet, in practice, psychological pitfalls hamper managers in applying these techniques correctly. The purpose of this text is to make students aware of potential psychological pitfalls, as they arise in the various decision tasks that financial managers confront, and to offer advice on how to mitigate the impact of these pitfalls.

The behavioral pitfalls discussed in this text are not unique to managers, but are prevalent across the general population. Many of these pitfalls were identified by

EXHIBIT 1.1 How Psychology Affects Financial Decisions

Psychological Phenomenon	Example of Faulty Financial Decision	Resulting Outcome for Firm
1. Biases		
Excessive optimism	Delay cost cutting during a business recession	Lower profits
Overconfidence	Make inferior acquisitions when cash-rich	Reduce firm value because risk underestimated
Confirmation bias	Ignore information that is counter to current viewpoint	Lower profits from delayed reaction to changing environment
Illusion of control	Overestimate own degree of control	Incur higher costs than necessary
2. Heuristics		
Representativeness	Choose wrong projects based on biased forecasts	Reduce firm value because net present value (NPV) not maximized
Availability	Choose wrong projects based on biased forecasts	Reduce firm value because of misjudged priorities and risks
Anchoring	Become fixated on a number and adjust insufficiently	Reduce firm value because of biased growth forecasts
Affect	Rely on instincts instead of formal valuation analysis	Reduce firm value because negative NPV projects adopted
3. Framing effects		
Loss aversion	Losses loom larger than gains of the same size	Foregone tax shield benefits because of aversion to debt
Aversion to a sure loss	Throw good money after bad in losing projects	Reduce firm value because of a negative NPV decision

psychologists Daniel Kahneman and the late Amos Tversky. Their work was recognized with a Nobel Prize in Economics, awarded to Kahneman in 2002, jointly with economist Vernon Smith who pioneered the use of experimental techniques to study markets.

Because psychologically induced mistakes can be, and often are, very expensive, studying behavioral corporate finance is vital. Exhibit 1.1 provides a thumbnail sketch of the main points in the chapter. The chapter discusses how 10 particular psychological phenomena lead managers to make faulty decisions, thereby reducing the values of their firms. Despite the psychological terminology, the 10 phenomena are intuitive and easily understood. Students need not have studied psychology previously in order to appreciate the importance of the concepts.

Like agency conflicts, behavioral phenomena also cause managers to take actions that are detrimental to the interests of shareholders. However, behavioral costs are the result of managers' mistakes, not the result of managers having different interests from investors. The distinction is important in that the two sources of cost typically require very different remedies. Remedies for agency conflicts tend to emphasize the manipulation of incentives. Remedies for behavioral pitfalls tend to emphasize training and process.

1.3   ILLUSTRATIVE EXAMPLE

In order to illustrate some of the psychological phenomena that underlie the study of behavioral corporate finance, consider an example, the situation at one specific firm, Sun Microsystems. Sun is known for producing servers, computers that perform complex functions such as transmitting Web pages over the Internet.

As you read the discussion about Sun in the nearby Behavioral Pitfalls box, try to identify two sets of concepts, first the psychological attributes of Sun's chief executive officer (CEO) Scott McNealy, and second the decisions made by Sun's managers. The manner in which psychological attributes impact managers' decisions about investment and financing lies at the core of behavioral corporate finance. Although most of the examples in this chapter involve decisions made by the CEO, the psychological traits described affect managers at all levels of the firm. Indeed, they affect most people, be they managers or not.

1.4   BIASES

bias
A predisposition toward error.

excessive optimism
People overestimate how frequently they will experience favorable outcomes and underestimate how frequently they will experience unfavorable outcomes.

The three categories of psychological phenomena discussed in this chapter are biases, heuristics, and framing effects. A **bias** is a predisposition toward error. This section discusses four particular biases: excessive optimism, overconfidence, confirmation bias, and the illusion of control.

Excessive Optimism

In general, managers have **excessive optimism.** They overestimate how frequently they will experience favorable outcomes and underestimate how frequently they will experience unfavorable outcomes.

The cover story in the July 26, 2004, issue of *Business-Week* is about Scott McNealy, the chief executive officer of high-technology firm Sun Microsystems. Sun is known as a leading manufacturer of servers and for having invented the Internet software programming language Java. The *BusinessWeek* article uses the following adjectives to describe Scott McNealy: optimistic, smart, acerbic, cocky, and combative. These are all psychological traits that influenced McNealy's business decisions.

McNealy was one of Sun Microsystem's founders, became its CEO in 1984, and had a history of being willing to take major risks in order to avoid disaster. During the 1980s, against the advice of his executives, he decided to substitute Sun's own microprocessors for those manufactured by Motorola. That decision turned out well for Sun.

During the 1990s, Sun's competitors produced servers that used Microsoft's Windows operating systems. McNealy instead chose to invest in servers that ran Sun's own software Solaris. That decision also turned out well, as Solaris came to be highly praised for its speed, reliability, and security. Sun's sales, profits, and cash holdings soared, and it dramatically increased its spending on a great many research and development projects.

Sun's fortunes changed with the onset of an economic recession in 2001. Wall Street analysts called for Sun to cut costs. However, McNealy was optimistic that the recession would be short-lived. In 2001, during a conference call with analysts, he said about business cycles: "We don't have rolling waves. We seem to have real edges." Instead of cutting costs during the recession, Sun invested heavily in new projects. In justifying that decision, McNealy stated: "The Internet is still wildly underhyped, underutilized, and underimplemented. I think we're looking at the largest equipment business in the history of anything. The growth opportunities are stunning."

Cisco Systems is the leading producer of router products used on the Internet. On March 8, 2001, Cisco announced that because the economic downturn looked like it would last much longer than expected, it was going to lay off 18 percent of its workforce. Some of Sun's executives wanted to follow suit. One stated: "When times are hard, you've got to shoot activities that aren't making money." However, McNealy refused to do so.

In an effort to cut costs, Sun's customers sought low-end servers. McNealy initially dismissed their concerns. Later, Sun spent $2 billion to acquire Cobalt, a manufacturer of low-cost servers. However, after the acquisition, Sun chose to limit Cobalt's budget, and McNealy later admitted that the acquisition was a mistake.

The economic downturn was much longer than McNealy had forecast. In the next three years, Sun lost a third of its market share, its sales fell by 48 percent, and its stock price fell from $64 in 2000 to about $4 in 2004.

Source: J. Kerstetter and P. Burrows, Sun: "A CEO's Last Stand," *BusinessWeek,* July 26, 2004. Reprinted by special permission from *BusinessWeek* © 2004 The McGraw-Hill Companies, Inc.

Delayed Cost Cutting and Value Loss

The *BusinessWeek* magazine article specifically included *"optimistic"* among the list of adjectives to describe Sun's CEO Scott McNealy's personal attributes. Most importantly, that excessive optimism affected his decisions as a manager. Excessive optimism led him to delay cost-cutting measures, which resulted in steep losses for Sun. In this regard, the general evidence suggests that people who report that economic conditions will improve are twice as optimistic as those who report that economic conditions will either stay the same or get worse.[1]

Do you think that McNealy was excessively optimistic when he predicted that the recession of 2001 would be brief, albeit with extreme changes (sharp edges)? The National Bureau of Economic Research (NBER) is officially responsible for determining when economic recessions begin and end in the United States. According to the NBER, the U.S. economy entered a recession in March 2001, and the recession lasted until November 2001, a period of nine months that was neither brief nor atypical.

The slowdown was longer for firms engaging in business investment. Sun Microsystems' customers are other firms. When those firms purchase Sun's servers, they are engaging in business investment. During the 2001 recession, investment fell for six consecutive quarters, twice as long as the period real gross domestic product (GDP) fell.

Scott McNealy's prediction that the recession of 2001 would be brief was excessively optimistic. Was his prediction necessarily biased? In other words, might Scott McNealy's prediction about the recession of 2001 have been reasonable, even though it was wrong after the fact?

Between World War II and 2000, the average length of a U.S. recession was 11.6 months. During those recessions, real gross domestic investment tended to fall for 12 months. The recession before 2001 occurred in 1990–1991 and featured three consecutive quarters of negative growth in real GDP. During the recession of 1990–1991, real gross domestic investment fell for 12 months.

What are we to conclude? There is nothing in the historical record to suggest that recessions would be brief affairs. The more reasonable conclusion is that Scott McNealy's prediction was biased in the direction of optimism and that his optimism led him to delay cost cutting, thereby destroying value at his firm.

Excessively Optimistic Sun Stockholders

During the stock market bubble between January 1997 and June 2000, irrational exuberance drove up the prices of both the S&P 500 and Sun's stock. Exhibit 1.2

EXHIBIT 1.2
Sun Microsystems'
Market Capitalization
1986–2003

Source: Center for Research in Security Prices.

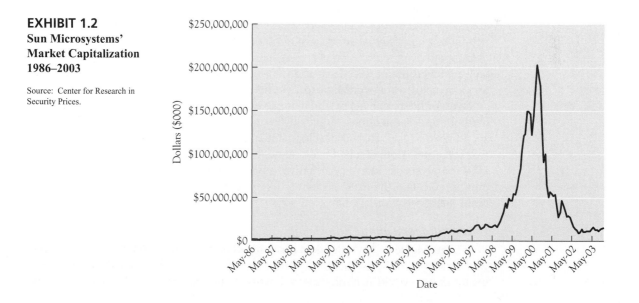

displays the market value of Sun's equity between 1986 and 2003. An investor who held the S&P 500 during this period would have seen his or her investment almost double. An investor who held Sun stock during this period would have seen his or her stock increase by more than fourteen fold. No firm the size of Sun has historically merited a price-to-earnings ratio (P/E) over 100. In March 2000, at the height of the bubble, Sun's P/E reached 119.[2]

It seems plausible that the spectacular rise in Sun's stock price encouraged some of the excessive optimism experienced by Sun's managers. In this text, considerable space is devoted to explaining why blindly trusting market prices can lead even the best-intentioned managers to make faulty decisions about investment policy, financing, and acquisitions.

Overconfidence

overconfidence
People make mistakes more frequently than they believe and view themselves as better than average.

In general, managers display **overconfidence** when it comes to difficult tasks and their own abilities. Overconfidence is a bias that pertains to how well people understand their own abilities and the limits of their knowledge. People who are overconfident about their abilities think they are better than they actually are. People who are overconfident about their level of knowledge think they know more than they actually know. This overconfidence does not necessarily mean that these people are ignorant or incompetent. It just means that in their own eyes they are smarter and better than is actually the case.

Some people use the term *overconfident* to mean optimistic. Overconfidence and excessive optimism often go hand in hand, but are not the same. Managers can be pessimistic, yet overconfidently so. The point is that overconfident managers are overly convinced that their views are correct.

Overconfidence about Ability

Among the adjectives used in the *BusinessWeek* article to describe Scott McNealy are *cocky* and *smart*. Cockiness is a symptom of overconfidence. Overconfident people can certainly be smart, just not quite as smart as they think they are. Moreover, people can learn to be overconfident, as a result of past successes.[3] McNealy had achieved major successes in the past, particularly in his decision to support Sun's own software over Microsoft's software.

Overconfident managers tend to make poor decisions about both investments and mergers and acquisitions, especially if their firms are cash-rich. Sun's increased spending on research and development in 2000 and its acquisition of Cobalt are cases in point. Both resulted in dramatic reductions in Sun's market value. In March 2004, analysts issued very negative reports about Sun. McNealy responded by pointing out that the firm was hardly likely to become distressed, given that it held more than $5 billion in cash.

Overconfidence about Knowledge

Was Scott McNealy overconfident about his knowledge of U.S. business cycles? He was certainly confident that the 2001 recession would be sharp-edged, by which he meant that it would feature a sharp downturn followed by a sharp upturn. Was it?

EXHIBIT 1.3
GDP Growth Rates
During U.S. Recessions
(Inflation Adjusted)

Source: Federal Reserve Bank of
St. Louis, Economic Data (FRED)
research.stlouisfed
.org/fred2/categories/22.

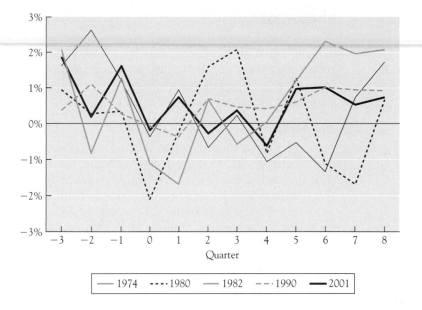

Exhibit 1.3 contrasts the manner in which GDP growth behaved in the quarters just before, during, and after a recession for all recessions between 1974 and 2001. Quarter 0 marks the onset of recession. The heavy line in the exhibit depicts the recession of 2001. Notice that it is neither briefer nor more sharp-edged than most of its predecessors. Moreover, there is no pattern suggesting that recessions were becoming increasingly sharp-edged. Scott McNealy was simply overconfident.

Confirmation Bias

confirmation bias
People attach too much
importance to information
that supports their views
relative to information that
runs counter to their views.

Managers who overlook information that disconfirms their views in favor of information that confirms their views are said to exhibit **confirmation bias.** Managers often only hear what they want to hear. They spend too much time searching for reasons to support why their views are right and too little time searching for reasons that might lead them to conclude that their views are wrong.

Turning a Blind Eye

Is there anything in the *BusinessWeek* magazine article to suggest that Scott McNealy exhibited confirmation bias? The article mentions that in late 2000, executives at Sun learned that the revenues of industry leader Cisco Systems were declining dramatically and began to suggest that a cost-cutting program be put in place at Sun. In March 2001, Cisco Systems laid off 18 percent of its workforce. However, this information did not confirm McNealy's view about recessions being short. Despite the recommendations of his upper-level executives, McNealy refused to approve any cost cutting at Sun. Scott McNealy exhibited confirmation bias, which led him to make decisions that dramatically reduced the value of his firm.

Illusion of Control

illusion of control
People overestimate the extent to which they can control events.

When a manager makes a decision, the outcome typically depends on a combination of luck and skill. In general, managers have an exaggerated view of how much control they exert over outcomes. The associated bias is known as the **illusion of control.** Psychological studies have found that an increase in perceived control leads to an increase in excessive optimism.

Not Made Here

Although not mentioned earlier, the *BusinessWeek* article describes a decision that Sun's managers had to make in 1997: whether to use their own microchips for Sun servers or to use Intel's chips. In 1997, Sun could purchase Intel's chips for 30 percent less than what it cost to produce its own comparable chips.

Despite the desire of some Sun executives to buy Intel chips instead of making their own, Scott McNealy felt that Sun's chip design group exerted enough control to close the gap. In a short meeting, McNealy ordered that Sun would not feature "Intel Inside." Seven years later, Intel chips were twice as fast as those produced by Sun. In retrospect, McNealy describes his decision about using Intel chips as one of his biggest regrets.

1.5   HEURISTICS

heuristic
A rule of thumb used to make a decision.

Most managers rely on heuristics to make decisions. A **heuristic** is a rule of thumb. This section describes some of the most common biases that result from the reliance on particular heuristics. These biases are known as representativeness, availability, anchoring and adjustment, and affect.

Representativeness

Managers often make judgments and predictions by relying on heuristics that make use of analogues and stereotypes. Psychologists refer to the underlying principle as **representativeness.** In asking about the extent to which an object or idea fits a stereotype, managers are asking how representative that object or idea is for the class to which it belongs. In general, people place too much reliance on representativeness, and representativeness-based thinking can result in bias.

representativeness
People make judgments based on stereotypic thinking, asking how representative an object or idea is for the class to which it belongs.

The Internet Represents the Overall Economy

Relatively speaking, Internet firms have a short history. During this history, the growth rate in sales of the typical or representative Internet firm featured extreme movements. Scott McNealy is quoted as having said in early 2001: "The Internet is still wildly underhyped, underutilized, and underimplemented. I think we're looking at the largest equipment business in the history of anything. The growth opportunities are stunning."

The *BusinessWeek* article reported that Scott McNealy believed that the Internet had fundamentally changed the U.S. economy and that the Internet was critical to a great many firms. Representativeness-based reasoning might lead someone to conclude that because of the growing importance of the Internet in the economy, and because Internet firms experience brief sharp swings in business conditions, the U.S. economy as a whole will experience brief sharp swings rather than rolling waves. In other words, representativeness-based thinking would have led Scott McNealy to conclude that the U.S. business cycle pattern would be sharp-edged instead of a rolling wave.

Availability

availability
People overweight information that is readily available and intuitive relative to information that is less salient and more abstract, thereby biasing judgments.

In general, managers employ an **availability** heuristic, in that they rely on information that is more readily available than information that is less readily available. Doing so predisposes their judgments to bias.

Out of Sight, Out of Mind

Sun played a principal role in a large suit against rival firm Microsoft that received national attention. The dispute had extended out several years and had become quite personal between Scott McNealy and Microsoft's founder Bill Gates. As such, it was in the forefront of McNealy's mind and highly salient.

Sun's upper-level executives communicated their concerns that the Microsoft suit had distracted McNealy from focusing on the needs expressed by Sun's customers. Customers themselves echoed this concern. They had been asking for low-end servers in order to cut costs during the downturn. With Microsoft on his mind, McNealy paid little attention to customers' requests. In April 2004, Sun and Microsoft announced that Sun had dropped its suit, in exchange for a cash settlement and technology agreement. In July 2004, Sun was offering low-end servers and McNealy was claiming that Sun was more focused than any of its competitors.

Anchoring and Adjustment

anchoring and adjustment
People form an estimate by beginning with an initial number and adjusting to reflect new information or circumstances. However, they tend to make insufficient adjustments relative to that number, thereby leading to anchoring bias.

Managers often develop quick estimates by beginning with an initial number with which they are familiar and then adjusting that number to reflect new information or circumstances. Just as a dropped anchor keeps a boat from drifting too far, the initial numbers with which managers begin can serve to anchor their judgments. The heuristic has come to be called **anchoring and adjustment.** The attendant bias is known as anchoring bias. When forming judgments, people have a tendency to become anchored on numbers in their heads and do not make sufficient adjustments relative to the anchor.

Anchored to Growth

During its most successful period, the turn of the century, Sun's earnings growth rate reached 50 percent per quarter, faster than competitors Microsoft, Intel, and Dell. That rate was not sustainable on a permanent basis. In forming forecasts going forward, the question is how to adjust relative to the 50 percent. If Sun's executives became anchored on the 50 percent, then even if they adjusted their forecasts of future growth downwards, they would be psychologically disposed to adjust insufficiently. That is the nature of anchoring bias. In this case, anchoring would have contributed to excessively optimistic forecasts of growth.

Affect Heuristic

affect
An emotional feeling.

affect heuristic
Basing decisions primarily on intuition, instinct, and gut feeling.

Most managers base their decisions on what feels right to them emotionally. Psychologists use the technical term **affect** to mean emotional feeling, and they use the term **affect heuristic** to describe behavior that places heavy reliance on intuition or "gut feeling." As with other heuristics, the affect heuristic involves mental shortcuts that can predispose managers to bias.

Acquisitions That Feel Right but Destroy Value

Michael Lehman joined Sun's board of directors in 2002. Before that he was Sun's chief financial officer (CFO). In 2000, Lehman described Sun's decision process for making acquisitions. He stated: "Now, in determining the price we are willing to pay for such acquisitions, we are not nearly as formal as the corporate finance textbooks suggest we perhaps ought to be. Our approach to acquisition pricing is more intuitive."[4]

Remember that intuition is based on affect. In contrast, the formal textbook approach to corporate decision making is based on the net present value (NPV) of the acquisition being positive, or at worst zero. When the NPV of an acquisition is greater or equal to zero, the fair value of that acquisition is at least as high as the number of dollars invested making the acquisition.

Lehman explained that the managers at Sun did not say to themselves: "For every dollar we invest, we're going to get at least an NPV of one dollar in return." (Lehman likely misspoke here, having used NPV when he meant PV.) He went on to say that instead of relying on DCF, the managers at Sun asked how an "acquisition will enhance our overall capabilities, and how that enhancement will contribute to our overall market value."

Intuition is important, make no mistake about it. Experience is valuable, and firms pay for experienced managers. Indeed, the emotions that managers feel are a manifestation of their minds making associations with the memories of past experiences. However, experience is not a substitute for careful analysis. Acquisitions that feel right might well feature negative NPV. Think back to Sun's experience with Cobalt.

1.6 FRAMING EFFECTS

frame
Synonymous for description.

framing effect
A person's decisions are influenced by the manner in which the setting for the decision is described.

prospect theory
A general psychological approach that describes the way people make choices among risky alternatives.

In this text the word **frame** is synonymous for description. Therefore a decision frame means the description of the decision task. A manager is vulnerable to a **framing effect** when his or her decisions are easily influenced by the manner in which the setting for the decision task is framed.

Framing is a critical aspect of **prospect theory,** the approach that Kahneman and Tversky developed to describe how people make decisions involving risk and uncertainty. The Nobel committee singled out prospect theory when announcing the award to Kahneman. Prospect theory features two notable framing phenomena with similar sounding names: loss aversion and aversion to a sure loss. In order to illustrate both effects, consider the history of Merck discussed in the nearby box, one of the best-known pharmaceutical firms in the world.[5]

In 1994 Judy Lewent, the chief financial officer of pharmaceutical firm Merck & Co., was one of the most respected CFOs in the United States. That year the *Harvard Business Review* published an interview with her, which they entitled "Scientific Management at Merck: An Interview with CFO Judy Lewent." However, in 2004, *CFO* magazine ran an article entitled "What Will Judy Do?" asking whether she would be able to keep her job. What happened?

The short answer to the last question is that in September 2004 Merck recalled its blockbuster drug Vioxx, a drug that had contributed 8.7 percent of the firm's global revenues that year. The long answer is more complicated and requires a short history of the firm.

According to *Fortune* magazine's annual reputation survey, Merck was one of America's most admired companies. In fact, for the seven straight years between 1986 and 1992, Merck ranked as America's most admired company. Merck gained its exalted status by producing a series of blockbuster drugs, such as Vasotec for the treatment of blood pressure, Prinivil for cardiac medication, Pepcid and Prilosec for ulcers, and Mevacor to lower cholesterol.

The year 1999 was auspicious for Merck. That year the five drugs mentioned earned Merck $4.38 billion in U.S. sales and royalties, at a time when its total net sales were $32.7 billion. At the same time, there were dark financial clouds on the horizon. Pharmaceutical products typically receive patent protection for a period of 17 years. By the end of 2001, all five of the major drugs mentioned were due to go off patent.

The pharmaceutical industry is also regulated. In the United States, the Food and Drug Administration (FDA) must approve all new drugs as being safe and effective. To establish safety and efficacy, pharmaceutical firms collect data for submission to the FDA, using clinical trials to test new drugs in small samples involving both animals and people.

In May 1999, the FDA approved Vioxx to treat pain. However, it asked Merck to conduct a new large postapproval trial in order to extend its study of the side effect profile of Vioxx in respect to stomach ulcers. The issue was important, in that existing painkillers that were already on the market, such as aspirin and naproxen (for example, Aleve), caused stomach irritation. Merck's earlier studies showed that Vioxx did not irritate people's stomachs.

Because aspirin reduces blood clotting, it reduces the incidence of heart attacks and strokes. Vioxx does not, a fact of which Merck's scientists and executives were well aware.

Surprisingly, Merck's postapproval study appeared to show that Vioxx actually caused heart attacks and strokes. However, the firm's executives resisted that interpretation and invested heavily in promoting the drug. Then, in September 2004 a new separate Merck study of colon polyps also found that Vioxx caused heart attacks and strokes. Merck's managers belatedly recalled the drug and prepared for the lawsuits to come.

Sources: Anna Wilde Mathews and Barbara Martinez, "E-Mails Suggest Early Vioxx Worries—As Evidence of Heart Risk Rose, Merck Officials Played Hardball; One Internal Message: 'Dodge!'" *The Wall Street Journal,* November 2, 2004; "Scientific Management at Merck: An Interview with CFO Judy Lewent," *Harvard Business Review,* Jan–Feb, 1994; Kate O'Sullivan, "What Will Judy Do?" *CFO Magazine,* December 3, 2004.

Loss Aversion

CONCEPT PREVIEW *Question 1.1*	Imagine a 50-50 risk where you lose $50 if a coin toss comes up tails, but win a different amount if a coin toss turns up heads. What is the lowest amount you would have to win and yet still accept the risk? For example, if you accepted the 50-50 risk between winning $500 and losing $50, would you still be willing to accept the risk if it was between winning $250 and losing $50? If you answer yes, would you still be willing to accept the risk if it was between winning $125 and losing $50? In other words, think about how *low* your win would have to be before you were indifferent between accepting and rejecting the opportunity to face the risk.

Most people make choices about risky alternatives by weighing potential gains against potential losses, adjusting for the odds. In a 50-50 situation, the odds attached to gain and loss are the same. Therefore, someone who rejects the risk in Concept Preview Question 1.1 when the gain is $50 attaches greater weight to the $50 loss than the $50 gain. The average response to Concept Preview Question 1.1 is $125. This response suggests that people experience the loss of $50 two and a half times (= 125/50) as acutely as a $50 gain. Psychologists refer to this phenomenon as **loss aversion.**

loss aversion
Psychologically, people experience a loss more acutely than a gain of the same magnitude.

Loss aversion leads people to behave in risk-averse fashion when facing alternatives that feature the possibility of both gain and loss. Some people are prone to treating repeated risks over time the same way as they treat one-shot deals, thereby behaving unduly conservatively. This phenomenon is known as **narrow framing.**

narrow framing
Treating a repeated risk as if it were a one-shot deal.

Loss Aversion Can Cause Debt Aversion

Traditional textbooks in corporate finance teach that debt can be used to shield investors from corporate taxes. Yet many firms appear to take on less debt than textbook theory suggests, thereby leaving tax shield dollars on the table.

As an example, consider Merck's debt policy. Has Merck been averse to debt? Exhibit 1.4 displays the time paths of three variables between 1983 and 2003, Merck's ratio of total debt to total assets, its ratio of long-term debt to equity, and its return on equity (ROE).

Exhibit 1.4 shows that Merck's total debt has typically been low, below 20 percent of its assets during the 20-year period 1983 through 2003. These ratios are based on book values, meaning Merck's financial statements. Financial textbooks suggest that decisions about debt be made using market values rather than debt values. In this regard, the market value of Merck's equity averaged six times the book value of its equity during the period. Therefore, in market terms Merck's debt was a much lower fraction of its assets than shown in Exhibit 1.4.

EXHIBIT 1.4
Merck's Capital Structure and ROE 1983–2003

Source: Compustat.

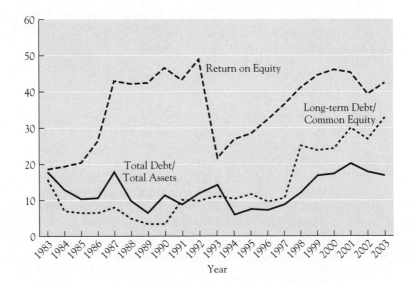

In the traditional approach to debt policy, managers balance the benefits of additional tax shields against the costs of possible future financial distress stemming from excessive debt. Firms such as Merck have significant intangible assets stemming from research and development. Those assets largely reside in the brains of its scientists and managers. As a result, Merck's executives would have to be concerned that the firm's scientists and managers might react to financial distress by leaving the firm, taking with them a large portion of the firm's intangible assets. A concern about losing intangible assets might reasonably lead the firm to shy away from taking on too much debt.

Such a concern is not hypothetical. After Merck withdrew Vioxx from the market, the price of its stock fell by more than a third over the next two months. That drop made Merck a strong takeover candidate, and its directors began to worry about talented managers leaving the firm. In response, Merck filed a new compensation plan for top executives with the Securities and Exchange Commission. The new plan featured one-time severance payments of up to triple executives' salary and bonus, along with other perquisites like health benefits, should Merck be acquired and the executives lose their jobs.

This change in compensation suggests that there are alternatives to addressing brain drain besides the assumption of lower debt. Moreover, it is important to ask whether in the late 1980s and throughout the 1990s the risk of distress was reasonable or instead was overblown. Between 1988 and 2001, Merck had a high tax bill, held a large amount in cash, and had several blockbuster drugs. Its high cash holdings (10 to 20 percent of sales) and blockbuster drugs with many years remaining of patent protection provided for low risk as far as bankruptcy was concerned.

By taking on more debt in the late 1980s and early 1990s, Merck could have reduced a tax bill that amounted to roughly 60 percent of its cash holdings. Yet Merck systematically lowered its debt ratio between 1988 and 1996. Was there some credible risk of bankruptcy that its managers perceived but investors did not? Or was the motivation for its debt policy more psychological?

One possibility is simply that Merck's managers chose a debt policy that was overly conservative because they were loss averse. In general, loss aversion leads managers to be reluctant to issue debt, even when issuing more debt would produce positive financing side effects for shareholders. Psychologically, the potential losses stemming from financial distress can loom larger than the potential gains stemming from tax shields.

Aversion to a Sure Loss

CONCEPT PREVIEW *Question 1.2*	Imagine that you have lost $74 and face a choice. You can accept the loss of $74, or face a risky alternative. If you accept the risky alternative, there is a 75 percent chance that your loss will be $100, and a 25 percent chance that your loss will be $0. Which alternative would you choose, the sure loss of $74 or the risk?

aversion to a sure loss
People choose to accept an actuarially unfair risk in an attempt to avoid a sure loss.

Most answer Concept Preview Question 1.2 by choosing the risky alternative. They do so in spite of the fact that the odds are against them, but they choose risk hoping to beat the odds, thereby breaking even. Such a person is said to be **averse to a sure loss.**

Hoping to Beat the Odds in Drug Sales

In 1999, the executives at Merck were watching the clock tick down, as five of their most successful products were due to go off patent in 2000 and 2001. One possible scenario was that the firm would be unable to find new products to replace the lost profits from the ones going off patent. Merck continued to be one of America's most admired companies throughout the 1990s, a state of affairs to which its executives had become accustomed. It is plausible to suggest that if the firm's profits declined, these executives would have difficulty adjusting psychologically from their days of past glory. As a result, they might have used past profitability as a **reference point** and framed the lower forecasted profit situation as a loss relative to that reference point.

reference point
Benchmark used to
measure gains and losses.

After the FDA approved Vioxx in May 1999, Merck's executives were hoping that its sales would help them to avoid entering the domain of psychological losses, meaning lower profits. However, the results from its postapproval clinical study, code named VIGOR (for Vioxx Gastrointestinal Outcomes Research), indicating that Vioxx might actually cause heart attacks and strokes, presented the executives with a dilemma involving two alternatives.

The first alternative was to promote Vioxx for a small market, namely people who needed pain relief, whose sensitive stomachs did not tolerate drugs like aspirin and naproxen, and who were not prone to heart problems. This alternative was akin to accepting a sure loss (meaning, lower profits). The second alternative was to try and beat the odds, hoping that the negative findings from VIGOR would not carry over to the general population. The second alternative involved promoting Vioxx as a general painkiller for the whole market, downplaying the cardiac side effect profile, and hoping for blockbuster sales.

People who view themselves in the domain of losses are much more prone to accept risks than people who view themselves in the domain of gains. Because of the looming patent expiration on its older drugs, Merck executives felt the pressure to make Vioxx a major success. They chose the risky alternative.

Researchers at Stanford University, Harvard University, and the Cleveland Clinic wrote scientific articles that raised concerns about Vioxx's safety. Merck challenged these concerns and continued to promote Vioxx as safe. In February 2001, the FDA issued a letter to Merck's CEO at the time, Ray Gilmartin, chastising the firm for deceptive promotional practices. In August 2004, a researcher from the FDA's drug-safety office presented data that showed that higher doses of Vioxx correlated with a tripled risk of a heart attack or sudden cardiac death. Merck responded by issuing a press release reiterating its confidence in the safety and efficacy of its drug.

Between 2000 and 2004, twenty-eight million people took Vioxx. After Merck finally withdrew Vioxx from the market, the British medical journal *The Lancet* wrote that the firm should have made that decision several years earlier. In December 2004, the best estimates were that the lawsuits against Merck would total $18 billion.

In February 2005, by a vote of 17 to 15, members of an FDA advisory panel recommended that Vioxx was safe enough to be sold in the United States, as long as its package label carried strict warnings about the risk of heart attacks and strokes. The vote led Merck to inform the FDA that it was considering requesting permission to reintroduce Vioxx.

In August 2005, a Texas jury rendered its verdict on the first of the Vioxx trials, finding Merck liable for the death of 59-year-old marathon runner Robert Ernst who had taken the drug. The jury award of $253 million jolted Merck executives, and Merck's market capitalization fell by 7.7 percent after the announcement of the jury's verdict.

Jury members indicated that they were particularly troubled that Merck executives had knowledge of Vioxx's negative side-effect profile before they placed the drug on the market, but took actions to conceal that knowledge from the public. Although Texas law requires the amount of the actual award to be much less than $253 million, and Merck planned to appeal the verdict, the outcome of the trial set an important precedent for the remaining Vioxx suits, which numbered 4,200 at the time. On August 22, 2005, *The Wall Street Journal* reported that after the verdict was announced, analysts' estimate of the value of Merck's legal liability increased to $30 billion, raising questions about Merck's long-term ability to survive.

1.7   DEBIASING

The psychological phenomena described in this chapter are systematic and persistent. Although they vary in incidence and degree from person to person, by and large the average responses are similar across different groups of people. What can be done to reduce these errors and biases? How can people debias?

debiasing
Reducing susceptibility to biases and framing effects.

Debiasing turns out to be an enormous challenge. Psychologists have repeatedly demonstrated that recognizing our errors and biases does not lead us to change our behavior automatically. The psychology that underlies errors and biases is remarkably resistant to change.[6] That is not to say that people cannot learn to avoid mistakes. People can learn. However, people learn slowly, and the task of debiasing requires great effort.

Debiasing is more difficult in some situations than in others. Situations where people receive quick, clear feedback about the results of their actions are more conducive to debiasing efforts than situations where the feedback is slow, and outcomes are influenced by many factors. Unfortunately, many of the tasks in corporate finance feature long lags between the time decisions are made and the time the outcomes occur, as well as sources of risk that can obscure the underlying biases.

Throughout this textbook, you will encounter tips and suggestions for mitigating bias. These tips and suggestions appear in boxes labeled Debiasing for Better Decisions. As you read these tips, remember to keep your expectations modest. Debiasing

Debiasing for Better Decisions

Errors or biases: Accepting an actuarially unfair risk.
Why does it happen? Aversion to a sure loss.
How does it happen? When faced with the prospect of a sure loss, people try to beat the odds.
What can be done about it? First, view decision tasks broadly, rather than narrowly, remembering that over the course of a lifetime, risks are faced repeatedly. Because of the law of averages, accepting an actuarially unfair risk as a policy is likely to produce inferior results over the long term. Second, reframe by resetting reference points in order to accept losses and treat sunk costs as sunk. Try using stock phrases such as "that's water under the bridge" and "don't cry over spilled milk" as helpful reminders.

is a process that rarely produces quick results. The tips and suggestions produce progress, but rarely miracles. In respect to corporate finance, managers make errors both individually and in groups. Mitigating bias at both levels requires the use of explicit procedures and the exercise of discipline. Debiasing requires major effort.

Consider an example of debiasing that builds on the earlier discussion about aversion to a sure loss. The example provides some advice on steps that managers can take to mitigate their vulnerability to faulty decisions that reduce value.

Summary

Heuristics, biases, and framing effects impede managers from making the best use of the traditional tools of corporate finance, causing them to make faulty decisions that destroy value. The main biases discussed in the chapter are excessive optimism, overconfidence, confirmation bias, and the illusion of control. Managers are inclined to choose negative net-present-value projects because they are excessively optimistic about the future prospects of their firms, overconfident about the risks they face, discount information that does not support their views, and exaggerate the extent of control they wield over final outcomes.

The main heuristics discussed relate to representativeness, availability, anchoring and adjustment, and affect. Managers are prone to make faulty decisions about uses of funds because they place too much reliance on stereotypic thinking when forming judgments, attach too much emphasis to information that is readily available, become overly fixated on numbers in their analyses, and place too much reliance on intuition.

The main topics discussed in the section on framing effects are loss aversion and aversion to a sure loss. Managers are inclined to make faulty decisions about investment policy and financing because they are unduly sensitive about potential future losses and find it difficult to accept losses that have already occurred.

Managers need to be aware that psychological phenomena also cause investor errors that can result in the mispricing of the securities issued by their firms. Avoiding bias, or debiasing, is a major challenge that generally requires a sophisticated, disciplined approach.

Additional Behavioral Readings

Bernstein, P., *Against the Gods: The Remarkable Story of Risk.* New York: John Wiley and Sons, 1996.

Belsky, G. and T. Gilovich, *Why Smart People Make Big Money Mistakes and How to Correct Them: Lessons from the New Science of Behavioral Economics.* New York: Simon & Schuster, 2000.

Gilovich, T., D. Griffin and D. Kahneman, *Heuristics and Biases: The Psychology of Intuitive Judgment.* Cambridge, UK: Cambridge University Press, 2002.

Key Terms

affect, *10*	debiasing, *15*	narrow framing, *12*
affect heuristic, *10*	excessive optimism, *3*	overconfidence, *6*
anchoring and adjustment, *9*	frame, *10*	prospect theory, *10*
availability, *9*	framing effect, *10*	reference point, *14*
aversion to a sure loss, *14*	heuristic, *8*	representativeness, *8*
bias, *3*	illusion of control, *8*	
confirmation bias, *7*	loss aversion, *12*	

Explore the Web

www.businessweek.com/magazine/content/04_30/b3893001_mz001.htm
This is the link to the cover story in the July 26, 2004, issue of *Business Week* pertaining to Scott McNealy and Sun Microsystems.

www.islandnet.com/~see/weather/history/icline.htm
This Web site describes the weather history of Galveston, Texas, the subject of the minicase at the end of the chapter.

http://www.pbs.org/now/transcript/transcript_neworleans.html
This Web site contains the transcript of the program *Now* "The City in a Bowl" about New Orleans' vulnerability to a disastrous hurricane, which aired on September 20, 2002.

www.ssem.com/investigations/vioxx/fda_letter_to_merck.html
This Web site contains the warning letter that the FDA sent to Merck in 2001.

Chapter Questions

1. Does the chapter present any information that would lead you to conclude that managers at Sun Microsystems were averse to a sure loss? Discuss.

2. During its most profitable years in the late 1990s, Sun did not carry any debt. In 1999, Sun paid $138.6 million in taxes. Compare the situation at Sun with the situation at Merck in respect to their debt policies.

3. Did Merck's managers exhibit confirmation bias in their assessment of Vioxx? Discuss this question.

4. At the beginning of 2001, Merck's CFO Judy Lewent predicted that Vioxx sales for the year would be between $3 and $3.5 billion. In June she qualified her prediction to say that although Vioxx sales would be closer to the lower end of the prediction range, four of their top five drugs would achieve the upper end of their prediction ranges. One month later, she stated that Merck's research pipeline was as productive as at any other time in the firm's history. However, in August the *Journal of the American Medical Association* published a study linking Vioxx to an increased risk of heart attack and stroke. Immediately thereafter, sales of Vioxx began to slow. In 2001 Vioxx sales were $2.3 billion. In 2002 Vioxx sales were $2.5 billion. In light of the graph of return on equity displayed in Exhibit 1.4, discuss whether the events just described reflect any behavioral biases.

5. Merck's VIGOR study used 8,000 subjects. Notably, Merck chose to include only subjects whose risk of experiencing a heart attack was low. Half the subjects in the study received Vioxx, and the other half received naproxen. Of those receiving Vioxx, 20 had heart attacks. Of those receiving naproxen, four had heart attacks. Many medical researchers believe that naproxen does not reduce the incidence of heart attacks. Suppose that this is the case. From the vantage point of 1999, discuss whether the study outcome was just a fluke, with Vioxx actually being no riskier than naproxen when it comes to heart attacks.

6. On November 2, 2004, *The Wall Street Journal* published an article describing the manner in which Merck's executives made decisions about Vioxx. *The Wall Street Journal* article pointed out that the November 2000 issue of *The New England Journal of Medicine* included an article describing the results of the VIGOR study. *The New England Journal of Medicine* article stated that Vioxx did not significantly increase the incidence of heart attacks among patients who did not appear to be at high risk of having a heart attack. Notably, Merck had excluded subjects whose risk of experiencing a heart attack was anything but low. In retrospect, the executive editor of *The New England Journal,* Gregory Curfman, told *The Wall Street Journal* that his journal did not have all the details that were available to the FDA. He stated that his journal concentrated its efforts on ensuring that the text of the article accurately represented the data presented in the article. The authors of the article were academics who received consulting contracts or research grants from Merck and employees of Merck. Can you detect any behavioral issues and agency conflict issues (meaning general conflicts of interest) in the preceding discussion?

www.mhhe.com/shefrin

Minicase

Hurricanes and Psychology: From Wall Street of the Southwest to The Big Easy

Galveston, Texas, is a deep-water port on the Gulf of Mexico. In 1900, by virtue of having the only deep-water port in the state, Galveston was the center of a very profitable cotton export trade. The city has an historic district known as The Strand. In 1900, The Strand housed many financial firms and was known as the Wall Street of the Southwest.

Galveston had a weather station that was part of the U.S. Weather Service. In 1895 one of its meteorologists, Isaac Cline, became the first person in the Weather Service to issue accurate freezing weather warnings to local farmers 24 to 36 hours in advance. Doing so had been an uphill battle for Cline. Willis L. Moore, the Chief of the Weather Bureau in 1895, had written to Cline that his scientific staff had concluded that the task of predicting freezing weather accurately for that long a period was impossible. Cline then repeated the success he had achieved with freezes to timely flood warnings.

Being a port city on the Gulf of Mexico, Galveston was vulnerable to serious tropical storms, having been struck at least 10 times during the nineteenth century. It was an island city, and its peak elevation was less than 9 feet above sea level. During 1875, tidal flooding prompted calls from the community for a seawall. In 1886 these calls were renewed after a hurricane destroyed the neighboring community of Indianola, Texas, and killed over 125 people.

The call for a seawall involved an ongoing debate. In the July 15, 1891, edition of the *Galveston News,* Isaac Cline published a two-page article about Galveston's vulnerability to damage from tropical storms. In the article he wrote: "It would be impossible for any cyclone to create a storm wave which could materially injure the city." He reasoned that rising surf would flow over Galveston into the bay behind it and onto the Texas prairie, leaving the city undamaged. He predicted that the coastline would break up the incoming surf. And he added a comment, stating that hurricanes rarely struck Texas, and those that did were weak.

By the turn of the century no seawall had been built in Galveston. In September 1900 telegraph reports reached

Galveston about a strong storm in the Caribbean. The *Galveston County Daily News* reported that the storm had moved into the Gulf of Mexico, but that nobody knew when or if it would reach land. In the early hours of September 8, water levels rose abruptly in Galveston. Of his own volition, Cline hoisted hurricane warning flags, without waiting for permission from the central office of the Weather Bureau. In doing so, he risked being dismissed from his position.

Cline also went to the shoreline itself to warn people. However, less than half the population evacuated the island. Indeed, sightseers came from Houston in order to view the dramatic surf.

For more than a century, the hurricane that struck Galveston on September 8, 1900, would stand as the deadliest natural disaster in U.S. history. It killed between 6,000 and 8,000 people, one-sixth of Galveston's population, and destroyed three quarters of the city. Cline lost his wife in the disaster and almost died himself.

In his report after the storm, Cline wrote: "I believe that a sea wall, which would have broken the swells, would have saved much loss of both life and property." In his autobiography, he included the following comment: "This being my first experience in a tropical cyclone I did not foresee the magnitude of the damage which it would do."

For the next century, residents of the gulf states and Florida witnessed many destructive hurricanes. In 1992 Hurricane Andrew set a damage record of $26.5 billion when it struck Florida and parts of Louisiana. In 2004 four hurricanes struck Florida, combining to cause $49 billion in damage and approximately 100 deaths.

The most powerful hurricane is deemed a category 5 storm, with a category 4 storm being somewhat weaker. On August 29, 2005, Hurricane Katrina, a category 5 storm that weakened to a category 4 storm, devastated New Orleans and other parts of the gulf coast in the most costly natural disaster in American history. The death toll exceeded 800 in Louisiana and 1,000 overall.

New Orleans had an interesting history with hurricanes consisting of floods from mid-strength storms and near misses with category 4 and 5 storms. Most of the city is below sea level and therefore was particularly vulnerable to the flood damage that a hurricane would cause. In 1965 New Orleans had a near miss with the worst of Hurricane Betsy, the first storm to cause more than $1 billion in damage in the United States, and in 1969 it had a near miss with Hurricane Camille, a category 5 storm that was the strongest ever to hit the United States. Because Camille missed the city, it caused much less damage than Hurricane Andrew.

Only after seeing the damage caused by Hurricane Andrew in 1992, did officials in New Orleans begin to fret about the risk that a category 4 or 5 hurricane would strike their city. New Orleans officials repeatedly, but unsuccessfully, beseeched the Federal Emergency Management Agency (FEMA) to establish a contingency plan to prepare for the possibility that a major hurricane would strike New Orleans. In 1998, the city had another near miss, with Hurricane Georges, which lost strength when it hit land and became a category 2 storm.

The American Red Cross placed a major hurricane striking New Orleans at the top of its list of potential natural disasters in the United States. The next two disasters were earthquakes along the New Madrid, Missouri fault, and along the San Andreas fault near San Francisco.

In 2001, FEMA finally began to develop a plan for New Orleans, and working with the Army Corps of Engineers, released a report in 2002. The events that were predicted by the report turned out to be remarkably accurate, except for loss of life. The successful evacuation of a million of the city's inhabitants before Katrina made land led the actual death toll to be much less than the 144,000 anticipated by the Red Cross. Still, tens of thousands of people would not, or could not, obey the mandatory evacuation order that preceded Katrina. Katrina breached New Orleans' levees, and the resulting flood trapped many people in their homes. For days tens of thousands of people were stranded in both the city's Superdome stadium and its convention center without food, water, sanitary conditions, and medical care.

In 2002 Walter Maestri, the director of Emergency Preparedness for Jefferson Parish, a suburb of New Orleans, explained that psychological reasons would lead federal government officials to underestimate the hurricane risk that New Orleans faced. Appearing on the public television program *Now* on September 20, 2002, he stated that despite having the risks explained to them, federal government officials were unable to grasp what the real effects would be. He suggested that these officials were preoccupied with the war on terrorism where the risks felt more real rather than hypothetical. As for himself, Maestri indicated that it was even difficult for him to imagine the French Quarter of New Orleans being totally destroyed by a hurricane. In most respects, the *Now* program would prove prophetic, describing as it did the chain of catastrophes that would occur, should a devastating hurricane strike New Orleans.

After the release of the 2002 report, the Army Corps of Engineers compiled a list of approximately $18 billion in projects that they deemed necessary to address New Orleans' structural weaknesses, among them a $188 million water pump. President Bush, who viewed the expenditure on the pump as extravagant, promptly fired the chief of the Army Corps for supporting the proposal. In June 2005, the New Orleans district of the Army Corps learned that its budget for 2006 was likely to be cut by 20 percent, to $272 million.

In the aftermath of Katrina, the emergency response by the federal government was slow, much slower than it had been after Hurricane Charley struck Florida a year earlier. Walter Maestri appeared on television to express frustration for having begged and pleaded, with the response to his pleas having been "Yeah. Yeah. Yeah."

A front page story in the September 6, 2005, issue of *The Wall Street Journal* suggested that FEMA's response to the aftermath of Katrina was much too slow because FEMA's focus had shifted from responding to natural disasters to preventing terrorism. After the events of September 11, 2001, FEMA had become part of the Department of Homeland Security, rather than continue as a separate agency. Describing Katrina and its aftermath in a press conference on September 4, Homeland Security Secretary Michael Chertoff stated: "This is really one which I think was breathtaking in its surprise . . . I will tell you that, really, that perfect storm of combination of catastrophes exceeded the foresight of the planners, and maybe anybody's foresight."

Case Analysis Questions

1. Identify which psychological phenomena described in the chapter played a role in the 1900 Galveston disaster.

2. Compare the psychological traits and experiences of Isaac Cline with those of Scott McNealy, chief executive officer of Sun Microsystems.

3. Use the concepts and examples developed in the chapter text to analyze the behavioral issues that arose in respect to hurricane Katrina that struck New Orleans in 2005. Do you see any common behavioral patterns in the situations that prevailed in Galveston and New Orleans before they were devastated?

Chapter **Two**

Valuation

The main objective of this chapter is for students to demonstrate that they can identify how heuristics and framing affect the way managers and analysts value firms.

After completing this chapter students will be able to:

1. Explain why some financial executives and analysts rely on valuation heuristics instead of textbook techniques that emphasize intrinsic value.
2. Describe the main heuristics that financial executives and analysts use to compute value.
3. Identify the biases that arise in connection with the use of valuation heuristics.
4. Identify the biases that arise in connection with the use of traditional textbook techniques that emphasize intrinsic value.

2.1 TRADITIONAL APPROACH TO VALUATION

Valuation centers on the constant-growth present-value perpetuity formula $PV = C/(r - g)$, where C is the first payment, future payments grow at rate g, and the discount rate is r. In the case of equities, the future cash flows consist of dividends, so that C is the expected future dividend payment D_1 one year hence. The discount rate r is the required return on equity, measured as an opportunity cost. It is the expected return that could be earned on the next best alternative with the same risk. The growth rate g is given by the long-term sustainable growth rate of the firm's equity. This variable has an associated formula, $g = (1 - d) \times ROE$. Here, d is the dividend payout ratio, equal to the ratio of dividends to earnings, and ROE is the expected return on equity. The term $1 - d$ is the plowback ratio, the ratio of retained earnings to total earnings.

An alternative approach to equity valuation focuses on a firm's growth opportunities. Valuation through growth opportunities involves decomposing equity value into two components: (1) the value of the firm when it pays out 100 percent of its earnings as cash dividends; and (2) the net present value associated with plowing back a portion of future earnings into the firm's future projects. The second component is called the firm's (net) present value of growth opportunities (PVGO or NPVGO).[1]

In the case of constant growth, the growth opportunities valuation formula takes the form $P_0 = E_1/r + PVGO$ (or $E_1/r + NPVGO$). In this last equation, P_0 is the value of the firm on a per-share basis and E_1 is the expected earnings per share (EPS) over the next year.

Growth opportunities are central to understanding the fundamental determinants of a company's price-to-earnings ratio (P/E). Specifically, the last equation for stock price can be rewritten as $P_0/E_1 = [r \times (1 - \text{PVGO}/P_0)]^{-1}$. The latter equation indicates that the forward-looking P/E ratio is an increasing function of the ratio PVGO/P_0. In other words, for given r, the higher the fraction of a firm's value that stems from its growth opportunities, the higher will be its P/E ratio.

2.2 VALUATION HEURISTICS

The valuation techniques taught in traditional finance textbooks are based on the computation of intrinsic or fundamental value. Do financial executives and security analysts rely on textbook techniques? If not, do they rely on heuristics, and if so, which ones? Does reliance on heuristics predispose financial executives and analysts to bias? These questions constitute the heart of this chapter.

Consider the first two of the three questions in the preceding paragraph. *Financial Executive* is the main publication of Financial Executives International (FEI), an international organization of financial managers. Its March/April 2002 issue contains an article describing several valuation techniques used in practice.[2] Some of the techniques described correspond to the traditional textbook discounted cash flow (DCF) approach. Some are non-DCF heuristics.

This chapter focuses on three common heuristics, named for ratios upon which they rely: P/E, PEG, and price-to-sales. Descriptions of all three are provided next. Later sections provide examples of how these are used by financial executives and security analysts.

P/E Heuristic

Valuation based on the P/E ratio involves the product of two terms: a P/E ratio and an earnings estimate. The P/E ratio is a forward P/E, having the form P_0/E_1, where P_0 denotes current price and E_1 denotes the forecast of earnings per share for the next year. Security analysts rely on the **P/E heuristic** more than any other technique.[3]

P/E heuristic
An approach to valuation based on multiplying a P/E ratio and an earnings forecast.

The valuation identity is given by $P_0 = P_0/E_1 \times E_1$. However, this relationship is also used to forecast price in the future. In order to forecast the price P_1 a year hence, apply the relationship $P_1 = P_1/E_2 \times E_2$. Of course, the challenge is to arrive at sensible forecasts of the P/E ratio that will apply a year hence and earnings per share two years hence.

PEG Heuristic

A firm's PEG ratio is defined as its P/E ratio divided by its expected earnings growth rate per year (actually $100 \times$ expected earnings growth rate). The premise underlying the use of PEG-based valuation is that the stocks of high-growth firms merit higher P/E ratios than the stocks of low-growth firms. Valuation based on the PEG ratio involves the product of three terms, the PEG ratio, an estimate of future earnings per share, and an estimate of expected earnings growth.

PEG heuristic
An approach to valuation based on multiplying a PEG ratio, an earnings forecast, and a forecast of the growth rate.

The valuation identity is given by $P_0 = \text{PEG} \times E_1 \times G$, where G is $100 \times$ growth rate. As with the P/E heuristic, the **PEG heuristic** can be used to forecast price P_1 a year hence. Doing so requires forecasts of the PEG ratio that will apply a year hence, earnings per share two years hence, and the growth rate that will apply over the forecast period.

price-to-sales heuristic
An approach to valuation based on multiplying a price-to-sales ratio and a sales forecast.

Price-to-Sales Heuristic

The **price-to-sales heuristic** has the same structure as the P/E heuristic, except that future sales are substituted for future earnings. The valuation identity is given by $P_0 = P_0/S_1 \times S_1$, where S stands for sales.

2.3   A CFO'S RELIANCE ON VALUATION HEURISTICS

In order to make the ideas about valuation heuristics and biases concrete, this chapter uses the case of one particular firm, eBay, as a vehicle for discussion.

The initial public offering (IPO) for eBay took place in September 1998. By the end of 2002 eBay was one of the most successful Internet companies in the world. A $100 investment in eBay stock at the time of its IPO would have grown to more than $640 by May 2003. In contrast, the return to both the S&P 500 and the Nasdaq Composite index during the same period was close to zero, if not negative.

On May 20, 2003, eBay's stock closed at $97.75, having risen by more than 44 percent from the beginning of the year. That increase gave eBay a market valuation higher than the market valuations of both General Motors and McDonald's. On that day the consensus analyst estimate of its earnings per share (EPS) for the coming four quarters was $1.56. That produced a forward P/E for eBay of 62.7.[4]

CONCEPT PREVIEW *Question 2.1*	After Internet stock prices had generally soared in May 2003, the *San Jose Mercury News* asked whether the rapid increase was due to solid fundamentals or 1999-style bandwagon investing. Investors were asking the same question. If you were a financial executive at eBay, what combination of traditional and heuristic valuation techniques would you use to answer this question?

Consider next how the financial executives at eBay, see nearby box, actually approached valuation at the time.[5,6]

Both eBay's chief financial officer and vice president for corporate finance were highly educated and experienced. Despite all the emphasis in corporate finance textbooks on discounted cash flow analysis, many financial executives rely on heuristics instead of the fundamental valuation techniques taught in textbooks. Heuristics are simpler to use: P/E, PEG, and price-to-sales require very few variables and involve

On April 1, 2003, Rajiv Dutta, eBay's chief financial officer (CFO) addressed a chapter meeting of Financial Executives International (FEI). During his presentation he discussed the manner in which eBay's executives respond to investors who suggest that the firm's stock is overvalued. He indicated that eBay's executives take skeptical investors through the following PEG-based analysis.

In March 2003, eBay's P/E ratio was 79, which some investors took to imply that its stock price was too high. However, Dutta suggested that a valuation based on P/E alone failed to factor in earnings growth. In this respect, he suggested comparing the stock of eBay to the stock of the large retail firm Wal-Mart, and using the PEG ratio as the valuation metric. According to *Fortune* magazine, Wal-Mart was the most admired company in America during 2003.

On May 20, 2003, eBay's forward-looking P/E ratio was 66.2, while Wal-Mart's P/E ratio was 22.7. On a P/E basis, eBay appeared to be over twice as expensive as Wal-Mart. However, Dutta pointed out that analysts were expecting eBay to grow by 42.5 percent, while they were only expecting Wal-Mart to grow by 14 percent. As a result, eBay's PEG was 1.56, which was actually lower than Wal-Mart's PEG of 1.62. By the PEG metric, eBay was actually cheaper than Wal-Mart, a point that eBay's CFO emphasized.

In May 2003 Mark Rubash, eBay's vice president for corporate finance and investor relations, explicitly stated that the firm's managers did not track return on equity and were uncertain about the value of their firm's cost of capital. Based on conversations with investors and perhaps analysts, they believed their cost of capital to be in the range of 11 to 12 percent. However, they claimed not to compute their cost of capital, say by using a textbook framework such as the capital asset pricing model (CAPM), or by factoring their historical return on equity into their valuation analysis. Given the high and accelerating growth rates they were witnessing during 2003, eBay's executives stated, frankly, that they had very little idea about the intrinsic value of their firm's stock.

For the record, on August 29, 2003, eBay split its stock 2-for-1, when it closed at $109.52 (presplit). On December 27, 2004, its stock price closed at $112.86 (postsplit). Wal-Mart closed 2004 at $52.79, almost exactly where it had been on April 1, 2003.

simple formulas. As such they have intuitive appeal, the basis for the affect heuristic. The DCF-based analyses taught in textbooks require far more detail than the heuristic techniques, involve more complex formulas, and are far less intuitive.

2.4   HOW ANALYSTS VALUE FIRMS: AN ILLUSTRATIVE EXAMPLE

Analyst Mary Meeker

Section 2.3 illustrated how the financial executives at eBay approached the value of their firm. Essentially, they relied on the PEG heuristic to assess whether or not their stock price seemed to be fairly priced. However, they did little analysis beyond that.

What about security analysts? One of their main tasks is to assess value. Do they rely on DCF? Do they use heuristics, and if so which ones? In the Spring of 2003, 24 analysts followed eBay. Among these, the most well known was Mary Meeker from the firm Morgan Stanley. Mary Meeker's analysis of eBay used a series of valuation techniques, each of which gave a different target price for eBay. Her April 2003 report offers a rich set of insights into how analysts apply these various techniques. Before describing the details, refer to the Behavioral Pitfalls box for some background information on Mary Meeker.

During the late 1990s Mary Meeker was a security analyst at Morgan Stanley and was one of the highest-paid analysts on Wall Street, having earned approximately $15 million in 1999 and $23 million in 2000. At the time, she placed very high valuations on some Internet firms, and as a result came to be called Queen of the Internet.

In 1998, *Time Magazine* interviewed Mary Meeker, asking her to justify the high valuations of Internet companies that prevailed at the time. She began by stating that the development of the commercial Internet was "the biggest new technology cycle ever."

Continuing, she pointed out that just as the traditional retailer Wal-Mart came to dominate the retail sector, Web-based counterparts would emerge and dominate Internet commerce. Mary Meeker described the phenomenon as the "Wal-Marting of the Web."

Wal-Mart had built its business by beating its competition in regard to convenience, product selection, and low prices. She argued that the Internet provided the opportunity for other firms to follow Wal-Mart, but on the Web.

In 2000, after a period of excessive optimism, if not irrational exuberance, the prices of many Internet stocks fell dramatically. This event has been described as the bursting of the dot-com bubble. In May 2002 *Fortune* magazine placed Mary Meeker's picture on their cover and asked if investors could ever trust Wall Street again.

In the wake of the collapse in stock prices, regulators from New York State's attorney general's office and the U.S. Securities and Exchange Commission launched a major investigation. Among those investigated was Mary Meeker. In 2003, the attorney general's office and the SEC criticized her valuations as excessive, but they did not bring charges against her.

On February 23, 2004, *The Wall Street Journal* ran a feature titled "Ah, the 1990s" updating the fates of key Wall Street personalities from the 1990s stock market bubble. Regarding Mary Meeker, the article notes that she was recently named Morgan Stanley's coleader of tech-sector research. In August 2004, Meeker told *Newsweek* and *CBS.MarketWatch.Com* that she was not going to be hiding out any more. The press duly noted that her stock picks were outperforming the market.

Sources: Mary, Meeker and Maryanne Murray Buechner, "Q&A: Morgan's Mary Meeker: Look for the Net's 'Top Dogs'," *Time*, April 1, 1998; E. S. Browning, "Ah, the 1990," *The Wall Street Journal*, February 23, 2004; Frank Barnako, "Mary Meeker Is Still a Believer," *CBS.MarketWatch.com*, August 23, 2004; Charles Gasparino and Susanne Craig, "Meeker Won't Face Securities-Fraud Charges," *The Wall Street Journal*, April 3, 2003; Charles Gasparino, "Climbing Back Up; Ready to Reign Again, Wall Street's Fallen 'Queen of the Net' Tells *Newsweek*: 'I'm not hiding out anymore,'" *Newsweek*, August 30, 2004.

Mary Meeker's Target Prices for eBay

At the time Mary Meeker released her April 2003 report, eBay's price was $89.22. Meeker's task was to develop a target price for eBay over the subsequent 12 months. In undertaking this task, she used all three valuation heuristics described earlier, as well as a discounted cash flow (DCF) computation.

Exhibit 2.1 provides a summary of the components of Mary Meeker's target price analysis. For each of the first three heuristics, Meeker computed a low, high, and intermediate guess, which she calls downside, upside, and base respectively. She then averaged these together with her DCF valuation to arrive at a target price of $106 per share.[7]

Exhibit 2.2 describes the assumptions and computations that underlie Mary Meeker's heuristic-based average target values displayed in Exhibit 2.1. In Exhibit 2.2, an E after a year (for example, 2004E) designates that the numbers are estimates, not actual values. In all cases target prices were computed for year-end 2004 and then discounted back to mid-2004. To arrive at her target price for December 2004, Meeker used a P/E value of 40 for 2005, the midpoint of 47 and 33

EXHIBIT 2.1
Summary of
Components in Mary
Meeker's Target Price
Analysis of eBay

Source: Mary Meeker and Brian
Pitz, "CQ1 Results: Tales of a
Growth Machine," Morgan Stanley
Analyst Report on eBay,
April 23, 2003.

Technique	Downside	Upside	Base
P/E	$74	$111	$ 84
PEG	45	91	68
Price-to-sales	97	210	147
Discounted cash flow			117
Average			$104
Upside adjusted average			$106

EXHIBIT 2.2
Valuation Methodologies in Mary Meeker's Target Price Analysis of eBay

Source: Mary Meeker and Brian Pitz, "CQ1 Results: Tales of a Growth Machine," Morgan Stanley Analyst Report on eBay, April 23, 2003.

			Year			
			2002	2003E	2004E	2005E
	EPS at 32% growth		$0.86	$1.14	$1.50	$1.98
	EPS at 38% growth		$0.86	$1.19	$1.64	$2.26
	GMS/share at 38% growth		$39.53	$54.55	$75.27	$103.88
	P/E		103	63	47	33

Method	P/E Ratio	PEG Ratio	Price-to-Sales Ratio	EPS	Growth	GMS Sales per Share	Target Price Dec 2004	Target Price (Discounted)
P/E	40			$2.26			$90	$84
PEG		1.5		1.50	32		72	68
Price-to-sales			1.5	2.26		$103.88	156	147

shown in the table. For sales, she used the gross global sales activity on all eBay Web sites, called gross merchandise sales (GMS).

As can be seen in Exhibit 2.1, Mary Meeker used a DCF approach, applied to eBay's free cash flows. This computation comes closest to the traditional textbook technique and is the only one of the four that purports to derive the target price in terms of intrinsic or fundamental value.

A firm generates positive free cash flows when its after-tax cash flows from operations are positive and it does not spend all those after-tax flows acquiring working capital and fixed assets. The difference between after-tax cash flow from operations and investment in working capital and fixed assets is paid out to the firm's owners.

Exhibit 2.3 displays the DCF valuation table from her April 2003 report. The heart of her DCF analysis consists of the forecasts for eBay's revenues (not shown in Exhibit 2.3), and its earnings before interest, taxes, depreciation, and amortization (EBITDA).

The free cash flows for eBay are in the third line from the bottom in Exhibit 2.3. Free cash flows are akin to dividends, but are paid to all investors, meaning debtholders and stockholders. Just as the present value of the future expected dividend stream comprises the value of the firm's equity, the present value of the firm's expected free cash flows comprise the value of the entire firm.

In her April 2003 report, Mary Meeker forecast free cash flows through the end of 2010. She used a terminal value to capture the free cash flows that would occur after 2010 and discounted these at a rate of 12 percent.[8] In Exhibit 2.3, she obtained her $65.3 billion terminal value in 2011 by assuming that free cash flows would grow at the rate of 7 percent from 2011 on, and then valued the future expected free cash flow stream beginning in 2011 using the constant-growth-rate perpetuity formula. Specifically, she forecast that free cash flows in 2011 would be $3,266,096 = 1.07 × $3,052,426. She then applied the perpetuity formula:

$$PV = \frac{\$3,266,096}{0.12 - 0.07} = \$65,321,907$$

Meeker computed the present value of the free cash flow stream by summing the discounted free cash flow values for every year between 2004E and the terminal year. As shown in Exhibit 2.3, that sum came to $36.5 billion. Then she added eBay's $2.3 billion cash holdings to arrive at the value of the firm as a whole and subtracted the value of eBay's $79 million in debt to arrive at the value of eBay's equity. The net result was $38 billion, which Meeker called eBay's "full value." Dividing full value by eBay's shares outstanding (330 million) lead to a target value of about $117 per share at year-end 2003.[9] In using this amount, she did not take the future value of the $117 to mid-2004.

EXHIBIT 2.3 **Free Cash Flow Computation in Mary Meeker's Target Price Analysis of eBay**

Note: Values given are in $ thousands.

Source: Mary Meeker and Brian Pitz, "CQ1 Results: Tales of a Growth Machine," Morgan Stanley Analyst Report on eBay, April 23, 2003.

	2000	2001	2002	2003E	2004E	2005E	2006E	2007E	2008E	2009E	2010E	2011E on
EBITDA	84,072	229,438	444,614	723,735	1,005,276	1,401,682	1,853,230	2,426,297	3,110,990	3,985,085	4,982,032	
Taxes	—	—	—	—	—	140,168	370,646	849,204	1,088,846	1,394,780	1,743,711	
Change in working capital	(47,582)	(41,091)	39,232	(26,792)	6,849	(58,695)	9,709	(52,096)	7,375	(53,278)	4,105	
Capital expenditures	49,753	57,420	138,670	188,908	190,000	190,000	190,000	190,000	190,000	190,000	190,000	
Free cash flow	(13,263)	130,927	345,176	508,035	822,125	1,012,819	1,302,292	1,334,997	1,839,519	2,347,027	3,052,426	65,321,907

Target Price—Dec 31, 2003

Present value eBay free cash flows	$36,478,759
Less debt	$79,592
Plus cash	$2,280,857
eBay's full value	$38,680,023
Shares outstanding ('000)	330,259
Discount rate	12%
Future growth rate	7%
DCF per share value	$117

2.5 BIASES

Biases and Heuristics

Was Mary Meeker's valuation analysis of eBay biased? At the end of June 2004, eBay's stock price reached $180 (on a presplit basis), well above Meekers' target price of $106. At year-end 2004 its stock price closed 2004 (pre-split) at $232, and its forward P/E for eBay was 70, well above Meeker's forecast of 47. Those facts alone in no way indicate that Meeker's analysis was biased.

Was $106 a biased target price to have established in April 2003 when eBay stock was trading at about $89.22? The rate of return associated with a target price of $106 lies above Meeker's discount rate of 12 percent. In this respect, $106 would be upwardly biased, if in April 2003 Meeker judged eBay's stock to have been fairly priced. Of course, in April 2003 Meeker might have judged eBay's stock to be undervalued.

Were the target prices associated with Meeker's individual heuristics biased? The P/E heuristic is the approach most favored by analysts. Meeker's range for the P/E target price was $74 to $111. Her base case estimate of $84 lies below the April 2003 price of $89.22 and therefore gives rise to a negative return.

The PEG heuristic produces a value range that is more negative and is therefore even worse. Unless Meeker judged eBay stock to have been overvalued at the time, it is safe to conclude that the P/E heuristic or the PEG heuristic, or both, produced downward biased estimates of future value.

Moreover, the assumptions that underlie the two techniques are not consistent. The P/E heuristic target price computation is premised on a growth rate of 38 percent, whereas the PEG heuristic target price computation is premised on a growth rate of 32 percent. Moreover, for her PEG calculation, Meeker appears to have used an EPS number of $1.50 for 2004 rather than 2005. Actually, she used $1.42 for EPS, which corresponds to $1.50 discounted back to mid-2004, but which she listed as expected cash earnings for the year 2003.

The target price range of $97 to $210 based on the price-to-sales ratio might well be biased upward. The average of this range produces a return of 63 percent, far above the required return (discount rate) of 12 percent.

Biases and Framing Effects

The DCF-based free cash flow computation is the only technique that purports to measure intrinsic value, the approach taught in textbooks. Meeker's DCF target price of $117 per share corresponds to a return of 25 percent and is upwardly biased. The bias stems from the manner in which Mary Meeker framed eBay's free cash flows.

There are multiple ways to define free cash flows. One definition, called sources of free cash flows, is cash flows from operations less the sum of new short-term debt, investment in working capital and fixed assets. Another definition, called the uses of free cash flows, is the sum of interest payments, dividends, and share repurchases, less the sum of new debt and new share issues. Uses of free cash flows are the cash flows that a firm pays to its investors, net of new financing. Notably, the sources of free cash flows must equal the uses of free cash flows.

Free cash flows are important because they form the basis for computing the fundamental value of the entire firm, not just its equity. The uses of free cash flows are what investors receive as owners of the firm. Therefore, the value of the firm is the present value of the firm's expected future free cash flows.

A firm that is all equity financed and internally funded will pay no interest, take out no debt, and refrain from issuing new shares or repurchasing shares. The uses of free cash flows of such a firm will consist exclusively of its dividends. Therefore, the fundamental value of the firm will be determined in accordance with the dividend discount model. That is, in this case the present value of future free cash flows equates to the present value of future dividends.

Did Mary Meeker misframe eBay's free cash flows in Exhibit 2.3? Notice that Exhibit 2.3 contains no reference to dividends, share repurchases, changes in debt, or stock issues. Instead free cash flows are computed using earnings and purchases of new assets. That is, Exhibit 2.3 purportedly displays eBay's sources of free cash flows.

As was mentioned previously, sources of free cash flows must be equal to uses of free cash flows. Now computing the uses of eBay's free cash flows (from financial statements available on the course Web site) is a straightforward exercise. In 2001, eBay paid $2.2 million in interest and $320,000 in dividends, it paid down debt in the amount of $21.9 million, and it raised $122 million in new equity including the exercise of employee stock options.[10] Taken together, eBay's free cash flows in 2001 amounted to −$97.6 million. Yet, Exhibit 2.3 records eBay's free cash flow computation for 2001 as a positive $130.9 million.

Remember, the two should be equal: $130.9 million is a far cry from −$97.6 million. This is the first hint that something is amiss.

Moreover, examine the free cash flow forecasts in Exhibit 2.3 extending out from 2003 through 2010. The entries are all large positive numbers, which are growing rapidly. Was Mary Meeker expecting that eBay would be paying out large cash dividends, engaging in major share repurchases, making large interest payments, or paying down large amounts of debt? Nothing in her report suggests anything of the kind.

Disconnect

In order to understand the disconnect between the −$97.1 million free cash flow and the $130.9 million in Meeker's analysis, consider how Meeker arrived at her $130.9 million figure. She began with eBay's EBITDA for 2001, its earnings before interest, depreciation, and amortization. For this entry she used $229.4 million (the operating income in eBay's income statement). She then subtracted cash taxes (eBay paid zero taxes in 2001), the change in net working capital (shown as $41.1 million), and capital expenditures (shown as $57.4 million). So, in Meeker's cash flow table,

$$\text{Free cash flow} = \text{EBITDA} - \text{Cash taxes} - \text{Change in working capital}$$
$$- \text{Capital expenditures}$$
$$= 229.4 - 0 - 41.1 - 57.4 = 130.9$$

Juxtaposition

Exhibit 2.4 displays the computation of eBay's free cash flows based on its statement of cash flows for 2001, juxtaposed with the free cash flows in Mary Meeker's

EXHIBIT 2.4
Contrasting Mary
Meeker's Free Cash
Flows and Textbook
Formula Free Cash
Flows for 2001

Note: Meeker uses EBITDA of
$229.4 in her report, which is very
close to the income statement item
Operating Income before
Depreciation. The sum of the first
three items in the column that
displays Meeker's figures sum to
$229.4. Her report provides the
aggregate figure, but not the
decomposition. As a general matter,
net income is after-tax, and eBay's
cash taxes in 2001 were $0.

	eBay's Statement of Cash Flows $ millions	Mary Meeker's Report $ millions
Sources of free cash flow		
Net Income (adjusted for cash flow from other income)	206.6	140.6
Depreciation	86.6	86.6
Interest	2.2	2.2
Change in net working capital − Change in short-term debt	−363.2	−41.1
Investment	−29.8	−57.4
Free cash flow	**−97.6**	**130.9**
Uses of free cash flow		
Interest	2.2	
Dividends	0.3	
Change in long-term debt − Change in short-term debt	21.9	
Stock issue − Other financing	−122.0	
Free cash flow	**−97.6**	

report. The figures are in millions of dollars. Notice that in Exhibit 2.4, Meeker's EBITDA figure of 229.4 appears as the sum of the first three items plus zero for taxes, $229.4 = 140.6 + 86.6 + 2.2 + 0$.

Pinpointing the Differences

The values of the items derived from eBay's statement of cash flows differ from those that appear in Meeker's report. The EBITDA number is different because EBITDA is an income statement item, not a cash flow item. The working capital item is different because Meeker excluded cash from working capital. And the capital expenditures item is different because investment includes items other than capital expenditures, such as acquisitions and sale of property, plant, and equipment.

Misusing the Numbers

Are the free cash flow figures that Meeker reported wrong? Yes, if the point is to compute the intrinsic value of the firm by computing the discounted value of its expected free cash flows. Recall that the value of the firm is the present value of the uses of free cash flow; that is, the net cash flows to the firm's investors. As can be seen in the bottom section of Exhibit 2.4, the uses of eBay's cash flows sum to −$97.6 million, the same as the sources of eBay's cash flows, as derived from eBay's statement of cash flows.

By far, the most significant contributor to the disparity between the −$97.6 figure and Meeker's $130.9 figure is working capital. During 2001, eBay increased its cash holdings by $322.1 (million). This amount was not paid out to eBay's investors. And free cash flows used in valuation are generalized dividends: they need to be paid out at the time they are recorded. Notably, $322.1 represents the difference between the working capital amount that Meeker used and the working capital amount based on eBay's statement of cash flows.

One of the main behavioral issues described in Chapter 1 concerns framing, the way that information is described. There is an important issue of framing here. Mary Meeker framed her free cash flow analysis in terms of sources of free cash flow, not uses of free cash flow. As a result, the uses of cash flow are not salient in her analysis, despite the fact that uses of cash flow lie at the heart of valuation analysis.

Why Misframing Causes Valuation Bias

The definition of free cash flows that Mary Meeker used is fairly common. Many financial journalists define free cash flows that way, and eBay's financial executives adopt the same definition though they do not use it for valuation. Yet the issue is important. The consequence of Mary Meeker having defined free cash flows as she did is that her DCF valuation of $117 per share for eBay will be too high.

To understand the nature of the bias better, consider a simple textbook style valuation of eBay. For sake of discussion, suppose that we accept Mary Meeker's earnings growth forecasts through 2010 (based on EBITDA in Exhibit 2.4) along with her assumption that eBay would grow at 7 percent after 2010. Exhibit 2.5 shows how eBay's earnings might hypothetically grow through the year 2011.

Suppose that eBay pays no dividends before 2010 and that when its growth rate stabilizes at 7 percent, as Mary Meeker assumed, its growth opportunities are zero. In this case, computing eBay's intrinsic value is straightforward, taking Mary Meeker's discount rate of 12 percent. At the end of 2010, the intrinsic value associated with eBay's future earnings would be

$$\$24,851 = \frac{E_{2011}}{r} = \frac{\$2,982}{0.12}$$

as recorded in the present value column of Exhibit 2.5. In accordance with the growth opportunities valuation formula, the value of a firm having zero growth opportunities does not depend on its dividend policy.

Because eBay is assumed to pay no dividends before 2010, its value in April 2003 will be based on the present value of the $24,851 in 2010 dollars. The $24,851

EXHIBIT 2.5
Illustrative Computation Table for Fundamental Value of eBay

Year	Earnings $ millions	Growth Rate (%)	Present Value $ millions
2002	$250		$10,037
2003E	407	63%	11,241
2004E	566	39	12,590
2005E	787	39	14,101
2006E	1,039	32	15,793
2007E	1,361	31	17,688
2008E	1,742	28	19,811
2009E	2,230	28	22,188
2010E	2,787	25	24,851
2011E	2,982	7	

would be worth $22,188 at the end of 2009, $22,188 = $24,851/1.12$. Discounting back to mid-2004 would lead to a value of $11,897 (= $12,590/1.12^{0.5}$) at that time.

According to Mary Meeker's report, in mid-2003 eBay held $2.8 billion in cash. If none of that cash were required to generate future earnings, then that cash would be added to $11,897 to arrive at $14,178, or $42.93 per share.

The amount of cash eBay would require to produce the earnings stream depicted in Exhibit 2.5 is critical. Quite plausibly, eBay will continue to add cash between 2004 and 2010. In that case, eBay's intrinsic target value might be more than $42.93 per share.

Cash and New Financing.   By leaving cash out of working capital in what she called free cash flows, Mary Meeker ostensibly controlled for additions to cash. However, a portion of those cash additions come from new equity capital, including the exercise of employee stock options. In 2001, eBay raised $122 million in new equity. That is an important reason why its free cash flows were −$97.6 million that year. In 2002, eBay raised $263 million in new equity and its free cash flows were −$262 million. In 2003, eBay raised $730 million in new equity and its free cash flows were −$714 million.

The shareholders of record in mid-2003 do not capture all the future cash flows to equity, including the contributions from new financing. Keep in mind that Mary Meeker did not include cash as part of working capital in her definition of free cash flows. In addition, she took the present value of her free cash flow stream and divided by the number of shares as of mid-2003. Doing so produced upward bias in the valuation because it implicitly assumed that contributions to future free cash flows from new financing would be completely appropriated by the shareholders of record as of mid-2003. The same remark applies to the illustrative textbook computation of eBay's intrinsic value described above. The computation implicitly assumes that eBay will be internally financed throughout.

In concluding this section, consider one final point. An important contrast between the traditional valuation just described and Mary Meeker's valuation involves the contribution to DCF from terminal value, the period after 2010. In the traditional approach based on the ratio E_{2011}/r, the present value of the terminal component is $11,897 million. In Mary Meeker's free cash flow approach, the present value of the terminal component is $29,548 million (= $65,322/1.12^7$). On a per-share basis, the difference amounts to $53.45, a substantial magnitude. The main explanation for this difference rests on Meeker's definition of free cash flows, coupled with the assumption that eBay's growth opportunities will be zero after 2010.

2.6   OTHER SOURCES OF BIAS

Growth Opportunities

CONCEPT PREVIEW *Question 2.2*	In traditional textbook valuation analysis, what factors determine whether the stock of a firm has a low P/E ratio or a high P/E ratio?

The answer to Concept Preview Question 2.2 can be found in Section 2.1 as well as in traditional textbooks. The two key variables that determine fundamental P/E are the required return (reflecting risk) and present value of growth opportunities.

Analysts rely heavily on the P/E heuristic to arrive at target prices. They rarely use techniques that emphasize growth opportunities (PVGO, NPVGO), despite the prominence of growth opportunity techniques in finance textbooks. This is not to say that analysts ignore growth, they most certainly do not. However, they are inclined to mistake growth in EPS for growth opportunities.

When a firm has zero growth opportunities, meaning PVGO is equal to zero, then its intrinsic forward P/E is $1/r$, where r is the required return. However, as PVGO becomes positive, P/E rises above $1/r$. As PVGO approaches P_0, P_0/E_1 rises to infinity.

Mary Meeker used a rate of 12 percent to discount eBay's future cash flows, thereby treating 12 percent as eBay's required return r. The intrinsic forward P/E ratio of a firm with zero growth opportunities and a required return of 12 percent is 8.33 ($= 1/0.12$). At the same time, Mary Meeker used a P/E ratio of 40 in her P/E valuation heuristic, suggesting that eBay had significant growth opportunities. Indeed, she titled her April 2003 report on eBay "Tales of a Growth Machine."

In order for a firm to have positive growth opportunities, its expected return on equity (ROE) must exceed its required return. Firms for which expected ROE equals r have zero growth opportunities.

In the time since eBay went public, how has that firm's actual ROE compared to its required return? In 1998, eBay's ROE was 2.84 percent. ROE rose to 4.76 percent in 2000, 7.03 percent in 2002, and was 10 percent in June 2004, a year after Meeker's report. In other words, from the time that eBay went public through June 2004, eBay did not earn its required return.

This is not to say that in mid-2003, eBay had zero growth opportunities and that a P/E ratio of 40 for 2005 was unjustified. What it does say is that it is important to identify the magnitude of growth opportunities explicitly and in a systematic fashion.

One question that the present chapter does not address is whether or not market values correspond to fundamental values. This important question relates to the concept of market efficiency, the subject of Chapter 5.

PEG and DCF

Although the PEG valuation relationship is an identity, it is used in a way that is at odds with textbook theory. As eBay CFO Rajiv Dutta explained when using PEG in connection with his own firm, the stocks of high-growth firms merit higher P/E ratios than the stocks of low-growth firms.

The PEG heuristic effectively assumes that the P/E ratio should vary inversely with the growth rate g. That is, P/E and g should be related through the relationship $P/E = Kg$ where K is a constant of proportionality.

It is plausible that firms with positive growth opportunities would tend to grow more quickly than firms that lack positive growth opportunities. After all, positive growth opportunity firms tend to feature higher values of ROE and in addition choose to plow back most if not all of their earnings. The long-term growth rate g is just the product of the plowback ratio and expected ROE. However, there is nothing in textbook theory that implies that P/E and g should be related through an equation such as $P/E = Kg$.

To see why P/E is not proportional to g, consider the case of a firm that has zero growth opportunities. Recall that in traditional textbook analysis the P/E ratio has the form $P_0/E_1 = 1/r$. When the plowback ratio is zero, g is zero. When the plowback ratio is 1, $g = ROE$. Regardless of whether g is equal to zero or equal to the ROE, P/E is $1/r$. Therefore, P/E does not vary in proportion to g, as required by the relation $P/E = Kg$.

The 1/*n* Heuristic

As displayed in Exhibit 2.1, Mary Meeker uses four techniques to establish a target price for eBay of $106 for mid-2004. Despite the enormous dispersion in values associated with P/E, PEG, price-to-sales, and DCF, Meeker simply averaged the numbers, which in her words, "combine to an average fair value of about $106."

1/*n* heuristic
A simple rule of thumb that assigns equal weight to all choices under consideration.

The **1/*n* heuristic** is a rule of thumb that assigns the same weight to each technique, as if they are all equally valid. In particular, textbook-favored DCF receives the same weight as the PEG heuristic, which has no basis in textbook theory. Relying on the $1/n$ heuristic might make sense if the biases associated with the various heuristics all tend to wash out.

There is no reason to expect that the biases from different heuristics will wash out. There is no reason why the P/E heuristic need generate downward bias, as it seems to in Meeker's P/E-based valuation of eBay. Other analysts covering eBay used different values than hers for P/E in their valuations. For example, a Prudential report on eBay, dated May 12, 2003, used a P/E ratio of 75. Analysts Mark Rowen, Aimee Landwehr, and Anne Wickland authored the Prudential report.[11] Notably, the Prudential analysts assessed the value of eBay stock at $108, not that different from Meeker's $106. Their valuations involved an EPS forecast of $1.43 for fiscal year 2003 and an EPS estimate of $2.15 for 2004.

Excessive Optimism

Financial executives and analysts who make biased forecasts of future earnings and P/E ratios will typically end up with biased valuations. On April 23, 2003, *The Wall Street Journal* published an article suggesting that the analysts following eBay were excessively optimistic about eBay's future revenue stream. The article pointed out that Mary Meeker's forecast for the period ending in 2010 was the most optimistic, followed by that of Safa Rashtchy, the author of the U.S. Bancorp Piper Jaffray report.[12]

The author of *The Wall Street Journal* article laid out several possible scenarios that might support the optimistic revenue forecasts. The scenarios involved the growth rates of eBay's active users and the associated revenue per user. The author of the article, Nick Wingfield, interviewed Safa Rashtchy and asked him to consider whether his 30 percent revenue growth forecasts for eBay were unduly optimistic. He reports Rashtchy reacted by reconsidering his assumption that eBay could grow at a 30 percent compounded rate between 2002 and 2010.

The EBITDA for eBay for 2003 and 2004 turned out to be higher than Mary Meeker's April 2003 forecast. Analysts became increasingly optimistic until January 20, 2005, when eBay announced that it missed analysts' consensus earnings forecast

---

Debiasing for Better Decisions

Errors or biases: Misvaluing stocks.

Why does it happen? Managers and analysts rely on crude heuristics to measure fundamental value, use biased forecasts of future cash flows, and misframe free cash flows.

How does it happen? Managers and analysts find heuristics based on P/E, PEG, and price-to-sales to be simpler and more intuitive than DCF. Moreover, managers and analysts are prone to using cash flows that reflect biases stemming from excessive optimism and misframing.

What can be done about it? Managers and analysts can:

- Develop both the uses of free cash flows as well as the sources of free cash flow, ensuring that these are equal.

- Apply a variety of valuation techniques that are firmly grounded in textbook theory, in addition to crude ratio-based heuristics.

- Check for consistency in the application of heuristics, to ensure that a common set of assumptions underlies the various valuation techniques being applied.

---

by a penny a share. At the time Meg Whitman, eBay's CEO, indicated that future earnings would be lower because of higher advertising costs and reinvestment. In response to the announcement, eBay's stock price fell by 20 percent to $81 per share.

Thereupon, Safa Rashtchy downgraded his recommendation on eBay from "outperform" to "market perform," stating that the stock was priced for perfection. He also lowered his earnings estimate for 2005 by 5.3 percent, but maintained his target stock price of $101 per share.

2.7 AGENCY CONFLICTS

It is important to keep in mind that analysts face conflicts of interest. Analysts are not necessarily objective evaluators, but instead are agents of financial organizations that seek to do business with the firms being covered. In respect to Morgan Stanley, that point is prominently noted in a text box on the first page of Mary Meeker's report.

The managers of firms prefer favorable coverage from analysts to unfavorable coverage. Therefore, analysts whose firms seek to do business with the companies that analysts cover have an incentive to generate favorable reports. This agency conflict may induce analysts to be excessively optimistic about their forecasts of earnings and cash flows. The agency conflict might also induce analysts to view valuation heuristics as alternative instruments that can provide numbers they want to deliver. In other words, excessive optimism and the reliance on heuristics may have an agency conflict component as well as a behavioral component.

Summary

Heuristics and framing impact the way managers and analysts value firms. Indeed, most rely on valuation heuristics involving P/E, PEG, and price-to-sales more than they rely on the valuation techniques taught in finance courses.

Several factors contribute to the reliance on valuation heuristics instead of the fundamental valuation techniques taught in textbooks. Heuristics are simpler to use: P/E, PEG, and price-to-sales require very few variables and involve simple formulas. As such they are relatively intuitive. The DCF-based analyses taught in textbooks require far more detail than the heuristic techniques, involve more complex formulas, and are less intuitive.

Although the equations upon which valuation heuristics are based are identities that hold by definition, their application is frequently subject to bias. The sources of these biases stem from poor assumptions made in respect to inputs for P/E, PEG, and price-to-sales. Biases in traditional discounted cash flow valuation arise in connection with the cash flows themselves, for example, excessive optimism, or misframing, as is the case with the way free cash flows are defined.

Finally, analysts face agency conflicts. They need to manage relations with the managers of the firms they cover. Hence, they might choose valuation heuristics strategically, in order to arrive at numbers that will please managers.

Additional Behavioral Readings

Martin, J. and J. W. Petty, *Value Based Management*. Boston: Harvard Business School Press, 2000.

Montier, J., *Behavioural Finance*. West Sussex, UK: Wiley, 2002.

Rappoport, A. and M. Mauboussin, *Expectations Investing*. Boston: Harvard Business School Press, 2002.

Wingfield, N., "Stock of eBay Acts Like . . . eBay, But How Can Shares Stay Lofty? The Bullish Projections Assume Gigantic Rise in Online Shopping," *The Wall Street Journal*, April 23, 2003.

Key Terms

$1/n$ heuristic, *33*
P/E heuristic, *21*

PEG heuristic, *22*

price-to-sales heuristic, *22*

Explore the Web

www.ebay.com
The Web site for eBay contains financial information about the firm, as well as serving as a gateway to the firm's transaction services.

www.morganstanley.com
The Web site for Morgan Stanley has an interesting section where institutional investors can view sample reports.

www.palm.com
The firm PalmOne was formerly the hardware division of Palm Inc.

www.palmsource.com
The firm PalmSource was formerly the software division of Palm Inc.

Chapter Questions

1. Mary Meeker's price-to-sales valuation for eBay was premised on the same assumption as her P/E-based analysis. In both analyses, she assumed that eBay's earnings per share would grow to $2.26 in 2005. Meeker assumed that earnings were 2.2 percent of gross merchandise sales (GMS), thereby implying that earnings of $2.26 per share were associated with GMS per share of $103.88. Yet the P/E-based heuristic and price-to-sales based heuristic produce very different target values for eBay's stock. Discuss what the two heuristics have in common and what features lead them to produce different valuations.

2. In the spring of 2003, analysts at Prudential established a target price for eBay, justifying the P/E values in their analysis by appeal to PEG. Their report stated that their assumptions of a P/E of 75 to multiply 2003 earnings, and a P/E of 50 to multiply 2004 earnings

    . . . equates to P/E/G ratios of 1.5 and 1.0, respectively, which we believe are reasonable, compared with those of other growth companies. We note that the S&P 500 currently trades at approximately 16.5 times forward-year earnings, equating to a P/E/G ratio of 1.3.

   Discuss the reasoning of the Prudential analysts.

3. In her report, Mary Meeker used a PEG ratio of 1.5 and assumed that the required return on eBay stock was 12 percent. She also assumed that the firm plows back all of its earnings. Suppose that the present value of eBay's growth opportunities amounted to zero in April 2003. Use the traditional textbook approach to compute the intrinsic value of PEG, and compare it to the value in Meeker's report.

4. The column "Ahead of the Tape" that appeared in the February 13, 2004, issue of *The Wall Street Journal* states that prudent investors prefer to value firms using free cash flow instead of EBITDA. The article explains that the typical definition of free cash flow is cash flow from operations minus capital expenditure, not EBITDA minus capital expenditure. Discuss these comments.

5. Analyst Safa Rashtchy's developed his 2010 forecast for eBay's revenue by assuming that its annual growth would be about a 30 percent compounded annual growth rate between 2002 and 2010. In the previous year, eBay's revenue had grown at the rate of 62 percent, and the firm forecast that its revenue would increase by 58 percent in 2003. Which, if any, of the behavioral elements described in Chapter 1 might have affected Rashtchy's long-term forecast?

6. Consider the following excerpt from a Prudential report on Wal-Mart, dated May 13, 2003.[13] The report states:

    We are maintaining our Hold rating on Wal-Mart as we believe the stock's current valuation of 28 times our 2003 EPS estimate of $2.01 adequately reflects the company's 13% 5-year EPS growth rate . . . Wal-Mart is currently trading at 28.2 times our 2003 EPS estimate of $2.01, a 57% premium to S&P 500. This is not far from the retailer's five-year average high premium of 59%. The stock is also close to its 52-week high of $59.30, achieved in May 2002. It is difficult for us to envision investors paying an even larger premium, particularly for 13% projected growth. We believe the stock will continue to hover around a 55% premium to the market multiple or 27.9 times. Using this valuation and our 2003 EPS estimate of $2.01 yields a 12-month price target of $56, up from $55.

   Discuss the merits of the valuation technique mentioned in this excerpt, with reference to the contents of the chapter. Base your discussion on the following questions.

   - Is using a heuristic necessarily wrong in respect to valuation?
   - Do you think eBay is an anomalous case, and are there situations where the use of heuristics makes sense?
   - Is valuation part science and part art?
   - What advice would you give financial managers when it comes to valuing their firms?

Minicase

Palm Inc.

In 2000 the firm 3Com spun out its personal digital assistant division as Palm Inc. On February 23, 2001, the financial services firm Telerate reported the following information about Palm.

- The closing price for a share of Palm was $21.69.
- Palm had 565,946,000 shares outstanding.
- Its book value of equity was $1,110,640,000.
- It held $742,888,000 in cash.
- Its trailing P/E was 181.
- Palm was an all-equity financed firm and had no debt.

During a presentation to investors, Palm's CFO Judy Bruner was asked two questions. (1) What is Palm's cost of capital? (2) What is Palm's return on equity likely to be over the next several years? Palm's CFO responded by saying that she thought that the firm's cost of equity was 16 percent and that her best estimate for ROE was 26 percent per year for the next six years.

The length of the horizon during which the expected ROE exceeds the required return on equity is called the CAP (an acronym for competitive advantage period). Assume that Palm's managers plan to maintain its dividend payout ratio at zero for six years, the length of the CAP.

The CFO of Palm also remarked that in view of recent volatility in the price of Palm stock, her firm was trying to understand how the market values Palm, relative to the right factors to value Palm. Its current price of about $22 was below the offer price of $38 that prevailed when Palm had gone public a year earlier.

Palm's CFO indicated that she focused on trailing P/E and price-to-sales, noting that these may send conflicting signals. For example, she indicated that the market assigned Palm a high P/E ratio (145 at the time) but, relative to other firms such as Handspring, a low price-to-sales ratio (8 at the time). (In 2001, Handspring was a separate firm, which competed with Palm. Palm acquired Handspring in 2003. Subsequently, the firm split itself into two, becoming PalmOne and PalmSource.)

Case Analysis Questions

1. On the basis of the data presented in the case, use the textbook techniques to compute the fundamental value of Palm on February 23, 2001. The file *Chapter 2 answer template.xls* (available on the book Web site, **www.mhhe.com/shefrin**) is a spreadsheet that is set up along the lines of the textbook valuation of eBay's stock.

2. Compare the ratio of the fundamental value per share that you computed in the previous question to Palm's market price per share (for February 23, 2001).

3. Compare Palm's market P/E on February 23, 2001, with the fundamental P/E you derive.

4. Analyze the approach that Palm's CFO took in trying to ascertain whether or not Palm was fairly valued in February 2001.

Chapter **Three**

Capital Budgeting

The main objective of this chapter is for students to demonstrate that they can identify the manner in which biases and framing adversely impact managers' forecasts of project cash flows and their decisions about project adoption and termination.

After completing this chapter students will be able to:

1. Explain why managers who avoid discounted cash flow analysis are prone to select low-value projects over high-value projects.
2. Explain why overconfidence and excessive optimism lead managers to adopt negative net-present-value projects.
3. Explain why the combination of aversion to a sure loss, regret, and confirmation bias leads managers to continue failing projects when they should terminate those projects.
4. Distinguish between the remedies appropriate to agency conflicts and the remedies appropriate to behavioral biases.

3.1 TRADITIONAL TREATMENT OF CAPITAL BUDGETING

The traditional approach to capital budgeting emphasizes different criteria for assessing project cash flows, including the manner in which project risk is incorporated into the analysis. The most important criterion that academics recommend for deciding whether or not to adopt a project is net present value (NPV). In theory, NPV measures the incremental fundamental value the project would create for the firm's investors, were it to be adopted.

The starting point for obtaining the project discount rate is typically the firm's cost of capital, the expected return that investors require in order to hold the firm's long-term debt and equity. In theory, the cost of capital is estimated as a weighted average of its constituent components, where the weights are market values. In practice, managers confront a series of challenges in deriving appropriate discount rates. These challenges involve having to rely on asset pricing models to estimate the cost of equity and having to adjust the cost of capital to reflect differential project risk, taxes, and transaction costs.

A close cousin of NPV is the concept of internal rate of return (IRR). Any discount rate that leads a project's cash flows to have an NPV of zero is said to be an

IRR for the project. Some managers may use IRR in deciding whether or not to adopt a project. A typical decision rule is to accept a project if it has an IRR that is at least as high as the required return r. Notably, a project may have more than one IRR. This can happen when there is more than one change in sign in the project's expected cash flow stream.

Some firms use a payback rule to evaluate project proposals. The payback period is defined as the length of time it takes for the sum of future cash flows to cover the initial investment. Traditional textbooks are often critical of the payback rule, as it is not value-based.

3.2   SURVEY EVIDENCE

Much of the evidence presented in this chapter is taken from survey data. The major surveys used are described by Exhibit 3.1.

Project Adoption Criteria

What do financial managers generally say about the criteria that they use to guide their capital budgeting decisions? To answer this question, consider evidence based on a survey of chief financial officers (CFOs) who belong to the organization Financial Executives International (FEI).[1] The survey evidence[2] tells us that although corporate practice has been moving in the direction of textbook theory, the overall picture is mixed.[3]

The FEI survey asked financial managers how frequently their firms use a host of techniques when deciding which projects or acquisitions to pursue. The top two choices identified by survey respondents were IRR and NPV. Specifically, 75 percent of CFOs reported that their firms use IRR and 75 percent reported the use of NPV.[4] On a scale of 0 to 4, where 4 is very important, the mean responses associated with both IRR and NPV were about 3.1.

Interestingly, 57 percent of CFOs reported using the payback rule. Academics are quite critical of the use of the payback rule for at least two reasons. First, the payback rule does not involve discounting and therefore ignores the time value of money.[5] Second, the payback rule attaches zero weight to cash flows that arrive after the payback period. Some argue that the use of the payback rule is rational for firms that are severely capital constrained.

EXHIBIT 3.1   Main Surveys Used in This Chapter

Group Surveyed	Survey Conducted by	Issues Surveyed
1. Financial executives	L. Gitman and P. Vandenberg	Use of capital budgeting evaluation techniques
2. Financial executives belonging to FEI	FEI/Duke University	Use of capital budgeting evaluation techniques
3. Financial executives and risk managers	Financial Executives Research Foundation, FM Global, and National Association of Corporate Treasurers	Sources of risk to earnings
4. Software project managers	Standish Group	Budgets, schedules, and features in software projects

The FEI survey found that the payback rule is used by older, longer-tenure CEOs without MBA degrees. However, the survey also failed to find a relationship between the use of the payback rule and degree of leverage, credit rating, or dividend policy. In consequence, the survey authors conclude that the use of the payback rule stems from a lack of managerial sophistication.

The Importance of Intuition

As previously mentioned, financial executives report that they use NPV and IRR with equal frequency. However, in corporate executive surveys that have been conducted since 1977, IRR or some variant of return has been cited much more frequently than NPV. Notably, these surveys were essentially conducted in large firms.

Consider some examples. For years Sun Microsystems, the manufacturer of servers described in Chapter 1, based its capital budgeting decisions on a measure the company called RONABIT (return on net assets before interest and tax). Applied Materials, one of the largest manufacturers of semiconductor manufacturing equipment, bases its capital budgeting decisions on a return measure the company calls ROOPA (return on operating assets). Xilinx, one of the major manufacturers of programmable chips, bases its decisions on ROIC (return on invested capital).

Why was the payback rule the predominant capital budgeting criterion for so long, and why do return measures seem to have an edge over NPV, the criterion emphasized in traditional textbooks in corporate finance?

Comparing NPV, IRR, and the payback rule, the payback rule is the most intuitive of the three measures and NPV is the least intuitive. The basic idea underlying the payback rule is very straightforward: how long a period it takes for the cumulative project cash flows to cover the initial investment. Return measures such as IRR, RONABIT, ROOPA, and ROIC come next. Most people interpret IRR as the rate of return from investing in the project. This may or may not be correct, but most people generally have reasonable intuition about what rate of return means, as in interest earned on bank deposits.

The concept of NPV is much less intuitive. Managers rarely think of NPV as the incremental wealth that a project generates for investors. They instead think about NPV in terms of its defining formula, which is abstract and unintuitive for most. Indeed many managers think of a zero NPV project as mediocre, as if it was just breaking even profitwise, rather than earning a competitive return.

Comfort is important. As was mentioned, 25 percent of the participants in the FEI survey reported using neither NPV nor IRR. People are more comfortable relying on criteria that they find intuitive than on criteria they find harder to understand.

3.3   THE AFFECT HEURISTIC

The remainder of this chapter describes how capital budgeting decisions are susceptible to biases stemming from heuristics and framing. For example, Chapter 1 introduced the concept of the affect heuristic. Managers who rely on the affect heuristic base their decisions not only on financial analysis, but also on whether the

In 1987, some of the engineers at the electronics firm Motorola conceived of the idea of using a global satellite system to build a worldwide telephone network, thereby enabling customers to place and receive calls from anywhere in the world. The engineers proposed the project in a presentation to top executives at Motorola: Robert Galvin (the CEO), John Mitchell, and William Weisz.

The initial presentation took about two hours. The proposed global satellite mobile telephone project was very ambitious, requiring a capital investment of several billion dollars.

What was Motorola's CEO Robert Galvin's reaction? Did he find the proposal attractive? Did he ask for a DCF-based analysis in order to assess the net present value of the proposed project?

In Robert Galvin's own words, "with no further review, the three of us approved the project on that first sitting." They asked for no cash flow forecasts.

Therefore, no discounting. No NPV. No IRR. Not even a payback analysis.

In other words, Motorola's executives substituted subjective judgment for rigorous financial analysis.

The project led to the creation of a new firm, to be called Iridium, with Motorola as its principal investor. Iridium was neither a small-scale project, nor a short-term project. It required an investment of $5 billion over 11 years, before generating revenues, making it one of the largest private-sector projects in the world.

During the 11-year investment period, Iridium's engineers achieved several technical successes. In November 1998, Iridium began to offer phone service to customers in remote locations. Yet, to the chagrin of its investors, the project proved to be a commercial failure. Within a year, Iridium had filed for bankruptcy protection and was sold to private investors.

Source: H. Wolinsky, "Iridium Failure Brought Motorola Back Down to Earth," *Chicago Sun-Times,* September 25, 2003.

decision they propose making feels right emotionally. That is a major reason why many firms continue to rely on payback, even when they compute IRR and NPV. Indeed, some managers rely exclusively on the affect heuristic, even for major projects.

Choice, Value, and the Affect Heuristic

The Iridium example, in the above Behavioral Pitfalls box, illustrates the perils of relying on intuitive judgment when making capital budgeting decisions. People's intuition about choice and value are not always the same.

CONCEPT PREVIEW *Question 3.1*	Imagine a bingo cage containing 36 balls, numbered from 1 to 36. Consider two risky alternatives whose outcomes depend on the number on a single ball drawn from the bingo cage. A. If the number drawn is 29 or less, you win $20; otherwise you win $0. B. If the number drawn is 30 or more, you win $90; otherwise you win $0. 1. What is the maximum amount you would be willing to pay for the opportunity to face alternative A? 2. What is the maximum amount you would be willing to pay for the opportunity to face alternative B? 3. If you could only choose one of these alternatives, which one would you choose, A or B?

Decisions about capital budgeting involve choices about uncertain cash flows. In Concept Preview Question 3.1, you are asked to consider two alternatives where the amount you might win or lose is an uncertain cash flow. Psychological studies have used this question to investigate how people make decisions and assign value when the outcomes are risky. The major conclusion from these studies is that people rely heavily on the affect heuristic, and that doing so leads them to attach a lower value to the alternative they choose than the alternative they reject.

In Concept Preview Question 3.1, alternative B offers a higher expected payoff ($17.50) than does alternative A ($16.10). Many people, typically 40 percent, assign a higher **willingness to pay** (WTP) to the riskier alternative B than the safer alternative A. Notably, many respondents typically assign a lower valuation to the alternative they choose than the alternative they reject. Psychologists suggest that this phenomenon, called **preference reversal,** occurs because people use a different mental process to make a choice than they do to assess value (WTP). Specifically, when choosing between alternatives A and B, the chance of winning generates more of an emotional (affective) response than the amount won. However, when assessing value, the reverse is true: amount won generates more of an affective response than the chance of winning.[6]

One interesting study redid Concept Preview Question 3.1 and changed the $0 outcome in alternative B to a loss of 50 cents. Although counterintuitive, that change made alternative B a more attractive choice than alternative A, thereby reducing the degree of the preference reversal. The study concluded that the 50 cent loss served as a more striking contrast for the $90 win than did $0, thereby increasing the affective response attached to the $90.

What is the takeaway? Decisions about project adoption and termination involve risk. Managers who do not base these decisions on NPV, but instead rely on subjective judgment, are prone to preference reversal, meaning they are prone to selecting projects with lower values in place of projects with higher values.

willingness to pay
How much a person or group is willing to pay to acquire something.

preference reversal
Choosing low-value alternatives over high-value alternatives.

3.4   OVERCONFIDENCE

As well as being vulnerable to preference reversal, managers who substitute subjective judgment for rigorous financial analysis tend to be overconfident. The general point about overconfidence is that it leads managers to be surprised more frequently than they had anticipated. In respect to capital budgeting, overconfidence leads managers to underestimate project risk.

Psychological Determinants of Overconfidence

There are two main contributors to overconfident decisions about capital budgeting. The first is perceived control. The psychological evidence indicates that increased perceived control is associated with lower perceived risk. This relationship turns out to be particularly strong among white males. White males who perceive risks as lower than others tend to trust experts and engineers more than others, especially when it comes to making the proper decisions about managing the risks from technology. Coming back to Iridium, recall that Motorola's executives adopted the satellite project on the basis of one two-hour meeting with a group of engineers and insufficient analysis of the attendant risks.[7]

The second contributor to managerial overconfidence is inadequate planning and risk management. When it comes to risk, out of sight is typically out of mind. Therefore people become more confident when they themselves have to generate a list of risks as compared to the list being generated for them. This is an example of availability bias. The general point is that failure to engage in adequate risk planning leads to overconfidence.

Evidence of availability bias comes from a 2003 survey of risk managers and financial executives, jointly conducted by the Financial Executives Research Foundation, the insurance organization FM Global, and The National Association of Corporate Treasurers.[8] The study found that risk managers and financial executives do not share the same view about the hazards that affect the earnings of their firms. Risk managers are more familiar with insurable risks, such as property-related hazards, whereas financial executives are more familiar with hazards associated with improper management.

In 2003, risk managers viewed the top risk as being due to fire and explosion, whereas financial executives viewed the top risk as being related to improper management and employee practices. Risk managers favored property-related hazards over other hazards, with the corresponding weights being 70-30. In contrast, financial executives gave 50-50 (equal weights) to property-related hazards and other hazards.

Illustrative Example of Overconfident Capital Budgeting

In respect to the Iridium project previously discussed, Motorola's executives underestimated the risk associated with the number of customers. Iridium's target market consisted of business executives who engage in frequent international travel. Its potential customer base comprised about eight million people. Despite 1½ million inquiries from potential customers, its subscriber base turned out to be a mere 20,000. Why the low number? The answer involves a series of *four* surprises.

1. *Indoors/outdoors.* Engineers discovered that their phones worked outdoors, but not indoors. This technical difficulty was totally unanticipated.
2. *Cellular competition.* In 1987, cell phones were expensive and used by only a few technically oriented individuals. A decade later, when Iridium took its service to market, cellular phones had become widespread in the general population. Interviewed in 2003, Robert Galvin stated: "I did not anticipate that by the time the Iridium product would finally be able to present itself to the world that the cellular telephone business would be so pervasive."[9]
3. *Size.* Iridium's telephone could not be made to be as small as a cellular phone. Cellular phones could fit in the palm of a user's hand. Iridium's phone was as large as a hand and required a long antenna. Users of cell phones viewed Iridium's phone as inconvenient.
4. *Cost.* Iridium's phones sold for over $3,000 each. At the time, the price of a cellular phone was about $100. Moreover, Iridium charged high rates for airtime, between $4 and $10 per minute.

3.5   EXCESSIVE OPTIMISM IN CAPITAL BUDGETING

Excessive optimism leads managers to develop upwardly biased forecasts of project cash flows. Some people believe that cost overruns are routine in the public sector, but not the private sector. The bottom line is that excessive optimism is a systematic bias that pervades project analyses in both sectors. Next, we review the evidence.

Excessive Optimism in Public-Sector Projects

Cost overruns in the military certainly have a long history. A study published in 1966 found the following ratios of actual costs to forecasted costs for the following series of items: missiles (4.9), bombers (3.0), fighter planes (1.7), and cargo tankers (1.2).[10] Notably, cost overruns continue to occur in respect to military spending. A front page article in the February 1, 2005, issue of *The Wall Street Journal* reported that the military costs of operations in Iraq were three times higher than the original $60 billion estimate.

One need not look far for civilian examples of excessive optimism. Boston's central artery/tunnel project, called the "Big Dig," is known to be the most expensive highway project in the United States. The Big Dig was approved in 1985 for $2.6 billion, but as the project neared completion in 2005, the final cost turned out to be closer to $15 billion. The Denver airport opened in 1995 a year behind schedule. The major delay was caused by problems with the automated baggage-handling system and cost the city of Denver approximately $1 million per day. For transportation infrastructure projects, actual costs have, on average, been 28 percent higher than estimated costs, and costs have been underestimated on 9 out of every 10 projects.[11] Moreover, cost underestimation does not appear to have decreased over the past 70 years.

Excessive optimism also afflicts revenue forecasts. Actual passenger traffic on European rail projects has been, on average, 39 percent less than had been forecast.

Excessive Optimism in Private-Sector Projects

Many studies document overruns in the private sector, in terms of both costs and time to completion. Only 42 percent of large systems projects, lasting at least a year, come in on budget. And only 37 percent come in on schedule.[12] For example, the ratio of actual costs to forecasted costs, for research and development in new chemical entities by one particular pharmaceutical firm, was 2.25. In the case of a second such firm, the corresponding figure was 3.66 for projects requiring large or medium[13] technological advances.[14] Studies of the mining industry suggest that the net present value of the average mining project has been negative.[15] Of course, there are also exceptions to the general rule of cost overruns.[16]

When it comes to sales forecasts, the evidence is mixed. Some studies found that sales forecasts for new products tend to be systematically optimistic.[17] Yet at least one study in the pharmaceutical industry found that on average, actual sales exceeded forecasted sales.[18]

A dramatic example of excessively optimistic revenue forecasts involves the Channel Tunnel (the Anglo-French tunnel). In the opening year of the Channel Tunnel, traffic was one-fifth of what planners had forecast.[19] Between 1987 and June 2005 shares of Eurotunnel, the firm that operates the Channel Tunnel, lost more than 95 percent of their value. There is a strong possibility that the firm will face bankruptcy in 2007.

Software projects may not be especially capital intensive, but because of their intangible character they may be especially vulnerable to excessively optimistic forecasts. Indeed in 1988 the publication *Computing* contained an article whose title asked: "Why do so many projects still miss deadlines and bust budgets?"[20] The first sentence of the article provided the answer, citing excessive optimism as the culprit.

In respect to software and information technology failures, the excessive optimism described in 1988 persists. Consider three dimensions on which software projects are typically evaluated: (1) budget, (2) schedule, and (3) functions and performance.

One study that has been ongoing since 1993 reports the following: In respect to budget, for all projects in their survey, the average cost overrun was 2.89 of the original cost estimate in 1994, declining to 1.45 in 2000. In respect to schedule, the average time overrun was 3.22 of the original time estimate in 1994, declining to 1.63 in 2000. In respect to functions and performance, of the originally specified features and functions, 61 percent were available on the released project in 1994, increasing to 67 percent in 2000.[21] The 2004 survey update found that 84 percent of software projects feature cost overruns, and only 29 are successful in respect to all three of the preceding dimensions.

In reports to executives about the status of ongoing projects, the degree of optimism does not appear to be constant across projects that feature different degrees of risk. Notably, status reports for low- and medium-risk projects appear to be excessively pessimistic, not optimistic. However, the opposite holds true in respect to high-risk projects. For high-risk projects experiencing difficulty on two of the three evaluation criteria previously mentioned (budget, schedule, and functions and performance), the most probable status report received by executives is that the project is performing well on all three criteria.[22]

Consider the largest and most highly publicized software failures between 1988 and 1998.[23] A study focusing on these failures identified the top two causes of these failures. The top cause is "project objectives not fully specified," and this is closely followed by "bad planning and estimating." In respect to the latter, the study stated that the most common problem in building software systems is underestimating costs. Fifty-five percent of the failures documented in the study involved no risk management. Although survey respondents indicated that 38 percent did make use of risk management, half claimed that they did not use the risk findings once the project was under way.

Psychological Determinants of Excessive Optimism

Excessive optimism in capital budgeting is widespread, pernicious, and has many causes. Mitigating excessive optimism requires an understanding of these causes. The main culprits are described next.

Control

Perceived control affects the degree of optimism (as well as the extent of overconfidence). And managers do exert control in that information technology systems, airports, and tunnels result from managers' decisions. However, excessive optimism is a side effect of control.

Familiarity and Representativeness

familiarity
Essentially a form of availability bias, where available information is familiar information.

People are prone to be excessively optimistic when they have **familiarity** with a situation and are able to picture themselves as representative of a successful person in that situation. For example, in the Iridium project, Motorola's executives were very familiar with wireless telephone communication and viewed themselves as representative of winners in the telecommunications industry.

Desirability and Wishful Thinking

desirability
One of the factors contributing to excessive optimism, commonly understood to be wishful thinking.

A British partner in the accounting firm KPMG, who specializes in infrastructure and government projects, suggests that planners often take as their forecast the most optimistic case, instead of a case that lies between the most pessimistic case and the most optimistic case.[24] This is wishful thinking; the more the **desirability** of the outcome, the more optimistic people become.

Anchoring and Adjustment, the Conjunction Fallacy

Successful outcomes in capital budgeting projects take place when a series of successful events occur in conjunction. Therefore success probabilities are often obtained by multiplying a sequence of probabilities.

When asked to multiply a series of numbers together, people often multiply the first few numbers and then extrapolate.[25] However, doing so leaves them vulnerable to anchoring and adjustment. That is, people often become anchored on the product of the first two or three terms in the multiplication sequence and then adjust insufficiently. In the case of a probability sequence, anchoring and adjustment leads to success probabilities being overestimated. This overestimation is an example of **conjunction fallacy,** in that it pertains to the probability of an event that occurs as the conjunction of several sub-events.

conjunction fallacy
Miscalculating the probability of an event that is defined as the conjunction or simultaneous occurrence of a series of separate events.

Agency Conflict Determinants of Excessive Optimism

To be sure, psychologically induced bias provides only part of the explanation for excessively optimistic project forecasts. The private interests of managers, such as the desire to engage in empire building, also serve as contributing factors. These private-interest issues give rise to agency conflicts. Agency conflicts are as pertinent to public-sector projects as to private-sector projects. In the traditional textbook approach, compensation policy is viewed as the key to dealing with optimistic forecasts that are agency-based. However, psychologically induced optimism might not be as amenable to compensation-based remedies. Some of the following examples illustrate this point.

Some people hold the view that excessively optimistic project forecasts stem entirely from agency conflicts. For example, Bent Flyvbjerg, Mette Skamris Holm,

Debiasing for Better Decisions

Errors or biases: Preference reversal, overconfidence, excessive optimism.

Why does it happen? Reliance on the affect heuristic, perceived control, familiarity, representativeness, anchoring, desirability.

How does it happen? Perceived control predisposes managers to be both overconfident and excessively optimistic. Familiarity, representativeness, anchoring, wishful thinking, in combination with the substitution of intuition for financial analysis, accentuate this predisposition.

What can be done about it? Managers can differentiate between the **inside view** that focuses on project details and the **outside view** that emphasizes general success rates. Managers who adopt the outside view attempt to recall as many projects as they can, both at their firm and outside their firm, that are at a stage comparable to their projects. They then need to ask themselves the following questions:

- What proportion came in under budget, at budget, and over budget?
- What proportion came in ahead of schedule, on schedule, and behind schedule?
- How do we rank our abilities relative to other managers?
- How thorough have we been in preparing cash flow forecasts?
- Are our forecasts too bold?
- Given how able we believe ourselves to be relative to other managers, and given the general success rates, are our capital budgeting forecasts reasonable or are we instead being excessively optimistic and overconfident?

inside view

Taking a perspective on a project by focusing on the details specific to that particular project.

outside view

Taking a perspective on a project by comparing the characteristics of a specific project with a large population of projects which are similar in nature.

and Soren Buhl study transportation projects in Europe. They take the position that agency conflicts, not psychological factors, explain forecast bias, referring to the prevalence of these biases as "lying."

Others disagree. Consider the following response by Paul Morrell, a partner at Davis Langdon & Everest.

> It really annoys me when Flyvbjerg talks about lying. To tell a lie, you have to know the truth and subvert it. It's not as if people are working out the true cost of a project and then lying about it. I'm sure deceit is sometimes a factor—construction represents a sizeable chunk of human endeavour, so nobody, least of all a social scientist, should be surprised to find that it demonstrates every kind of human behaviour, from honest effort to outright villainy.

In a similar vein, John McCready, head of regeneration at the accounting firm Ernst & Young, stated: "I worked on the Channel Tunnel, and the forecasts were not cooked deliberately to make them too optimistic. The engineers designed the tunnels before they designed the trains, so later there were a lot of design changes for health and safety reasons."

What is the point? Managers who use incentives alone to deal with excessively optimistic cash flow forecasts, because they believe that optimism stems from agency conflicts alone, are likely to experience unpleasant surprises.

3.6 RELUCTANCE TO TERMINATE LOSING PROJECTS

Once projects are adopted, managers face subsequent decisions about whether to continue these projects or terminate them. What makes the follow-on decision especially important is the presence of excessive optimism. If excessive optimism is systematically at work in capital budgeting, then managers will undertake more negative net-present-value projects than they anticipate. As a result, they will have to face the question of whether to abandon failing projects more frequently than they anticipated.

Interestingly, although survey evidence shows that 97 percent of firms use cost-of-capital techniques to evaluate new projects, the same survey shows that only 73 percent do so when deciding whether or not to abandon existing projects.[26] However, the issue here is not whether firms use cost-of-capital techniques when deciding whether or not to abandon projects. The issue is whether firms make negative net-present-value decisions by delaying the decision to abandon failing projects.

Aversion to a Sure Loss

As in the discussion about project adoption, avoiding DCF and NPV analysis means that capital budgeting decisions involve subjective judgment. And subjective judgment leads managers to be vulnerable to behavioral biases. In the case of project termination decisions, the most important bias is aversion to a sure loss.

CONCEPT PREVIEW

Question 3.2

1. Suppose that you faced a situation where you had to choose between a sure loss of $7,400, and a risky alternative that featured a 75 percent chance to lose $10,000 and a 25 percent chance to lose nothing. Would you choose to accept the sure loss of $7,400 or choose the risky alternative? Yes or no?

2. Suppose that you had an opportunity to choose a risky alternative where there was a 25 percent chance you could win $7,400, but a 75 percent chance you would lose $2,600. Would you be willing to accept the risk? Yes or no?

As discussed in Chapter 1, breaking even is a key issue. In Concept Preview Question 3.2, part 1, both the risk-free alternative and the risky alternative are framed in the domain of losses. Most people are averse to accepting a sure loss and therefore choose the risky alternative in this situation.

However, suppose that the person who faces the choice described in Concept Preview Question 3.2, part 1, could come to terms with that loss. Coming to terms with the loss, psychologically, means that he or she treats the $7,400 as an irrelevant

sunk cost
An expenditure made in the past that is irrevocable.

sunk cost. Having done so, he or she then frames the question as between choosing a risk-free $0, or facing a 25 percent probability of a $7,400 gain and a 75 probability of a $2,600 loss.

Notice that this choice is exactly what Concept Preview Question 3.2, part 2, offers and that almost everyone rejects the risky alternative. Loss aversion typically

In 1946, Masaru Ibuka and Akio Morita founded Sony. In 1961, Sony began to develop a color television receiver based on the Chromatron picture tube. Ibuka led a two-year effort to develop a commercial prototype and process technology. By September 1964, Ibuka's team had succeeded in developing a prototype. However, they had not developed a commercially viable manufacturing process.

Ibuka committed Sony to mass-produce color television sets before his engineers had developed a cost-effective mass-production process. A chronicler of the events indicated that Ibuka alone was confident. He had the product announced and displayed in Sony's showroom. Consumer reaction was enthusiastic.

Sony invested in a new facility to house the production assembly. Ibuka announced that the color television would be Sony's top priority. He placed 150 people on its assembly line.

To Ibuka's chagrin, the production process yielded only two or three usable picture tubes per thousand produced. The retail price of Sony's color television set was $550, but the cost of production was more than double that amount. There was a sharp difference of opinion within the Sony leadership about the appropriate course of action. Morita wanted to terminate the project. However, Ibuka refused.

Sony continued to produce and sell Chromatron sets, eventually selling 13,000 sets, each one at a loss. In November 1966, Sony's financial managers announced that Sony was close to ruin. Only then did Ibuka agree to terminate the project.

Source: John Nathan, *Sony: The Private Life*. Boston: Houghton Mifflin Company, 1999.

leads people to choose a risk-free $0 over an expected loss of $100 ($= 0.25 \times 7,400 - 0.75 \times 2,600$). However, aversion to a sure loss leads them to choose an expected loss of $7,500 ($= 0.75 \times 10,000 + 0.25 \times 0$) over a sure loss of $7,400.

What are we to conclude? People who accept losses reset their reference point so that they no longer perceive the status quo to be in the domain of losses. As a result, loss aversion typically induces them to reject the actuarially unfair alternative, whereas aversion to a sure loss leads them to choose the actuarially unfair alternative.

Escalation of Commitment

escalation of commitment
The tendency to throw good money after bad.

There is research documenting that managers often put more money into a failure for which they feel responsible than into a success.[27] This phenomenon is known as the **escalation of commitment.** Apparently, decision makers who feel responsible for a failure are inclined to be more retrospectively oriented than those who were not responsible for a failure. Retrospective means that they search for evidence to confirm that their prior decision was a reasonable course of action.

Visibility

visibility
How salient a project or activity is to others.

One very important finding is that the size of the sunk cost does not alter the tendency of managers to be retrospective or to escalate the level of expenditure. However, the **visibility** of the decision that resulted in failure does impact both. In this respect, think about a manager like Masaru Ibuka. See Behavioral Pitfalls box above. He was seen as a champion for a project that was prone to being viewed as a highly visible failure. Someone in this position is likely to be especially retrospective.

Regret

regret

This emotion occurs when people imagine having taken a different decision than the one they actually took, one that would have turned out favorably rather than unfavorably.

After an unfavorable outcome that stems from a past decision, many people experience the emotion of **regret.** This emotion occurs when people imagine having taken a different decision than the one they actually took, one that would have turned out favorably rather than unfavorably. In order to avoid experiencing regret, many managers will put off terminating losing projects, so as not to have to admit to having made a mistake.

Agency Conflicts at Sony

The behavioral influences driving Ibuka's actions represented a threat to the wealth of Sony's other shareholders. Morita sharply criticized Sony's engineers for wasting money in order to indulge their own scientific curiosity, and encouraging Ibuka to pursue a nonprofitable technology. Tensions rose as Morita's planners and accountants began to attend brainstorming sessions that the engineers held to grapple with Chromatron's technical problems.[28]

Ibuka's reluctance to terminate the Chromatron project caused the wealth of Sony shareholders (including Morita) to be sacrificed to the desire of some managers to indulge their curiosity. The traditional manner in which to address the agency conflicts between managers and owners is to use equity in order to align the incentives of managers with shareholders. However, Masaru Ibuka was a Sony founder and major shareholder. Being rewarded as a major shareholder did not prevent him from succumbing to the sunk cost fallacy in his actions as a manager. There is no doubt that incentives are important. However, the Sony example illustrates that incentive effects by themselves do not eliminate the impact of behavioral elements. It is a mistake to believe that monetary incentives alone can mitigate behavioral bias.

3.7 CONFIRMATION BIAS: ILLUSTRATIVE EXAMPLE

Notably, over half of the publicized failures mentioned in Section 3.5 began to display serious symptoms during system development, and a quarter showed these symptoms during initial planning. Downplaying information about project problems is a form of confirmation bias. Consider an example from the pharmaceutical industry, presented in the Behavioral Pitfalls box on the next page.

Behavioral Bias and Agency Conflicts at Syntex

John Fried threw good money after bad, trying to beat the odds. And the odds of success are low to begin with. The Tufts Center for the Study of Drug Development reports that for every 5,000 medicines tested, 5 are tested in humans and 1 reaches the market. Between 1979 and 1991, the cost of developing a new drug rose from approximately $54 million (in 1976 dollars) to $231 million (1987 dollars).

Like Sony's Ibuka, Syntex's John Fried was a major shareholder in his firm. In addition, he was vice chairman. His financial interests were aligned with shareholders. Yet he decided to throw good money after bad in a losing project. As in the Sony case, the message here is that behavioral biases can dominate financial incentives.

Syntex Inc. was a pharmaceutical corporation that was registered in Panama in 1944 and headquartered in Palo Alto, California, until 1995, when it was taken over by Roche Holding Ltd.

In 1977, Gabriel Garay, a senior Syntex researcher with a Ph.D. in pharmacology, led a team that created a new drug, enprostil. Enprostil was designed to turn off production of stomach acid and thereby heal stomach ulcers.

At the time, approximately 23 million people worldwide had ulcer problems. Enprostil was conservatively forecast to generate sales of $50 million to $100 million a year. Syntex's managers hoped that these sales would help offset the expiration of the patent on its major product, Naprosyn, an anti-inflammatory drug. The patent for Naprosyn was due to expire in December 1993. At the time, Naprosyn accounted for half of Syntex's sales and more than half of its operating profit. This made the enprostil project highly visible.

After Syntex invested in the research-and-development phase of enprostil, researchers in Garay's laboratory found that enprostil tended to make blood platelets clot in the test tube, posing a possible risk of stroke or heart attack. An internal Syntex memo from Garay's laboratory warned that in intravenous form, enprostil could provoke a blood clot (thromboembolism) that was possibly crippling or even fatal. Moreover, independent researchers found that enprostil significantly increased damage caused from ingesting alcohol.

The decision maker who bore ultimate responsibility for the enprostil project was John Fried, the President of Syntex's research division and also the vice chairman of the corporation. Fried characterized Garay's memo as inflammatory, speculative, and irrelevant. He ordered that the memo be rewritten. In 1986, researchers reported that several dogs involved in some enprostil animal studies had died. Fried stated that he was not surprised by the dog deaths because the drug had been administered rapidly and because the tests had also used other chemicals.

In 1987, researchers reported having discovered the mechanism underlying enprostil, and that this mechanism was known to cause clotting and spasms in veins and arteries, thereby further raising the danger of possible strokes or heart attacks in patients. Fried commented that the enprostil team was going around in circles instead of going forward meaningfully. He expressed concern that their efforts were potentially wasting the FDA's time.

In February 1988, the FDA met with Syntex and told them that side effects made it unlikely enprostil could win broad market approval as a treatment for common ulcers. Shortly afterward, Syntex withdrew its application.

Sources: Marilyn Chase, "A Matter of Candor: Did Syntex Withhold Data on Side Effects of a Promising Drug?" *The Wall Street Journal,* January 8, 1991; Reproduced with permission of Dow Jones & Co Inc in the format textbook via copyright clearance center.

"Has Syntex Run Out of Steam? Wall Street Is Impatient with Sluggish Sales and Few New Products," *Business Week,* July 12, 1993. Reprinted by special permission from Business Week © 2003 by The McGraw-Hill Companies, Inc.

To be sure, firms also suffer from traditional agency conflicts, such as the consumption of perquisites. Syntex's 1992 proxy statement indicates that Paul Freiman, Syntex's CEO at the time, had received perquisites valued at $98,304, approximately 10 percent of his total compensation. These perquisites had tripled in value from the previous year. The financial press noted that Freiman had been making frequent personal trips to Brazil on Syntex's corporate jet. At the same time, he had been in the process of divorcing his wife of 36 years and appearing in public with a woman from Brazil.[29]

As a general matter, granting CEOs personal use of corporate aircraft destroys value. The stocks of firms that have granted this perquisite have underperformed the stocks of firms that have not granted this perquisite by 4 percent a year, a differential far in excess of the associated aircraft costs.[30] Instead the costs are more closely

Debiasing for Better Decisions

Errors or biases: Reluctance to terminate failing projects.

Why does it happen? Aversion to a sure loss, regret, and confirmation bias.

How does it happen? People become risk-seeking when facing the prospect of a sure loss. People experience regret, which makes it difficult for them to admit to having made a mistake. People also overweight information that confirms their views and underweight information that disconfirms their views.

What can be done about it? Managers can ask themselves particular questions, or ask others to ask them the following questions:

- Can I clearly define what would constitute success or failure for this project?
- Has my definition of what would constitute success or failure changed since the time the project began?
- Do I have trouble hearing other people's concerns about the project?
- Am I more concerned about the welfare of this project than I am about the organization as a whole?
- If I took over my job for the first time today and found that this project was under way, would I support it or terminate it?

correlated with the CEO's outside interests as measured, say, by long-distance golf club memberships.

In one respect, the actions of both Paul Freiman and John Fried caused the wealth of Syntex's shareholders to decline. In another respect, there is a significant difference between the two situations. The appropriate way to reduce agency conflicts of the sort associated with the actions of Paul Freiman is to correct the distortions in his compensation package. However, there are no compelling reasons to think that John Fried's actions were the result of distorted incentives.

Summary

Biases and framing adversely impact the behavior of managers when they formulate forecasts of project cash flows and make decisions about both project adoption and project termination. Managers who do not undertake discounted cash flow analysis for the purpose of capital budgeting are vulnerable to preference reversal, in that they select low-value projects over high-value projects. Overconfidence leads managers to underestimate project risk. Excessive optimism leads managers to establish cash flow forecasts that are upwardly biased. The combination of aversion to a sure loss, regret, and confirmation bias leads managers to continue a failing project when they should terminate the project.

Managers display excessive optimism for many reasons. Managers typically exaggerate the degree to which they can control events. They might establish forecast ranges but set expected cash flows at the top end of the range. If the success of a project depends on the conjunction of several events, then anchoring may lead managers to overestimate the probability of the conjoined event that defines success.

In forming their own judgments about project success, managers may become anchored on the forecasts of those proposing the project and fail to adjust sufficiently from that anchor.

These issues pertain to the inside view. Managers might be able to mitigate excessive optimism by adopting an outside view.[31] However, adopting an outside view does not come naturally to managers.

Behavioral impediments are not the same as agency conflicts. The remedy for agency conflicts involves the alignment of incentives between principal and agent. Behavioral phenomena need to be addressed using debiasing techniques.

Additional Behavioral Readings

Flynn, J., P. Slovic and C. K. Mertz, "Gender, Race, and the Perception of Environmental Health Risks," *Risk Analysis,* vol. 14, no. 6, 1994, pp. 1101–1198.

Graham J. and C. Harvey, "The Theory and Practice of Corporate Finance: Evidence from the Field," *Journal of Financial Economics,* vol. 60, nos. 2–3, 2001, pp. 187–243.

Lovallo D. and D. Kahneman, "Delusions of Success," *Harvard Business Review,* July 2003, pp. 56–60.

Slovic, P., M. Finucane, E. Peters and D. MacGregor, "The Affect Heuristic." In T. Gilovich, D. Griffen, and D. Kahneman (eds.), *Heuristics and Biases: The Psychology of Intuitive Judgment.* New York: Cambridge University Press, 2002.

Key Terms

conjunction fallacy, *46*	inside view, *47*	sunk cost, *48*
desirability, *46*	outside view, *47*	visibility, *49*
escalation of commitment, *49*	preference reversal, *42*	willingness to pay, *42*
familiarity, *46*	regret, *50*	

Explore the Web

www.standishgroup.com
The Standish Group is a consulting firm that conducts studies on the capital budgeting practices of various organizations and posts summary updates of its studies on its Web site.

csdd.tufts.edu
The Center for the Study of Drug Development at Tufts University posts key information associated with the development costs for new drugs.

faculty.fuqua.duke.edu/~charvey/Research/Working_Papers/W62_How_do_CFOs.pdf
This site contains an article entitled "How Do CFOs Make Capital Budgeting and Capital Structure Decisions?" by John Graham and Campbell Harvey. The article was published in the *Journal of Applied Corporate Finance,* volume 15, number 1, Spring 2002.

Chapter Questions

1. Despite the growing popularity of cellular phones during the middle and late 1990s, Iridium undertook a $180 million promotional campaign to launch its product. It ran advertisements in *The Wall Street Journal, Fortune* magazine, and 37 airline magazines. It also launched a major direct-mail campaign in 20 markets and in 20 languages. Discuss any behavioral issues associated with Iridium's promotional expenditures.

2. In 1999 Iridium declared bankruptcy and was sold to private investors. Suppose that you were to learn that by the end of 2003, Iridium had gone out of business. How surprised would you be? How would you imagine that the events surrounding Iridium's liquidation

took place? Now suppose instead that you were to learn that by the end of 2003, Iridium had turned cash flow positive. How surprised would you be? How would you imagine that the events surrounding Iridium's turnaround took place?

3. Consider Robert Galvin's approach to evaluating the satellite project proposal. The text suggests that in not developing discounted cash flow analysis, Galvin's approach was flawed. In hindsight, Iridium was a failed project for Motorola, and even positive NPV projects can turn out to be failures after the fact. Can you provide a critique of the behaviorally based argument and suggest some reasons why in foresight it might have been entirely rational for Robert Galvin to have proceeded in the way that he did?

4. Consider the contention that excessive optimism and overconfidence are important characteristics of leadership. Might these traits help managers initiate and complete daunting projects that they would otherwise reject or abandon? Discuss this contention.

5. Consider the responses to a survey conducted of geologists working in the mining industry.[32] The survey put the following question to the geologists: "If an economic deposit was discovered tomorrow, how many years would pass before it could be put into production? Consider only typical problems, planning permission, objections, engineering studies, etc." In responding, the geologists provided a range, from 5 to 10 years. Historically, the typical project has taken 10 years. Discuss whether the geologists' responses exhibit any behavioral biases.

6. One of the points made in the discussion about the construction of the Anglo-French tunnel is that engineers designed the tunnels before they designed the trains, so there were many design changes because of health and safety. Are there any behavioral issues associated with these design changes?

Additional Resources and Materials for Chapter 3 Are Available at www.mhhe.com/shefrin

Minicase

CompuSys

In the early 1980s, the manufacturing division of CompuSys, a large computer company, began to develop an expert system called Config.[33] Config was designed to help the company's sales representatives produce error-free configurations prior to providing price quotations. Traditionally, configuration errors had been causing significant problems for the firm's sales representatives. Hopes ran high among the project's leaders, Tom Jones and George Smith, who planned to base Config on one of their earlier successful projects called Verifier.

Jones and Smith invited a small group of sales representatives to join the project team. Between November 1981 and January 1982 this group experimented with a prototype of Config and registered a series of complaints. They pointed out that Config did not integrate with the system that salespeople normally used to prepare price quotations, that it was slow, and that it was not user-friendly.

Jones and Smith promised to address these complaints and have Config operational in sales offices during 1983.

In 1982 the project team prepared a discounted cash flow analysis that indicated a net present value of $43.9 million (20 percent discount rate) for the five-year period FY82–FY86. Operating and development costs for the project were projected at $10.4 million between FY82 and FY86.

At the end of 1983, Config was still not operational in the firm's sales offices. Sales representatives involved in the project complained vigorously that the engineers had not responded to their complaints. Yet engineers on the team continued to be enthusiastic. The project team agreed to continue with the project and move forward with a full-scale implementation of Config. In 1985, the project engineers finally managed to link Config and the price quotation system used by the sales representatives. However, those representatives who used the system found it more time consuming to produce price quotes than the representatives who did not use the system.

Notably, a second financial analysis was undertaken in 1985, and it showed the net present value of Config to be $55.7 million, discounted at 20 percent, for the five-year period FY85–FY89.

Retrospectively, CompuSys executives described the reactions of Tom Jones and George Smith:

> When we have done surveys of people in the field, the information we got wasn't what Jones and Smith wanted to hear, but their denial has been so powerful. Their response has been: "Wrong answer, we don't like that answer." They never listen to negative feedback. When I approach Smith with negative feedback from the field, he gets defensive about it. He says: "Well, that's hearsay." So we have to go out and conduct additional surveys. Sometimes he asks us to go back and survey the same individuals again, and even if the information is still negative, Jones and Smith find some way to put a positive spin on it.

A third financial analysis conducted in 1987 indicated that the net present value of Config was at least $41.1 million for the five-year period FY87–FY91.

By 1990, Config had yet to catch on with the sales force. Many executives outside of manufacturing were arguing that Config should be abandoned. The following remarks were typical:

> I wrote three whistle-blowing memos to three vice presidents. I couldn't stop it. It was a sacred cow project.

> There were some very strong champions inside. My arguments fell on deaf ears.

> I pointed out that based on the usage patterns, I didn't think anybody would miss Config very much if we fumed it off tomorrow.

If CompuSys has spent millions on this project, we have really missed the boat. I argued that we should pull the plug on this effort immediately.

> The people responsible for developing Config are trying to breathe life into something that should be allowed to die. We have proof today that Config is not successful. It has failed miserably. The problem is nobody is willing to kill it.

On the other side, one manager who had been on the project team since its inception argued for its continuation, saying: "I don't think we want to get rid of Config. I don't want to just throw out 10 years of work."

In 1992, Tom Jones died, and George Smith left CompuSys. A new vice president evaluated the Config project and concluded: "What are we doing? We're spending a lot of money on something that nobody really wants. Stop." And so the project was terminated. Subsequently, managers provided their impressions about why Config had been adopted and why it continued. One manager stated:

> What I saw were Jones and Smith building upon a previous success with the Verifier project and saying we can hit that home run again. I think it was a combination of optimism which you could call undue or not and a sense that this was a new technology that we were applying to this problem and that experimenting with it could yield the results that we wanted even if we couldn't see them in front of us at the moment. So there was a kind of technological optimism.

A second manager offered the following view:

> Even though we sometimes got a cold reception from Sales, it continued to be funded anyway as an R&D project. As long as Tom Jones was in charge, Config never got reviewed. It didn't get into the official budget review process until 1992. Senior management had developed so much faith in the technology that they continued to fund it regardless of what the data said.

Case Analysis Questions

1. Draw up a list of the behavioral features you perceive in the case of Config, and indicate where in the case these features occur. If you perceive there to be multiple occurrences of a particular feature, list each occurrence separately.

2. Discuss any parallels between the case of Config and examples described in the chapter.

Chapter **Four**

Perceptions about Risk and Return

The main objective of this chapter is for students to demonstrate that they can identify the manner in which managers, investors, and analysts perceive the relationship between risk and return.

After completing this chapter students will be able to:

1. Identify managers' perceptions about the characteristics that underlie risk and return.
2. Explain why heuristics based on affect and representativeness lead managers and investors to associate higher expected returns with lower risk.
3. Analyze how representativeness leads managers, investors, and market strategists to form biased judgments about the market risk premium.
4. Describe conditions under which the heuristic "one discount rate fits all" destroys value.

4.1 TRADITIONAL TREATMENT OF RISK AND RETURN

In the traditional approach to corporate finance, managers rely on a combination of financial theory and data to arrive at discount rates in order to discount project cash flows and value the securities issued by their firms.

The typical starting point for the analysis of risk and return is the capital asset pricing model (CAPM), which provides a theory for determining the expected return that investors require in order to hold a security. Underlying the CAPM is the notion that investors are risk averse and require compensation in the form of a risk premium for bearing risk. In this respect, the beta of an individual stock measures the amount of risk that justifies compensation in the form of a higher expected return. The main tenet of the CAPM is that the risk premium on a stock is the product of beta and the market risk premium. For individual stocks, this tenet can be expressed in terms of a graph known as the *security market line*. The security market line features a positive linear relationship between beta on the x-axis and expected security return on the y-axis.

Between 1926 and 2000, stocks returned about 13 percent per year, 9.1 percent more than the return on investing in treasury bills. The 9.1 percent figure serves as the starting point for estimating the market risk premium. There is no uniformly accepted estimate for this premium. For example, textbook authors Richard Brealey, Stewart Myers, and Franklin Allen express their opinion in the form of a range, believing the market risk premium lies between 6 and 8 percent.[1] The range suggested within the academic literature, including textbooks, is even wider: −10 percent to 20 percent. Not surprisingly, surveys that financial economists have conducted reveal considerable disagreement about the magnitude of the market risk premium.[2]

The CAPM provides one theory for determining required returns. The CAPM features a single factor to measure risk, the market premium. A more general theory uses several factors to determine required returns. Other examples of factors besides the market premium relate to market capitalization (size), the ratio of book-to-market equity, and momentum. For example, the Fama-French model includes three factors: the market return, a factor reflecting the differential performance of the stocks of small cap firms to the stocks of large cap firms, and a factor reflecting the differential performance of value stocks to growth stocks. Empirical analysis shows that realized returns have been higher for small-capitalization stocks than for large-capitalization stocks. Stocks that feature low book-to-market equity are called growth stocks. Stocks that feature high book-to-market equity are called value stocks. Empirical analysis shows that historical returns have been higher for value stocks than for growth stocks. Empirical analysis has also shown that short-term historical returns have been higher for recent winners than for recent losers.

4.2   RISK AND RETURN FOR INDIVIDUAL STOCKS

In the traditional textbook approach to capital budgeting, managers use a single factor model such as the CAPM or a multifactor model as the basis for establishing discount rates. In practice, managers rely on a variety of techniques that include the traditional approach but also include heuristic techniques that leave them vulnerable to bias. This section describes the biases that stem from reliance on representativeness and the affect heuristic. In order to study these biases, consider the following example.

Example

Intel and Unisys are two technology firms. In April 2000 Intel was the world's largest manufacturer of microprocessors and one of the most prominent manufacturers of computer chips. Unisys specialized in large-scale business applications technology.

Consider how these two firms compared in terms of the various characteristics associated with long-run return performance. Exhibit 4.1 provides summary data about beta, market value of equity, book value of equity, the ratio of book-to-market equity, retained earnings, past returns, and past sales growth for the two firms.

In April 2000, analysts were predicting that Intel would announce increased earnings and sales, with sales increasing by as much as 10 percent from the $7.1 billion level achieved a year earlier. Unisys had just announced that revenue in the first quarter declined to $1.66 billion from $1.81 billion a year earlier.

EXHIBIT 4.1
**Comparison Data for
Unisys and Intel**

Note: Data are for April 2000.
Source: Center for Research in
Security Prices and Compustat.

	Unisys	Intel
Beta	1.33	1.04
Market value of equity ($ billions)	$8.003	$441.860
Book value of equity ($ billions)	$2.088	$36.103
Book-to-market equity	0.26	0.08
Balance sheet retained earnings ($ billions)	($1.62)	$25.22
Prior 6 month return	−67.6%	215.6%
Prior 1 year return	92.8%	222.3%
Prior 3 year return	60.2%	56.2%
Past 5 year growth rate of sales	0.8%	21.2%

**CONCEPT
PREVIEW**

Question 4.1

- On a scale of 0 to 10 how would you rate the quality of Unisys as a company, where 0 is worst and 10 is best?
- On a scale of 0 to 10 how would you rate Unisys in terms of financial soundness, where 0 is insolvent and 10 is solid as a rock?
- On a scale of 0 to 10 how would you rate Unisys' stock in regard to long-term investment value, where 0 is no value and 10 is extremely high value?
- What percentage rate of return would you expect to earn on Unisys' stock if you purchased it in April 2000 and held it for one year?
- On a scale of 0 to 10, where 0 is risk-free and 10 is extremely speculative, how would you rate the riskiness of Unisys' stock?
- Having answered these questions for Unisys, go back and answer them for Intel.

Risk, Representativeness, and Bias

Consider a manager who relies on the representativeness-based heuristic "stocks of good companies are representative of good stocks." How would such a manager use this heuristic to answer Concept Preview Question 4.1?

A manager who relied on representativeness would judge that Intel is a better company than Unisys. Why? Because Intel's products are everywhere, changing the world in ways that are obvious. The same cannot be said for Unisys' products. Over the prior five years, Intel's sales had grown much more rapidly than those of Unisys. Intel was a large firm. Its book value of equity principally consisted of retained earnings, the reflection of past earnings gains. Unisys had a much smaller market capitalization than Intel. Its book value of equity featured large negative retained earnings, the reflection of past losses. Of the two companies, Intel appeared to be more financially sound.

Managers who rely on representativeness to judge stocks would judge the stock of Intel to be a better stock than that of Unisys. This means that managers would say that Intel's stock offered better long-term investment value than Unisys' stock. What does *better value* mean?

Presumably better value means either higher expected returns, or lower risk, or both. Managers who rely on representativeness will be inclined to expect higher returns from better stocks. In this respect, Intel's stock had earned a much higher return than Unisys' stock over the prior year and had performed almost as well over the prior three years.

As to risk, managers who rely on representativeness will be inclined to view the stocks of financially sound companies as safe stocks and the stocks of companies that are not financially sound as risky stocks. As a result, managers who rely on representativeness will be inclined to view Intel as a safer stock than Unisys.

Taking the previous two paragraphs together, consider this question. Do managers expect higher returns from safer stocks? Traditional finance teaches that risk and return are positively related, that higher expected returns are associated with higher risk. Representativeness induces managers to view the relationship as going the other way.

Evidence That Executives Rely on Representativeness

Consider evidence that managers judge the stocks of good companies to be representative of good stocks. Every year since 1982, *Fortune* magazine has surveyed executives about corporate reputation.[3] The *Fortune* survey consists of eight questions, of which three are of special interest. These three survey questions ask about (1) the quality of the company's management, (2) the long-term investment value of its stock (LTIV), and (3) the financial soundness of the company.

In effect, quality of management can be understood as a proxy for the goodness of the company, while long-term investment value can be understood as a proxy for the quality of the company's stock. Using these proxies and comparing the responses to these two questions enables us to test the hypothesis that managers judge that good stocks are stocks of good companies. For the responses to the actual *Fortune* survey, the correlation coefficient turns out to be 90 percent. The high degree of correlation constitutes evidence that managers judge the stocks of good companies to be good stocks.

Notably, the correlation coefficient between quality of management and financial soundness is 85 percent. In other words, managers judge good companies to be safe companies. As for the company's stock, the correlation coefficient between LTIV and financial soundness is 91 percent, suggesting that managers also judge good stocks to be the stocks of financially sound companies.

Most respondents to the *Fortune* magazine survey are executives who are asked to rate companies in their own industry. The executives' responses indicate that they view good stocks to be the stocks of good companies, and good companies to be safe companies. That is, the responses of executives feature the classic hallmarks of representativeness.

Sign of Relationship between Risk and Return

The *Fortune* magazine survey does not ask executives for their assessments of risk and their expectations about future returns. In order to elicit direct information about risk and return, a small supplementary survey has been administered to separate groups of managers and investors. The supplementary survey has been run annually since 1997. It includes the same questions asked in the *Fortune* magazine survey, but adds the direct questions about risk and return that appear in Concept Preview Question 4.1. As in the regular *Fortune* survey, each participant in the supplementary survey is asked to make judgments about 8 to 10 stocks. Notably, Intel and Unisys are among the stocks included.

Even though the participants in the supplementary survey are not participants in the *Fortune* magazine survey, the responses from the supplementary survey are typically close to the responses in the survey conducted by *Fortune* itself. This statement even holds for the survey results that *Fortune* does not report when it publishes its list of most admired companies in America. This means that the *Fortune* survey results are replicable.

What do we learn from the additional questions in the supplementary survey, the questions that ask directly about risk and return? We learn that managers judge the relationship between risk and return to be negative. They expect higher returns from safer stocks. Year after year, only a few respondents provide return expectations that are positively correlated with their risk assessments. For example, in respect to Unisys and Intel, few respondents assign a higher expected return to the stock they judged to be riskier.

Recall that a cornerstone principle of the CAPM is that expected return is positively related to risk, where risk is measured by beta. To be sure, the variable used in the supplementary survey to measure risk is not as precise as the return standard deviation or beta. In a way, this is a benefit, in that it allows respondents to factor in whatever variables they feel determine risk. At the same time, the risk variable is arbitrary. For this reason, consider the relationship between expected return and beta. The graph of expected return against beta is called the security market line.

Those who participate in the supplementary study are provided with financial data about the firms in question. These data include the beta of each firm's stock. Plotting the average expected returns against beta and fitting a straight line reveals a relationship that is decidedly negative. Exhibit 4.2 displays a typical estimate of the perceived security market line.

Exhibit 4.2 displays actual responses from a group of respondents who were surveyed in the autumn of 2004, along with a regression fitted to their responses. This group completed Concept Preview Question 4.1 for 10 firms that included Unisys and Intel. Notably, these respondents were all finance professionals. On average, they judged that Intel was a better firm than Unisys, and that relative to Unisys stock, Intel stock offered higher long-term investment value, a higher expected return, and lower risk.[4]

The Affect Heuristic

Psychologists have found that the tendency to view risk and reward as being opposite is a general phenomenon.[5] They suggest that people form emotional impressions of activities, where impression reflects degree of goodness, or affect. Having a positive affect connotes something that is good, whereas having a negative affect connotes something that is bad.

EXHIBIT 4.2
Expected Return versus Beta

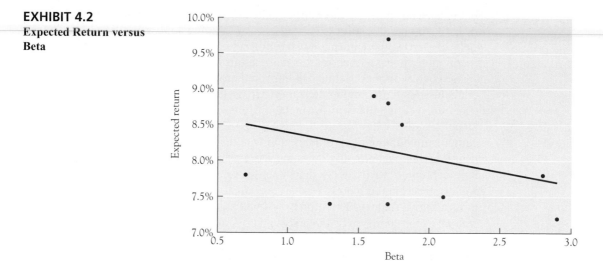

Evidence suggests that in their minds, people assign affective labels or tags to images, objects, and concepts. These tags exert a strong influence on their decisions. Moreover, imagery is important, in that the strength of affective responses typically depends on the sharpness of the mental image. That might explain why during the dot-com bubble in the late 1990s, managers who changed the names of their firms to feature the "dot.com" phrase saw an immediate increase in the price of their firms' stocks.[6]

Managers form opinions of companies, as in the case of *Fortune* magazine's corporate reputation score. In terms of affect, the most admired company has the highest positive affect. As was discussed in Chapter 1, people often use an affect heuristic, basing their decisions on affect rather than explicit analysis.

Heuristics, Biases, and Factors

Evidence from the *Fortune* magazine corporate reputation survey, along with the supplement that includes direct questions about risk and return, suggests that executives use heuristics to assess risk and return. The heuristics rely on a combination of representativeness and affect and predispose executives to bias.

The affect heuristic is a mental shortcut that people use to search for benefits and avoid risks. Benefits are associated with positive affect, whereas risks are associated with negative affect. Because of its unidimensional feature, reliance on affect leads to a negative relationship between benefits and risks. As a result, affect and representativeness reinforce each other when it comes to risk and return. Both lead managers to view the relationship between risk and return as being negative.

Consider the factors related to size and book-to-market equity that play central roles in the traditional Fama-French three-factor framework. Analysis of executives' responses to both the *Fortune* magazine survey and the supplementary survey reveals that executives associate low book-to-market equity and high market capitalization to both good stocks and good companies. And they do so consistently, year after year.

That is, executives judge large firms to be good firms. Executives judge firms with low book-to-market equity to be good firms. In doing so, executives also judge the stocks of large firms featuring low book-to-market equity to be good stocks.

Executives expect stocks associated with low betas, large market capitalization, and low book-to-market equity to earn higher returns than stocks associated with high betas, small market capitalization and high book-to-market equity. Yet the evidence suggests that the empirical relationships go the other way. That is, executives' perceptions display bias.

Interestingly, evidence from the supplemental survey does suggest that executives view stocks associated with low betas, large market capitalization, and low book-to-market equity to be less risky than stocks associated with high betas, small market capitalization, and high book-to-market equity. These associations are in accordance with traditional theory. Therefore, the major bias associated with executives' perceptions would appear to be that they view risk and return as being negatively related to each other. In this regard, executives strongly associate higher long-term investment value with safer stocks: the correlation coefficient between risk and LTIV is about −90 percent. Executives also associate LTIV positively with expected return, but the strength of the relationship is weaker than it is with perceived risk.

Analysts' Return Expectations

Consider the security analysts whose job it is to forecast future earnings and target prices for stocks. Like executives, analysts' expectations of future stock returns (implied by the target prices they establish) appear to be related to beta, size, and book-to-market equity.[7] Do analysts perceive the relationship between risk and return differently from executives? The answer is yes, they do.

The data used to answer the last question come from two sources, First Call and Value Line. The firm First Call Corporation collects the daily commentary, earnings forecasts, target prices, and stock recommendations of security analysts, portfolio strategists, and economists at major U.S. and international brokerage firms.[8] Data pertaining to analysts' one-year return expectations for the study discussed here come from First Call and were collected between November 1996 and December 2001. Data pertaining to analysts' three-year return expectations were based on *The Value Line Investment Survey.*[9]

What do these data tell us? Unlike executives, analysts expect high-beta stocks to earn higher returns than low-beta stocks. That is, analysts treat the relationship between beta and expected return as being positive. The scatter plot in Exhibit 4.3 is the counterpart to the plot displayed in Exhibit 4.2, with one exception: The responses in Exhibit 4.3 are from analysts who cover the technology sector containing the stocks in question. Notice that these analysts generally perceive the relationship between expected return and beta to be positive.[10]

Holding beta constant, analysts also expect smaller-capitalization stocks to earn higher returns than larger-capitalization stocks. In contrast, executives rate large-capitalization stocks higher than small-capitalization stocks in terms of long-term investment value.

What about book-to-market equity? On this dimension, the evidence on one-year expectations actually suggests that analysts behave like executives. Analysts expect

EXHIBIT 4.3
Expected Return versus Beta

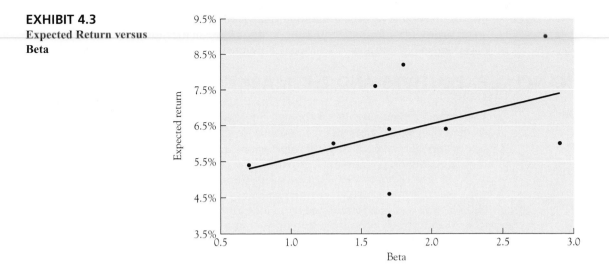

growth stocks to earn higher returns than value stocks, or at best to perform about as well. In this respect, analysts' return expectations are the mirror opposite of the historical pattern for realized returns.

Excessive Optimism and Agency Conflicts

The average return expectation in the First Call data is 26 percent, double the value associated with Value Line. The analysts tracked by First Call appear to be excessively optimistic. Why? Most of the analysts tracked by First Call face agency conflicts. The financial firms they work for would like to do business with the companies they follow. Because companies like favorable coverage, analysts have an incentive to

Debiasing for Better Decisions

Errors or biases: Managers misjudge the relationship between risk and return.
Why does it happen? Combination of reliance on representativeness and affect heuristic.
How does it happen? Managers view the stocks of good companies as representative of good stocks and associate positive feelings with these companies. Good companies feature both high returns and low risk. Therefore in considering the stocks of firms one by one, they tend to rate stocks of good firms as featuring both high future returns and low risk.
What can be done about it? After providing judgments of risk and return on a stock-by-stock basis, compare stocks on a relative basis to elicit the implied risk-return relationship. Many managers hold the general belief that risk and return are positively related to each other. However, they do not frame their judgments transparently enough to ascertain whether those judgments feature risk and return being positively related or negatively related.

produce favorable reports. In addition, analysts depend on the managers of firms they cover to provide information. In sum, analysts have an incentive to provide favorable coverage, in order to curry favor with corporate managers.

4.3 FINANCIAL EXECUTIVES AND THE MARKET RISK PREMIUM

Most managers and investors form their impressions of market risk and return based on their own experiences and their own sense of market history. Few regularly consult historical market data. What impressions do managers and investors generally form about market movements?

CONCEPT PREVIEW *Question 4.2*	The S&P 500 was first formulated as an index in 1926. Consider the 78-year period from 1926 through 2004. Define an up-year as a year when the total return on the S&P 500 was positive. Define a down-year as a year when the total return on the S&P 500 was zero or less. Without consulting historical data, write down your best responses to the following three questions: 1. For what fraction of the years 1926 through 2004 was the total return on the S&P 500 positive? 2. Focus on the years that followed an up-year. Some were up-years, and some were down-years. What fraction corresponded to up-years? 3. Focus on the years that followed a down-year. Some were up-years and some were down-years. What fraction corresponded to up-years?

The S&P 500 goes through periods that are bull markets and periods that are bear markets. Is the S&P 500 "hot" during a bull market and "cold" during a bear market? If the market is truly hot during a bull market, then the S&P 500 is more likely to have an up-year next year if last year was up. Similarly, if the market is truly cold during a bear market, then the S&P 500 is more likely to have a down-year next year if last year was down. On the other hand, if these probabilities do not depend on past outcomes, then past performance provides no guide to future performance.

The S&P 500 featured a positive return in approximately two out of three years during the period 1926–2004. Moreover, two-thirds of the time an up-year followed an up-year. Similarly, two-thirds of the time an up-year followed a down-year. In other words, the probability with which an up-year occurred was approximately two-thirds, regardless of whether the prior year was an up-year or a down-year.

The bottom line is that for annual returns, the S&P 500 did not experience hot and cold periods, even though it did give rise to bull markets and bear markets.

Die-Rolling

The occurrence of up- and down-years for the S&P 500 is akin to die-rolling. Imagine that your professor rolls a die. If the die turns up 3 through 6, you win $1. However, if the die turns up 1 or 2, you lose $1. Therefore, the probability of winning $1 is two-thirds, and the probability of losing $1 is one-third.

Imagine that you play this game and win $1 five times in a row. Call this a streak (or run) of five. Are you on a hot streak? What is the probability that you will win $1 the next time? Is it two-thirds, or is something different from two-thirds?

The answer is that the probability of winning $1 is two-thirds, the same as the situation if you had lost $1 five times in a row. The past outcome offers no guidance to future performance.

If you were to play the roll-a-die game just described, you would experience long streaks when you would win and long streaks when you would lose. On average, the longest winning streak turns out to be eight, and the longest losing streak turns out to be four. If you counted the number of times a win was followed by a loss, and a loss was followed by a win, the average number would be about 37. On average the number of streaks for the die-rolling game is about 37, and its standard deviation is about 4.5.

It is striking to see how closely the up-years and down-years for S&P 500 returns resemble die-rolling. The S&P 500 exhibited 37 streaks during the period 1926–2004. The longest streak of up-years occurred between 1982 through 1989 inclusive and was eight years. This may surprise some people, because that interval contains 1987, the year the stock market crashed. However, 1987 was an up-year for the S&P 500 overall, in that it returned 2 percent (including the dividend yield). The longest streak of down-years occurred from 1929 through 1932 inclusive, a streak of four years. In short, the pattern of up-years and down-years in the annual returns to the S&P 500 is absolutely typical of die-rolling.

Extrapolation Bias: The Hot-Hand Fallacy

base rate information
Information pertaining to the general environment.

singular information
Unique information directly related to a situation or object.

extrapolation bias, or the hot-hand fallacy
Unwarranted extrapolation of past trends in forming forecasts.

Most people do not think of S&P 500 annual returns as being analogous to rolling a die. Most people are unaware of the historical statistics just described. Historical statistics constitute examples of what psychologists call **base rate information.** Base rate information is typically abstract and not readily available. Therefore most people base their judgments about risk and return on information that is more available, such as recent events. Psychologists call this type of information **singular information.**

Psychologists suggest that people who overweight recent events are prone to extrapolating recent trends when forming forecasts. Therefore, during a bull market such people will expect high returns from stocks. During a bear market, they will expect low returns from stocks. If such extrapolation is unwarranted, the resulting bias is called **extrapolation bias.** Another name for extrapolation bias is the **hot-hand fallacy,** a term arising from basketball.

Some people who rely on representativeness identify the environment for which recent events are representative as being the underlying environment. During a bull market, people believe that the environment is one in which stock prices naturally go up. During a bear market, people believe that the environment is one in which stock prices naturally go down.

When the true environment is like the die-rolling game, people who are prone to extrapolation bias will make biased forecasts. In regard to the S&P 500 up- and down-years, people who are prone to extrapolation bias will be excessively optimistic during bull markets and excessively pessimistic during bear markets.

Biased Financial Executives' Estimates

Survey evidence from Financial Executives International suggests that financial executives succumb to extrapolation bias when estimating the market risk premium.[11] The higher the market return has been in the prior quarter, the higher their forecasts of the equity premium over the subsequent year. In addition, overconfidence leads financial executives to underestimate market risk.

Representativeness also affects the manner in which financial executives form their forecasts of future volatility. The higher the market return has been in the prior quarter, the lower are their forecasts of market volatility over the subsequent year. Notably, the combination of these beliefs leads financial executives to respond as if they believe that at the level of the market, expected returns and risk are negatively related. Of course, in this respect they are consistent, in that they also believe the risk-return relationship to be negative when it comes to individual stocks.

Interestingly, financial executives surveyed were overconfident in respect to risk. Typical market estimates for volatility are in the neighborhood of 20 percent. Financial executives' forecasts of volatility were in the neighborhood of 6 to 7 percent. Remember that overconfidence leads people to be surprised more frequently than they anticipated. Overconfidence leads people to establish confidence intervals that are too narrow.

In regard to optimism, the average financial executive estimated the equity premium to be between 1 and 3 percent. This range is well below the range specified by the authors of one well-known corporate finance text mentioned earlier and within the wide range proposed by textbook authors generally.

4.4   INVESTOR BIASES IN ESTIMATING THE MARKET RISK PREMIUM

Individual Investors and the Hot-Hand Fallacy

Individual investors exhibit the same type of bias as financial executives when it comes to the market risk premium. The financial firm UBS, together with the Gallup polling organization, has been surveying individual investors since 1997. Those surveys provide strong evidence that individual investors form return expectations in the same manner as corporate executives. Individual investors succumb to extrapolation bias. After the market has gone up, they become increasingly optimistic. After the market has gone down, they become less optimistic or even pessimistic. Exhibit 4.4 is a scatter plot displaying investors expected returns in the UBS/Gallup data against the prior 12-month return. Clearly the relationship is strongly positive.

Professional Investors and Gambler's Fallacy

Like individual investors, professional investors' return expectations are biased. However, the biases of professional investors differ from those of individual investors. While individual investors have very little knowledge of base rate information, professional investors are well acquainted with key base rate information pertaining to market returns.

EXHIBIT 4.4
**Expected Return
UBS/Gallup Survey
versus Prior Return
S&P 500**

Sources: UBS/Gallup Survey
(**www.ubs.com**) and Center for
Research in Security Prices.

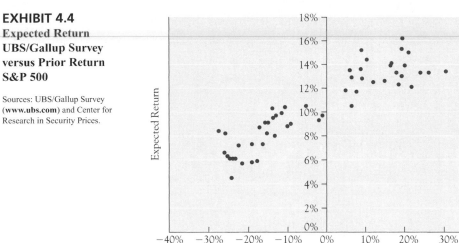

Consider how a manager who relies on representativeness and utilizes base rate information will be inclined toward bias. Take the case of up- and down-years for the S&P 500. As was mentioned earlier, the probability of an up-year is two-thirds. Think about the outcomes over three consecutive years. With the probability of an up-year being two-thirds, a representative outcome over three years will feature two up-years and one down-year.

Representativeness leads people to view three-year outcomes featuring two up-years and one-down year as being more likely than they actually are. This is because representativeness leads people to overfocus on stereotypes. At the same time, representativeness leads people to view sequences that feature long streaks, such as eight consecutive up-years, or four consecutive down-years, as being less likely than they actually are. This is because these sequences are not viewed as representative of a situation where the probability of an up-year is two-thirds.

The key point is that when people are familiar with the base rate for the S&P 500, representativeness will lead them to view long streaks as being unlikely. Therefore, representativeness predisposes such people to be overly prone to predict reversals. Psychologists call this phenomenon **gambler's fallacy.** Gambler's fallacy gets its name from the tendency of gamblers at a craps table to believe that a 7 or 11 is due, if neither have been rolled recently.

gamblers' fallacy
The tendency to overweight the probability of an event because it has not recently occurred at a frequency that reflects its probability.

Wall Street Strategists

Wall Street strategists make their living forecasting movements in the broad market and the economy. Unlike individual investors, strategists do not ignore base rates. However, this does not mean that they use base rate information appropriately. Exhibit 4.5 displays the expected change in the S&P 500 for professional investors, relative to the prior change in the S&P 500. Unlike the positive relationship for individual investors displayed in Exhibit 4.4, for professional investors the relationship

EXHIBIT 4.5
Professional Investors Forecasted Change in S&P 500 versus Prior Change in S&P 500 1990–2003

Sources: Livingston Survey (**www.phil.frb.org/econ/liv**) and Center for Research in Security Prices.

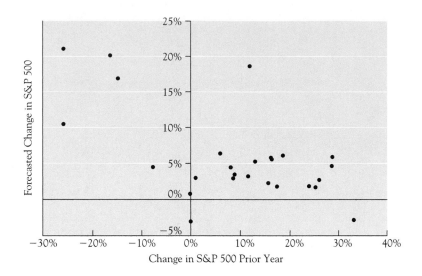

is negative. That is, Wall Street strategists' estimates of the market risk premium exhibit gambler's fallacy.

Wall Street Analysts

Just as Wall Street strategists succumb to gambler's fallacy when forecasting the overall market, Wall Street security analysts succumb to gambler's fallacy when forecasting the future prices of individual stocks. Over investment horizons between 3 and 12 months, short-term winners are likely to continue as short-term winners, and vice versa. This phenomenon has been called the momentum effect.[12] The momentum effect is strongest when using prior six-month returns to forecast subsequent six-month returns.

Interestingly, analysts' beliefs about momentum are 180 degrees wrong. Relative to prior year returns, analysts expect short-term return reversals. From the behavioral perspective, analysts appear to display gambler's fallacy in respect to short-term returns. From the traditional perspective, analysts judge recent winners to be safer than recent losers.

4.5 EXECUTIVES, INSIDER TRADING, AND GAMBLER'S FALLACY

The manner in which financial executives make personal portfolio decisions about the securities issued by their firms provides important insights into their thought processes. What do the patterns of their insider trades reveal?

Like security analysts, financial executives appear to be guided by gambler's fallacy in their insider trading activity. That is, financial executives tend to sell the stocks of their own firms when those stocks have featured high positive appreciation in the previous year. In contrast, executives hold, or even purchase, the stocks of their firms when those stocks have featured low price appreciation in the previous year.

Debiasing for Better Decisions

Errors or biases: Managers, investors, and analysts exhibit either hot hand fallacy or gambler's fallacy.

Why does it happen? Reliance on representativeness to combine base rate information and singular information.

How does it happen? Those who exhibit hot hand fallacy overweight recent events and underweight base rates. They form forecasts by asking for which environment is the most recent event representative. Those who exhibit gambler's fallacy overweight base rate information, in the sense that they believe that small samples must be representative of the base rate information.

What can be done about it? Carefully identify both the base rate information and the singular information. Use statistical forecasting techniques, and contrast the outcomes with forecasts based on intuitive judgments. Based on the contrast, ascertain whether the intuitive judgments fail to make appropriate use of either the base rate information or the singular information.

Typically, growth stocks have experienced high price appreciation in the previous year and value stocks have experienced low price appreciation. That is, price appreciation in the previous year is negatively correlated with book-to-market equity. If we sort stocks into deciles according to book-to-market equity, then for the period between 1992 and 2000, the prices of the bottom decile (growth) stocks appreciated by 80 percent, whereas the prices of the top decile (value) stocks declined by 5 percent. The associated correlation coefficient between price appreciation and book-to-market equity decile is about −93 percent. Therefore, executives appear to engage in insider selling when the stocks of their firms are growth stocks and engage in holding or insider buying when the stocks of their firms are value stocks.[13]

Section 4.2 discussed how representativeness and the affect heuristic lead executives to attach higher expected returns and lower risk to growth stocks than to value stocks. Yet when it comes to insider trading, executives appear to sell growth stocks relative to value stocks. Are these patterns inconsistent? As psychologists have found, people routinely display preference reversal, where their value judgments and choices go in opposite directions. This point was also discussed in section 3.3 of chapter 3. Return expectations and risk assessments are judgmental activities. Trading is a choice activity.

Like their judgments discussed previously, executives' trading choices are not particularly effective. Even though executives' insider trades feature the sale of growth stocks and the purchase of value stocks, those trades fail to earn economically significant abnormal returns. That is, the predictions of reversals implicit in executives' insider trades are unwarranted, in line with gambler's fallacy.

4.6 SURVEY EVIDENCE ON PROJECT DISCOUNT RATES

The remainder of this chapter does not address the question about how the relationship between risk and return is determined in the market. Instead, the focus is on how perceptions about the relationship between risk and return impact managers' decisions.

In theory, managers discount project cash flows at a rate that reflects the systematic risk of those flows. If those flows comprise a series of components, all featuring different levels of risk, then in theory managers should discount each component separately, using its own discount rate. Survey evidence from Financial Executives International indicates that, in practice, most managers use a "one size fits all" heuristic.[14]

The survey asked the following question of CFOs: "How frequently would your company use the following discount rates when evaluating a new project in an overseas market?" The list included

- The discount rate for the entire company.
- A risk-matched discount rate for this particular project (considering both company and industry).
- The discount rate for the overseas market (country discount rate).
- A divisional discount rate (if the project line of business matches a domestic division).
- A different discount rate for each component cash flow that has a different risk characteristic (e.g., depreciation versus operating cash flows).

The ordering of these items actually corresponds to the rating order provided by respondents. The survey found that 59 percent of CFOs use the discount rate for the entire company, that is, a "one size fits all" heuristic. Fifty-one percent indicated that they would use the second highest rated item, a risk-matched discount rate. Notably, the survey authors report that large firms are more likely to use risk-matched discount rates than are smaller firms. Fewer than 10 percent vary the discount rate across component cash flows.

To be sure, the simple heuristic "one discount rate fits all projects" leads to bias. Its application leads to risky projects being favored over safer projects, all else being the same. As in the traditional framework, risk should be defined as being systematic. However, estimating the systematic component of project risk is quite challenging, and availability bias tends to induce managers to focus on idiosyncratic risk as a result.

Summary

In theory, managers use the relationship between risk and return to make capital budgeting decisions and to value securities. In practice, managers appear to rely on representativeness when forming judgments about risk and return. In doing so, they are prone to view the stocks of good companies as representative of good stocks and to believe that risk and return are negatively related.

Representativeness, reinforced by the affect heuristic, leads managers to hold erroneous beliefs, associating higher returns with large-capitalization growth firms than with small-capitalization value firms. Representativeness also appears to lead managers to hold the erroneous view that the relationship between the one-year equity premium and future volatility is negative.

Representativeness leads financial executives, individual investors, and Wall Street strategists astray in their estimates of the market risk premium. Financial executives and individual investors are prone to hot hand fallacy, whereas Wall Street strategists are prone to gambler's fallacy. Representativeness affects Wall Street analysts, leading them to succumb to gambler's fallacy in their return forecasts for individual stocks. Gambler's fallacy also appears to influence executives' insider trades, leading them to sell shares in their firms after a year of high stock price appreciation, and to hold or purchase shares after a year of low stock price appreciation.

The majority of corporate financial managers report that they use a single discount rate when making capital budgeting decisions. Almost half report that they do not adjust discount rates to reflect the manner in which differences in project risk impact differences in project expected returns.

Additional Behavioral Readings

Celati, L., *The Dark Side of Risk Management: How People Frame Decisions in Financial Markets.* London: Prentice-Hall, Financial Times, 2004.

Finucane, M., A. Alhakami, P. Slovic and S. Johnson, "The Affect Heuristic in Judgments of Risks and Benefits," *Journal of Behavioral Decision Making,* vol. 13, 2000, pp. 1–17.

Shefrin, H., "Do Investors Expect Higher Returns from Safer Stocks than from Riskier Stocks?" *Journal of Psychology and Financial Markets,* vol. 2, no. 4, 2001, pp. 176–181.

Key Terms

base rate information, *65*	gambler's fallacy, *67*	singular information, *65*
extrapolation bias, *65*	hot-hand fallacy, *65*	

Explore the Web

cbs.sportsline.com/nba/story/7298245
Example illustrating the use of the hot-hand concept in the popular press.

www.hs.ttu.edu/hdfs3390/hothand.htm with a link to
www.hs.ttu.edu/hdfs3390/hh_hist.htm
Professor Alan Reifman's sites devoted to the hot-hand phenomenon in professional sports as well as the history of the phenomenon.

www.duke.edu/~charvey/Research/indexr.htm
Duke University survey of perspective of chief financial officers in regard to equity premium and volatility.

faculty.fuqua.duke.edu/~charvey/Research/Professional_Materials/
     PM39_Expectations_of_equity.ppt
PowerPoint presentation summary of the survey results from Duke University.

www.mhhe.com/shefrin

Chapter Questions

1. During a presentation in February 2001, the CFO of Palm Inc. was asked how frequently her firm assesses and uses its cost of capital. In response, she stated that Palm computes its cost of capital "from time to time." As far as computing the expected return on individual projects, she stated: "We do try to do this once in a while, but probably not as much as you might think we do." Discuss this remark in the context of the chapter.[15]

2. A *Barron's* article documents the history of Jim Chanos from the short-selling firm Ursus Partners.[16] Jim Chanos's career history has featured both successes and failures. In 1982, when he was 24 years old, he issued a sell recommendation on the stock of annuity firm Baldwin-United, on which other analysts were very positive. Thirteen months after issuing his sell recommendation, Baldwin-United filed for Chapter 11, and its market value of equity declined by $6 billion. In 1983, Chanos's successful call was the subject of a front-page story in *The Wall Street Journal*. During the bull market of the 1990s short-selling led Chanos's firm to lose 75 percent of its value. The *Barron's* article quotes a hedge fund manager as comparing Chanos to a major league baseball player who, in his first season achieves a batting average of 400 and expects to repeat the success every season. Discuss the baseball batting average analogy in the context of the psychological phenomena described in the chapter.

3. The author of the *Barron's* article discussed in Question 2 suggests that Jim Chanos might have suffered from hubris and let success get to his head. Is this suggestion consistent with any of the behavioral biases described in Chapter 1?

4. In 1999, the S&P 500 returned 21 percent, closing out a streak of five consecutive stellar up-years. Then in 2000, the S&P 500 returned −9.1 percent. In 2001, the S&P 500 returned −16.1 percent. At the end of 2001, Wall Street strategists who were interviewed by *Barron's* forecast that the S&P 500 would increase by 21 percent in 2002. In 2002, the S&P actually returned −23 percent. The average strategist's forecast for 2003 was for an increase of 15.3 percent. Do these forecasts reflect any psychological biases?

5. At various points in the chapter, evidence is presented suggesting that managers behave as if they view risk and return as being negatively related. Can you suggest reasons why the evidence may be faulty or unreliable insofar as reaching the conclusion that managers perceive risk and return as going in opposite directions?

Minicase

Intel and eBay

Between March and July 2000, Intel's stock price rose rapidly, to the point where in July Intel's market capitalization was above $500 billion, making it the largest firm in the world. Then on Thursday, September 21, 2000, Intel issued a press release indicating that its revenue for the third quarter would grow between 3 percent and 5 percent, not the 8 to 12 percent that analysts had been forecasting.

In response to this news, Intel's stock price dropped by 30 percent over the next five days. Intel's chairman, Craig Barrett, commented on the reaction, stating: "I don't know what you call it but an overreaction and the market feeding on itself."

An academic study found that at the time, virtually none of the analysts following Intel used discounted cash flow analysis to estimate the fundamental value of Intel's stock.[17] Instead, the study points out that analysts react to bad news in the same way that a bond-rating agency reacts to bad news. Just as a bond-rating agency would downgrade the firm's debt, analysts downgrade their stock recommendations. After Intel's press release, approximately one-third of the analysts following the firm downgraded their recommendations. Some of the recommendation changes were extreme. Notably, the cumulative return to Intel's stock, relative to the S&P 500, displayed a negative trend for the period September 2000 through September 2002.

In what some might see as a replay of history, consider an event that took place at the online firm eBay during January 2005. Between the end of 2002 and the end of 2004, eBay's shares increased by over 200 percent. During December 2004, eBay's stock price peaked at $118, and its forward P/E ratio was 73. At the time, the firm's market value was $81.7 billion. Fourth-quarter earnings for eBay grew by 44 percent to $205.4 million, or 30 cents a share.

Just as Intel had announced that its earnings growth would be lower than forecast, eBay's actual earnings for the fourth quarter of 2004 fell a penny below analysts' consensus forecasts. Meg Whitman, eBay's CEO, stated that future earnings would be lower because of higher advertising costs and reinvestment.

In response, eBay's stock price fell from $103 to $81 per share. The firm's market value fell to $56 billion. Many analysts immediately downgraded eBay's stock. Rajiv Dutta, eBay's CFO, issued a public statement to say that his concern was managing eBay's long-run prospects, not its stock price.

On January 26, 2005, James Stewart wrote about eBay in his *Wall Street Journal* column "Common Sense." Stewart indicated that he would consider purchasing eBay stock in the wake of its decline. While acknowledging that eBay could not grow at a stratospheric rate forever, Stewart noted that eBay is in the process of transforming world commerce and has a natural monopoly. Were he to own just one Internet stock, Stewart said, eBay would be that stock.

Case Analysis Questions

1. Discuss whether the analysts following Intel appear to have been influenced by any psychological phenomena, both generally and in their reaction to Intel's announcement in September 2000.

2. Discuss whether James Stewart's assessment of eBay reflects any psychological phenomena.

3. In what ways are the events described at Intel and eBay similar and in what ways are they different?

Chapter **Five**

Inefficient Markets and Corporate Decisions

The main objective of this chapter is for students to demonstrate that they can identify the psychological phenomena that obstruct market efficiency and the associated implications for managers' behavior.

After completing this chapter students will be able to:

1. Differentiate among the different definitions of market efficiency.
2. Identify pricing phenomena involving reversals and price drift that lie at the heart of the market efficiency debate.
3. Explain how the limits of arbitrage can interfere with market efficiency even in the presence of smart money.
4. Describe the implications of the market efficiency debate for corporate financial decisions involving project selection, earnings guidance, stock splits, and new equity issues.

5.1 TRADITIONAL APPROACH TO MARKET EFFICIENCY

The risk premium for a security is the additional expected return, over and above the risk-free rate, that investors require in order to compensate them for risk. When the additional expected return exceeds the risk premium, investors are said to earn a positive abnormal return.

The efficient-market hypothesis holds that investors cannot expect to make abnormal returns because market prices correctly reflect the information available to the market as a whole. As a concept, market efficiency is subtle and involves three different versions: (**1**) weak-form efficiency, (**2**) semistrong-form efficiency, and (**3**) strong-form efficiency. Each form pertains to the extent to which market prices correctly reflect particular information.

Weak-form efficiency pertains to information in past prices, semistrong-form efficiency to all publicly available information, and strong-form efficiency to all information including the information held by insiders. When prices are weak-form efficient, there are no trading rules based on past prices alone that enable investors to earn abnormal returns on a consistent basis. Similar statements apply to semistrong-form efficiency and strong-form efficiency. Efficient prices preclude consistent nonzero abnormal returns from being earned.

In the traditional framework, rational investors or smart money constantly monitor markets for abnormal profit opportunities. Therefore, the argument goes, smart money will quickly spot any opportunities that arise and begin to exploit them. Such exploitation, the buying of underpriced securities and selling of overpriced securities, is known as (risky) arbitrage. Notably, arbitrage will eliminate the opportunities as smart money bids up the prices of underpriced securities and bids down the prices of overpriced securities. Therefore, in the traditional view, inefficiencies will be small, temporary, and unpredictable.

The efficient-market hypothesis evolved from statistical studies of market price movements that concluded that such movements were essentially random and unpredictable. In 1965, Eugene Fama formalized this observation into the definition of market efficiency. Fama pointed out that in an efficient market, prices correspond to intrinsic (or fundamental) value.[1]

In practice, the notion of market efficiency involves an asset pricing model such as the capital asset pricing model (CAPM) or a multifactor model. Proponents of market efficiency view factors relating to size and book-to-market equity as proxies for risk. That is to say, they see the stocks of smaller firms as riskier than the stocks of larger firms. Likewise, they consider value stocks (associated with high book-to-market equity) to be riskier than growth stocks (associated with low book-to-market equity). This is because a firm whose market value of equity lies below its book value of equity is more likely to be facing financial distress than a firm whose market value of equity lies above its book value of equity.

Notably, some pricing phenomena do not require a risk-based explanation. For example, market efficiency implies that stock splits will not affect the market values of firms because such splits only represent a cosmetic change, with no impact on intrinsic value.

The main message from traditional textbooks is that corporate managers should trust market prices, as far as publicly available information is concerned. This means that managers should not believe that the securities of their firms are mispriced, unless as managers they have private information to the contrary. For example, the traditional approach warns managers to abstain from issuing new shares because they believe the stocks of their firms to be overvalued, and conversely to abstain from repurchasing shares because they believe the stocks of their firms to be undervalued.

5.2 THE MARKET EFFICIENCY DEBATE: ANOMALIES

An issue of great debate between finance traditionalists and behaviorists is whether or not markets are efficient. Traditionalists contend that markets are efficient in the sense that departures from efficiency are temporary, small, and infrequent. Behaviorists contend that because of the behavioral phenomena described in this book, there are particular circumstances in which departures from efficiency are likely to be large and occur for long periods of time.

Empirical patterns that appear to be puzzles from the perspective of market efficiency have come to be called *anomalies*. For the most part, traditionalists and behaviorists agree about the statistical properties of these anomalies. However, they disagree on the interpretation of those properties. This section describes some of the major empirical phenomena and discusses the different interpretations provided by traditionalists and behaviorists. Notably, the anomalies described in the following involve particular circumstances. It is important to understand that even behaviorists would not make the jump to conclude from the evidence that markets are generally inefficient.

Long-Term Reversals: Winner–Loser Effect

winner–loser effect
Extreme past losers tend subsequently to outperform the market, and extreme past winners tend subsequently to underperform the market.

Historically, stocks whose returns have been worst over a three-year period have tended subsequently to outperform the market over the subsequent five years by about 30 percent. Conversely, stocks whose returns have been best over a three-year period have tended to underperform the market over the subsequent five years by about 10 percent. On a cumulative basis, losers outperform winners by about 40 percent over five years. In summary, stock returns appear to exhibit long-term reversals. This finding is known as the De Bondt–Thaler **winner–loser effect.**

Behaviorists suggest that the winner–loser effect occurs because representativeness leads investors to exhibit extrapolation bias in respect to prior earnings. In the behavioral perspective, investors overreact to stocks that have been past losers, causing those stocks to become undervalued. By the same token, investors overreact to past winners, causing those stocks to become overvalued.

As a result, past losers subsequently earn positive abnormal returns when future earnings growth tends to be better than expected. By the same token, past winners subsequently earn negative abnormal returns when future earnings growth tends to be worse than expected. In this respect, the behavioral interpretation of the winner–loser effect is inconsistent with weak-form market efficiency.

The traditional interpretation of the winner–loser effect is that the phenomenon reflects differential risk rather than mispricing. Specifically, past losers are riskier than past winners, so over time the returns to past losers will tend to be higher than the returns to past winners. In particular, the winner–loser phenomenon is statistically subsumed by the three factors in the Fama–French model described in Chapter 4. Those factors reflect overall market risk, firm size, and book-to-market equity.

Recall that in the traditional perspective, the stocks of smaller firms are riskier than the stocks of larger firms, and because they are more financially distressed, value stocks are riskier than growth stocks. Hence, on average, when small-cap stocks outperform large-cap stocks and value stocks outperform growth stocks, past losers earn positive abnormal returns and past winners earn negative abnormal returns.

Momentum: Short-Term Continuation

momentum
Recent losers tend subsequently to underperform the market, and recent winners tend subsequently to outperform the market.

In the short-term, returns feature **momentum,** not reversal. Historically, a portfolio formed by holding the winners from the past six months and shorting the losers from the past six months earned more than 10 percent per year. The pattern is especially pronounced among small-cap stocks.

underreaction
The percentage change in
market price in response to
an event is too small.

overreaction
The percentage change in
market price in response to
an event is too large.

Behaviorists view short-term momentum as evidence against weak-form efficiency and propose three possible explanations for its occurrence. The first explanation is that analysts and investors **underreact** to new information. A second explanation is that subsequent to a news event and the initial market reaction, overconfident investors **overreact** to later events. For example, if there is good news about a stock and its price rises as a result, overconfident investors will then tend to overreact to good news that occurs subsequently. This second increase constitutes momentum.

A third explanation for momentum is based on investors who behave in accordance with prospect theory. In the event of good news about a stock, risk aversion predisposes investors to sell the stock at a gain relative to the original purchase price, thereby retarding the increase in price. By the same token, when there is bad news about a stock, aversion to a sure loss predisposes investors to hold their losers, thereby retarding the price decrease. However, as new investors enter the market and establish different reference purchase prices, market prices will tend to move toward fundamental value in the long run. As a result, the retardation only affects the speed of adjustment, not the end result. Therefore, the subsequent movement toward fundamental value appears as momentum. Statistically, the disposition to sell winners early and hold losers longer provides a strong explanation for momentum.

The traditional explanation of momentum holds that short-term winners are riskier than short-term losers. However, the Fama–French three-factor model is unable to subsume momentum as it does the De Bondt–Thaler winner–loser effect, a point that Fama and French acknowledge. For this reason, some traditionalists add the return difference between short-term winners and short-term losers (momentum) as a fourth factor to the Fama–French model.

Post-Earnings-Announcement Drift

Analysts forecast earnings. When a firm announces that its earnings have exceeded the consensus analyst forecast, the outcome is said to be a positive surprise. When a firm announces that its earnings have fallen below the consensus analyst forecast, the outcome is said to be a negative surprise.

Empirically, stock prices do not appear to adjust immediately to earnings surprises. Instead stock prices adjust slowly, exhibiting drift. This phenomenon has come to be called **post-earnings-announcement drift.**

**post-earnings-
announcement drift**
The stocks of firms giving
rise to positive earnings
surprises experience
positive drift after the
announcement, while the
stocks of firms giving rise
to negative earnings
surprises experience
negative drift after the
announcement.

Historically, it turns out that over the 60 days following an earnings announcement, the stocks of firms that registered the largest positive surprise returned 2 percent more than the stocks of firms with similar characteristics that did not register a surprise. Likewise, the stocks of firms that had the largest negative surprise returned 2 percent less than their peer group. The effect was more than twice as large in the case of small-cap and medium-cap firms.

Post-earnings-announcement drift is a phenomenon that illustrates both short-term continuation and long-term reversal. Post-earnings-announcement drift features momentum for a year after the first earnings surprise, but reversal after a year. In other words, momentum continues for up to 12 months and is then followed by reversal.

Given that earnings constitute nonprice public information, behaviorists interpret post-earnings-announcement drift as evidence against semistrong-form efficiency.

They suggest that part of the explanation for the phenomenon is that analysts underreact to the information in earnings announcements. Studies have consistently demonstrated that analysts underreact in adjusting their quarterly earnings forecasts after earnings surprises. As a result, a positive earnings surprise tends to be followed by a positive earnings surprise, and a negative earnings surprise tends to be followed by a negative earnings surprise. However, positive surprises tend to be followed by negative surprises a year later, and vice versa.

Traditionalists typically interpret post-earnings-announcement drift in the context of their overall critique of the studies documenting overreaction and underreaction. Their interpretation emphasizes that overreaction and underreaction are the results of random variation consistent with market efficiency. In 1998 Fama pointed out that empirically, findings of overreaction occur about as frequently as findings of underreaction.[2]

Although not fully resolved, the market efficiency debate has been shifting through time. In October 2004 *The Wall Street Journal* ran a front page story suggesting that the debate had begun to shift in favor of the behavioral position.[3] For example, during 2004, Fama and French began to question whether size and book-to-market return effects are actually due to risk.[4]

5.3   LIMITS OF ARBITRAGE

Arbitrage is the process of exploiting mispricing, essentially buying low and selling high. The intuition underlying the efficient market perspective is rooted in arbitrage, that smart investors will quickly take advantage of mispricing caused by irrational investors, thereby rendering the mispricing small and temporary. Behaviorists counter that because mispricing can become worse before it gets better, smart investors must accept additional risk in attempting to exploit mispricing. The additional risk will limit smart investors from trading as aggressively as they otherwise might, thereby reducing some, but not all, of the mispricing. Behaviorists call this phenomenon the **limits of arbitrage.**

limits of arbitrage
Smart investors do not fully exploit mispricing because of the attendant risks that the mispricing will become larger before it becomes smaller.

Pick-a-Number Game

Consider a game, called the pick-a-number game, whose purpose is to provide insight into the concept limits of arbitrage.

CONCEPT PREVIEW

Question 5.1

Imagine yourself in a contest, where you are to choose a whole number between 1 and 100 as your entry. The winner will be the person whose choice comes closest to two-thirds of the average entry. What number would you enter?

In 1997, the *Financial Times* ran this game in earnest. Readers were invited to submit choices, and a substantial prize was offered for the winning entry. The winning entry was 13. In classroom settings, the winning submission is often higher than 13. For graduate students a typical winning entry is 22 or higher. For under- graduates, a typical winning entry is 38 or higher.

How do people think about playing this game? Were everyone to submit 100, the winning entry would be 67. Someone who predicts that everyone else would select the highest plausible entry, namely 67, should consider entering a value close to 44, two-thirds of 67. But in doing so, he or she might ask why others might not be think- ing along the same lines, why everyone else might not enter 44 as well. Continued thinking along these lines would lead a person to consider revising his or her entry to 30, then to 20, and in subsequent rounds to 13, 9, 6, 4, 3, 2, and 1.

Clustering

Regardless of whether the participating group consists of students, professional investors, or subscribers to the *Financial Times,* the range of responses to Concept Preview Question 5.1 is wide. The responses often cluster around the values 67, 44, 30, 20, and 13, 9, and 1. Therefore, people do appear to think along the lines just described. Yet, those who predict 1 rarely win. Why? Because most people only go part way along the sequence described, stopping at 30 or 20, but not going all the way down to 1.

If everyone thought the game through in the described fashion, then everyone would eventually be induced to enter 1. If a person thinks that everyone else will enter 1, then he or she too should enter 1.

The Point

The pick-a-number game is an analogy for a financial market. A person who thinks the game through is a smart player, the analogy of a smart investor. A person who does not think the game through is the counterpart of a normal investor who is subject to bias.

Consider how a smart player would set out to win the game. Would he or she always enter a 1? Of course not. If most of the other players are not smart, then they will typically enter numbers much higher than 1. Therefore a smart player will have to assess the analytical propensities of the other players, and base his or her entry on that assessment. In the case of the *Financial Times* contest described, the winning entry was 13, not 1. An entry of 1 was a losing entry, not a winning entry.

Think about the limits of arbitrage in the context of this game. In order to bring the average of the entries as close to 1 as possible, where 1 corresponds to intrinsic value, a smart player should enter 1. However, doing so is not rational unless all the other players choose 1. Therefore, the desire to win will limit the smart player from behaving in a way that brings the average entry as close to the intrinsic value as possible.

To summarize, there are three concepts to take away from this discussion of the pick-a-number game. First, playing the game skillfully requires an understanding of the errors to which the other players are susceptible. Second, the appropriate course of action is different when the other players commit errors than when they do not. Third, skilled play by the winner does not necessarily bring the outcome close to what would occur if few players committed errors.

Implications for Managers' Decisions

In general circumstances, managers might do well to trust market prices, either because they are efficient or because managers lack the skills required to identify the inefficiency. At the same time, the point of the chapter is to indicate that there are special circumstances under which market mispricing will impact managers' decisions about investment policy and raising funds. These circumstances combine systematic behavioral phenomena and the limits of arbitrage. The remainder of the chapter discusses market efficiency in respect to three types of managerial decisions: investment policy in combination with earnings guidance, stock splits, and going IPO. At issue is how market inefficiency, or the perception of market inefficiency, impacts these decisions.

5.4 MARKET EFFICIENCY, EARNINGS GUIDANCE, AND NPV

Financial managers routinely disclose information to security analysts in a process called *guidance.*[5] Among the most important information that managers disclose is the managers' own forecasts of what future earnings per share will be for their firms. For this reason, managers are able to influence stock prices by choosing to disclose information to analysts and investors.

Net present value (NPV), when properly computed, measures incremental intrinsic value. In an efficient market, price equals intrinsic value. This important point, made by Eugene Fama, underlies the rationale for encouraging corporate managers to maximize NPV. In an efficient market, maximizing NPV is equivalent to maximizing market value.

When prices are inefficient, maximizing NPV based on cash flows might not be the same as maximizing the market value of the firm. As a result, market inefficiency can present financial managers with a dilemma.

Evidence from a survey of chief financial officers indicates that the majority view earnings rather than cash flows as the key variable upon which investors rely to judge value.[6] Because the market reacts very negatively when a firm misses an earnings target, a strong majority of managers are willing to sacrifice fundamental value in order to meet a short-run earnings target. Survey evidence finds that over half of managers would avoid initiating a very positive NPV project if doing so meant missing analysts' target for the current quarter's earnings.

The relationship between investment and earnings can also be direct in that managers can use expenditures on research and development (R&D) to affect earnings. For example, if managers are concerned that the firm's actual earnings will fall below analysts' earnings expectations, they tend to postpone planned expenditures for R&D. Notably, R&D expenditures are expensed rather than capitalized.[7] In this respect, consider the example presented in the following Behavioral Pitfalls box.[8]

During 2000, furniture manufacturer Herman-Miller was evaluating a potential Web-based project. The firm had put together a business plan for the project, with projected financial statements over a three- to five-year horizon. An accounting issue arose in connection with the project, because the initial investment had to be expensed rather than capitalized. Therefore the project, despite having positive net present value, would adversely impact net income in the short-term.

The managers at Herman-Miller said to themselves: "Maybe we shouldn't do it this year." Brian Walker, the president of Herman-Miller North America then asked the group: "How would we view this if it was capitalized and not expensed on the income statement?" He reported that members of the group looked at each other and said: "If it were capital and not expense, we'd do it; the problem was [that] it was hitting EPS."

Herman-Miller's CFO, Elizabeth Nickels, described the balancing act her firm faced, in the following terms: "Much of the outside world still looks at EPS, whether you like it or not, and the question is, how do you balance between the two?" Herman-Miller dealt with this balancing act by reevaluating and reprioritizing other expenditures in order to free up capital for the new project.

Walker also offered the following observation, contrasting his firm with Internet firms:

> For dot.coms, it appears that the market has implicitly capitalized a lot of those costs. The market views their negative earnings as investments in the future. It's more difficult for a traditional Old Economy company trying to participate in the New Economy, because when it affects my earnings, it's more difficult for Wall Street to say, "We'll give you a break on this."

Source: G. Millman, "Capital Allocation: When the Right Thing Is Hard to Do," *Financial Executive,* September/October 2000, pp. 29–40. Reprinted by permission of *Financial Executive* copyright 2000 by Financial Executives Institute, 200 Campus Park Drive, Florham Park, NJ, 07932-0674.

5.5 STOCK SPLITS

Proponents of market efficiency urge managers to trust market prices.[9] For example, according to the efficient-market view, a firm that splits its stock should not expect to see an abnormal change in its market value of equity. However, it turns out that there is positive drift associated with stock splits.[10]

Firms that split their stocks earn an average abnormal return of 7.93 percent in the first year, and 12.15 percent in the first three years. The three-year effect seems to be concentrated in value stocks. For growth stocks, the effect does not extend beyond the first year. What is especially interesting is that firms that decide to split their stocks tend to feature pessimistic coverage by analysts in respect to earnings forecasts.[11] In addition, firms that announce stock splits are much less likely to experience a decline in future earnings, relative to firms with comparable characteristics.

Example: Tandy's Stock Split

Tandy Corporation operates the Radio Shack stores. In May 1999 Tandy Corporation announced a two-for-one stock split. In making the announcement, Leonard Roberts, Tandy's CEO, stated that he believed Tandy's stock price to be undervalued, even though it had increased 81.5 percent since the beginning of the year. He also indicated that he expected that the digital revolution would continue to fuel growth in Tandy's sales and profits, especially for wireless phones.

Chuck Hill, the research director for First Call Corporation, which tracks corporate earnings, offered two interesting comments in respect to Tandy's stock split. First, he stated that he believed that Tandy would not have undertaken the split if it had concerns about a downturn in the near future. That statement reflects the general finding that firms that announce stock splits are much less likely to experience a decline in future earnings, relative to firms with comparable characteristics.

Second, Hill suggested that the lower stock prices would generate interest among individual investors, even though institutional investors held 72 percent of Tandy's stock. His reason? The stock price will look cheap even though the intrinsic value of the firm will be unchanged. Hill noted that stock splits often make a difference, even though the logic is questionable.[12] Notably, Tandy's stock outperformed the S&P 500 (by 11.3 percent) one year after the stock split.

5.6   TO IPO OR NOT TO IPO?

hot issue market
Demand for new issues is relatively high.

initial underpricing
The offer price is too low, resulting in a large first-day price pop.

long-term underperformance
New issues earn lower returns than stocks with comparable characteristics against which they have been matched.

EXHIBIT 5.1
Number of Offerings and Average First-Day Returns 1980–2003

Source: Jay Ritter's Web site, **bear.cba.ufl.edu/ritter**.

Three Phenomena

IPO decisions take place against the backdrop of three phenomena: a **hot issue market, initial underpricing,** and **long-term underperformance.**[13] To say that managers like to issue new equity in a hot issue market is to say that they prefer to issue equity when the number of new issues is relatively high. To say that a new issue is initially underpriced is to say that the offer price is too low, resulting in a large first-day price pop when the stock is traded publicly for the first time. To say that the stocks of new issues feature long-term underperformance is to say that new issues earn lower returns than stocks with comparable characteristics (size and book-to-market equity) against which they have been matched.[14]

In order to understand these phenomena, and the way they have changed over time, begin with Exhibit 5.1.[15] This exhibit displays two monthly series for the time period 1980–2003, the number of offerings and the average first-day return to an

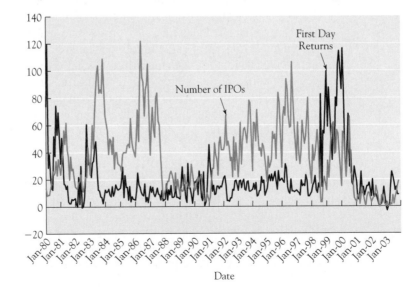

EXHIBIT 5.2

Comparison IPO Returns and Firms Matched by Size and Book-to-Market Equity 1970–2002

Source: Jay Ritter's Web site, **bear.cba.ufl.edu/ritter**.

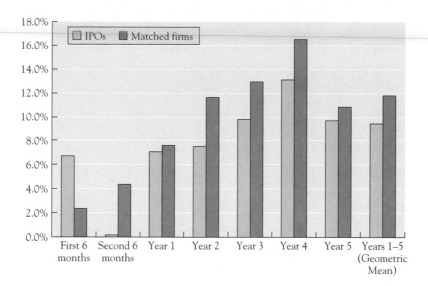

IPO (in percent). Notice how the number of IPOs occurs in waves, giving rise to so-called hot and cold issue markets.

The first-day return has also been highly volatile over time. In this respect, look at four distinct subperiods: the 1980s (1980–1989), the 1990s (1990–1998), the so-called bubble period (1999–2000), and the postbubble period (2001–2003). The average first-day return was about 7 percent in the 1980s, 15 percent in the 1990s, 65 percent during the bubble period, and 12 percent in the postbubble period.

Exhibit 5.2 displays the general finding about long-term underperformance for the period 1970–2002. Notice that during the first six months, the returns of issuing firms were higher than the returns of comparable firms that were similar in size and book-to-market equity, but did not issue new shares. However, beginning six months after the new issue, the shares of issuing firms began to underperform the shares of similar firms that did not issue new shares. Over a five-year horizon, IPOs underperformed by 2.4 percent a year ($= 0.118 - 0.094$). The degree of long-term underperformance has not been steady over time. In the 1980s it was 2.8 percent, and in the 1990s it was 5.2 percent.

IPO Decisions

All three IPO phenomena discussed reflect decisions made by financial executives. Consider the nature of these decisions in relation to the concept of market efficiency.

Hot Issue Markets

Imagine the financial executive of a privately held firm that does not plan on raising external funds for at least two years. When the firm needs external funds, the executive plans to raise those funds through an IPO. Suppose that the current market is a hot issue market. Should the executive move up the firm's plans to take the firm public to try to take advantage of the hot issue market?

The traditional efficient-market based advice is that managers should not try to time markets. In contrast, the typical advice from financial executives is to try to exploit hot issue markets. On May 20, 2004, *The Wall Street Journal* quoted George Rathmann on this issue. Rathmann was the first chief executive officer of biotechnology firm Amgen. He drew an analogy between deciding whether or not to go IPO and deciding whether or not to accept hors d'oeuvres at a cocktail party when the tray comes around. His advice? Take the hors d'oeuvres when the tray comes around, whether you are hungry or not.[16]

Initial Underpricing

Financial executives' decisions play an important role in the extent of initial underpricing. The IPO offer price is typically determined in a pricing meeting between the firm's executives and the underwriters taking the firm public, just before the stock begins to trade publicly. The existence of initial underpricing suggests that on average, executives agree to an offer price that is too low, that they do not bargain hard enough, and consequently they leave money on the table.

Risk. If markets are efficient, the initial underpricing reflects compensation for risk, not the fact that executives do not bargain hard enough. That is, investors purchasing the shares at the offer price face risk in buying the shares of a new firm. Therefore, they are only willing to purchase those shares if the offer price is low enough.

Psychology and Changing Underpricing. Exhibit 5.3 shows that the magnitude of underpricing increased throughout the 1990s and soared during the bubble period, 1999–2000. Why were executives increasingly willing to leave so much money on the table, especially during the bubble period? There are several possible explanations: changing risk, behavioral phenomena, and agency conflicts. Behaviorists contend that there is no strong evidence that changing risk conditions could explain the dramatic amounts of money left on the table during the bubble period.[17] However, they do suggest that there are strong reasons to suspect that behavioral phenomena and agency conflicts were key.

EXHIBIT 5.3
Amount Left on Table 1990–2003

Source: Jay Ritter's Web site, **bear.cba.ufl.edu/ritter**.

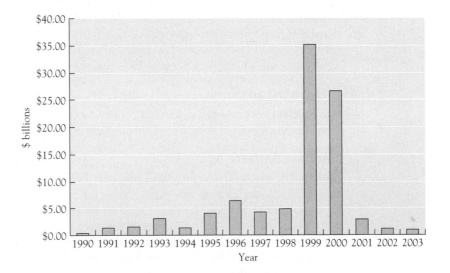

Imagine two people, Ginger and Jane, who have each just received parking tickets that will cost them $50 apiece. As it happens, both Ginger and Jane have won office lotteries for $75. Ginger won her office lottery the month before she received her parking ticket. Jane won her office lottery the same day she received her parking ticket. Both Ginger and Jane feel the pain of their parking tickets.

1. Who do you think feels the pain more intensely? You may answer Ginger, Jane, no difference, or no opinion.
2. Suppose that instead of receiving a parking ticket that will cost her $50, Ginger learns that she missed out on winning $50 in another office lottery because she was absent from work that day. Which do you believe would cause Ginger more pain, receiving the $50 parking ticket or having missed winning $50 in an office lottery?

Concept Preview Question 5.2 offers two lessons. The first lesson is that most people feel that Ginger experiences the pain from receiving her parking ticket more than Jane feels the pain from receiving hers. Presumably, Jane can mentally offset her $50 loss with the $75 lottery win and view herself as $25 ahead at the end of the day. However, that mental operation is much more difficult to do for Ginger, who is less likely to associate the $75 gain with the $50 loss because the gain occurred a month earlier. Therefore, Ginger is likely to view herself as being down $50 at the end of the day because of the parking ticket, instead of up $25.

The second lesson from Concept Preview Question 5.2 is that Ginger feels the $50 loss from the parking ticket more than she feels having lost out on winning $50 in the office lottery. Generally, people experience a cost that is out of pocket more intensely than an opportunity cost.

Consider an IPO example to illustrate the behavioral phenomenon just described.[18] VA Linux Systems (now VA Software) sells computers that run the Linux operating system, an alternative to Microsoft's Windows. When the firm planned to undertake an IPO, it filed with the SEC and established a file range for its offer price of $11 to $13 a share. VA Linux went public on December 9, 1999, issuing 4.4 million shares at an offer price of $30 to raise $132 million. That day VA Linux set a new record for initial underpricing, closing its first day at a price of $239.25, for a return of 698 percent.

Based on the difference between its offer price and its stock price at the end of its first day, VA Linux left $920.7 million on the table. Had the offer price been $239.25 instead of $30, the firm would have only needed to issue 551,724 shares to raise $132 million, not 4.4 million shares. As a result, the original shareholders ended up owning about 9 percent less of the firm. See Exhibit 5.4.

Was VA Linux's huge first-day return gain predictable? Based on other recent IPOs, a large first-day gain was predictable, although certainly not the record amount set. As Exhibit 5.1 shows, throughout the bubble period the magnitude of underpricing had been large. Several months earlier, on August 11, the share price of Red Hat Inc., a distributor of Linux, tripled on its first day of trading. By the time

EXHIBIT 5.4
Money Left on Table for VA Linux IPO

Source: Jay Ritter's Web site,
bear.cba.ufl.edu/ritter.

Midpoint file range in initial prospectus	$12.00
Offer price	$30.00
Price close on first day of trading	$239.25
Number of shares held prior to IPO	35,307,419
Number of shares issued in IPO	4,400,000
Amount raised by IPO	$132,000,000
Number of new shares issued if no underpricing	551,724
Percent of firm retained by initial investors	88.9%
Percent of firm retained by initial investors if no underpricing	98.5%

VA Linux went public, Red Hat shares had risen twentyfold and were trading at $286.25. Andover.net Inc., another firm with a significant Linux component, had gone public a few days before VA Linux, and its share price had more than tripled.

In agreeing to initial underpricing, VA Linux's chief executive, Larry M. Augustin, agreed to owning 2 percent less of the firm than he would have if the offer price had been set at $286.25. As was mentioned, the original investors collectively gave up 9 percent.

Think about the changes to Augustin's personal wealth during the IPO process. When VA Linux went public, Augustin owned 6.6 million shares. Based on the midpoint of the $11 to $13 file range specified in the initial prospectus, he might have expected his shares to be worth $12 each. Therefore, the $30 offer price constituted a mental gain of $18 per share, a total wealth gain of about $119 million. And the record first-day return increased Augustin's wealth by another $1.4 billion.

As in Concept Preview Question 5.2, the money left on the table is not experienced as painfully if it occurs in conjunction with some other gain, and moreover, is framed as an opportunity cost. Although giving up 9 percent of a firm is not small change, it is difficult to imagine a CEO feeling too badly when his personal wealth has just increased on successive days by $119 million and $1.4 billion. Those gains are not only tangible, but take attention away from the money left on the table because of initial underpricing. Moreover, the amount of money left on the table is an opportunity cost, not an out-of-pocket cost.

Evidence indicates that CEOs who are satisfied with the psychological balance of gains and losses described above use the same underwriter for their first seasoned equity offering as their IPO.

Agency Conflicts and Changing Underpricing. Every year, the publication *Institutional Investor* ranks security analysts. Analysts achieving the highest rank are accorded star status. Notably, investment banks that underwrite IPOs employ analysts, with investment banks employing all-star analysts tending to gain market share in the underwriting business. Presumably this is because firms who choose an underwriter to take them IPO factor in analyst coverage in the aftermarket (post-IPO).

In exchange for taking a firm public, an investment bank typically charges an underwriting fee that amounts to 7 percent of the gross offering. Underwriters do not charge firms directly for analyst coverage. However, firms might pay indirectly for analyst coverage by agreeing to initial underpricing. That is, a firm might accept a lower offer price in exchange for coverage by an all-star analyst, believing that such coverage will promote higher stock prices in the future.

Underwriters might capture the benefits of initial underpricing indirectly rather than directly. They do so circuitously by allocating hot IPO shares, those that are likely to feature a large first-day return, to clients who will do a lot of business with their firm. To illustrate, consider a real example involving the investment bank Credit Suisse First Boston (CSFB).[19] A CSFB customer received an IPO allocation of 13,500 shares of VA Linux, which he sold on the first day for a profit of $3.3 million. The customer then sold two million shares of Compaq through CSFB, paying a commission of $0.50 a share, or $1 million in total. The customer then repurchased the two million shares of Compaq from another brokerage firm, paying only $0.06 a share in commissions. Overall, the customer paid $1.2 million in commissions, but came out $2.1 million ahead. CSFB captured $1 million of the $3.3 million in underpricing associated with the customer's allocation.

Investment banks extended the process of allocating hot IPO shares to favored customers. The practice came to be called *spinning* and was eventually banned as part of a legal settlement initiated by Eliot Spitzer, the New York Attorney General. Spinning exploits agency conflicts. An underwriter would spin hot IPO shares by allocating them to the personal accounts of financial executives whose investment banking business the underwriters wished to attract. Investment banker Frank Quattrone of CSFB attracted the most attention for the practice, and the brokerage accounts he set up for corporate executives came to be called *Friends of Frank* accounts.

On March 7, 2003, the *San Jose Mercury News* published a list of 63 executives who had Friends of Frank accounts. The median executive earned $538,000 from his or her account. An agency conflict arises when the executive of a firm that is planning to go public chooses to use CSFB and agrees to initial underpricing in exchange for large future allocations in his or her Friend of Frank account. The executive gains that benefit by imposing the underpricing cost on his or her own firm's investors. For its part, CSFB comes to be known for underpricing, and its Friends of Frank accounts attract a steady stream of executives to provide underpriced IPOs for its revolving-door scheme.

Frank Quattrone was tried for obstructing justice when he forwarded an e-mail message to CSFB employees suggesting that they delete documents. The e-mail was sent shortly after federal investigators began to focus on IPO practices at CSFB. In September 2004, Quattrone was found guilty and sentenced to an 18-month prison term, which he appealed. A year earlier, the National Association of Securities Dealers had barred him from the securities industry for life.

Long-Term Underperformance

The stock of VA Linux closed in 2002 at a price of $0.91 per share, providing a dramatic example of all three IPO phenomena. Although proponents of market efficiency suggest that long-term underperformance can be explained by factors such as size and book-to-market equity, Exhibit 5.2 provides evidence that this is not the case.[20] Although size and book-to-market equity explain some of the returns to IPOs, there appears to be a separate new-issue phenomenon.

Dilemma

The three IPO phenomena present executives with something of a dilemma. Maximizing market value in the short-term might well require going IPO in a hot issue

Debiasing for Better Decisions

Errors or biases: Executives agree to offer prices that are too low.
Why does it happen? Executives exhibit framing bias, emphasizing in-pocket gains over opportunity losses, and agency conflicts.
How does it happen? In the case of large revisions relative to the file range, executives overweight gains relative to the midpoint of the file range in relation to money left on the table from initial underpricing.
What can be done about it? Executives need to identify all the benefits and costs associated with going IPO, and think explicitly about treating opportunity costs in the same way as out-of-pocket costs.

market and paying for all-star analyst coverage by means of initial underpricing. However, doing so might involve exploiting excessive optimism on the part of current investors. If so, then there is reason to expect long-term underperformance, as the market eventually corrects itself.

What then should managers do? Maximize the interests of short-term investors over those of long-term investors, vice versa, or try to balance the two? There is no easy answer to this question, although anecdotes such as the one involving Herman-Miller suggest that managers are prone to strike a balance.

To the extent that market prices revert to fundamental value in the long-term, maximizing long-term value corresponds to the conventional approach based on NPV. To the extent that the impact of size, book-to-market equity, and momentum on expected returns stems from behavioral mispricing rather than fundamental risk, discount rates used for the long-term should be based on a single-factor CAPM approach.

The preceding statements should not be interpreted to mean that managers compute NPV correctly. Doing so requires that managers prepare unbiased forecasts of cash flow, the market risk premium, and risk. The evidence presented throughout this text suggests that managers' forecasts exhibit systematic bias.

Summary

Market efficiency is a subject of great debate among financial economists. The traditional approach holds that markets are efficient, whereas proponents of behavioral finance hold that in special circumstances market prices tend to be inefficient.

The debate about market efficiency has centered on a series of anomalies, such as the winner–loser effect, short-term momentum, post-earnings-announcement drift, stock split drift, and the new-issues puzzle. The traditional approach contends that these phenomena can be explained by compensation for risk. Proponents of behavioral finance suggest that these phenomena reflect market mispricing.

The notion of arbitrage is central to the debate between proponents of market efficiency and proponents of behavioral finance. Traditionalists contend that the actions of arbitrageurs render price inefficiencies small and temporary. Behaviorists contend that arbitrage is limited and that as a result market prices can deviate from intrinsic values substantially and for long periods of time.

Managers appear to behave as if they believe markets are inefficient. For example, they indicate that they would reject positive NPV projects if accepting those projects would lower their firm's EPS. They split their stocks, even though doing so has no value when markets are efficient. And they time IPOs to take advantage of hot issue markets.

Behavioral explanations alone do not explain managerial behavior in respect to IPOs. Agency issues also contribute to explaining initial underpricing and long-term underperformance, two other IPO phenomena.

Additional Behavioral Readings

Fox, J., "Learn to Play the Earnings Game (and Wall Street Will Love You)," *Fortune*, March 31, 1997.

Lamont, O. and R. Thaler, "Can the Market Add and Subtract? Mispricing in Tech Stock Carve-Outs," Working Paper, University of Chicago, 2000.

Loughran, T. and J. Ritter, "Why Has IPO Underpricing Changed over Time?" *Financial Management*, vol. 33, no. 3, 2004, pp. 5–37.

Key Terms

hot issue market, *82*	momentum, *76*	underreaction, *77*
initial underpricing, *82*	overreaction, *77*	winner–loser effect, *76*
limits of arbitrage, *78*	post-earnings-	
long-term	announcement drift, *77*	
underperformance, *82*		

Explore the Web

www.fullerthaler.com/Strategies.html
The Web site for the money management firm Fuller & Thaler, whose funds seek to exploit the winner–loser effect (Behavioral Value Fund) and post-earnings-announcement drift (Behavioral Growth Fund).

www.dfaus.com
The Web site for Dimensional Fund Advisors (DFA), whose philosophy reflects the views of efficient-market theory, viewing size and book-to-market equity as proxies for risk.

www.nasdr.com
Search for SEC litigation release 17327, documenting the manner in which Credit Suisse First Boston captured a portion of the value generated by initial underpricing.

Chapter Questions

1. In April 2003, analysts at Morgan Stanley and Prudential had set 12-month target prices of $106 and $108 for the firm eBay. At that time, eBay's stock price was $89.22 and the consensus forecast for eBay's EPS was $1.45. Subsequently, eBay split its stock two-for-one. Its actual EPS turned out to be $0.82 (postsplit, corresponding to $1.64 on a presplit basis). On April 30, 2004, eBay's stock price closed above $82 ($164 on a presplit basis), and the consensus analyst EPS forecast for the subsequent 12 months was $1.18 (postsplit). Discuss whether the stock of eBay was efficiently priced in April 2003. (In answering this question, you may wish to refer to the discussion in Chapter 2.)

2. Consider the comments of Brian Walker, the president of Herman-Miller North America, who was quoted in the chapter as having said: "For dot.coms, it appears that the market has implicitly capitalized a lot of those costs. The market views their negative earnings as investments in the future. It's more difficult for a traditional Old Economy company trying to participate in the New Economy, because when it affects my earnings, it's more difficult for Wall Street to say, 'We'll give you a break on this.'" Discuss Walker's remark in the context of the concepts developed in the chapter.

3. For many years, the large retail firm Wal-Mart chose not to provide guidance. The firm's legendary founder, Sam Walton, wrote in his autobiography that he did not care what the market thought. Beginning in 1994, Wal-Mart's earnings announcements generated a string of negative surprises. In the resulting post-earnings-announcement drift, Wal-Mart's cumulative abnormal return relative to the S&P 500 drifted down for the subsequent four years. Wal-Mart's situation changed dramatically in 1998. An article appearing in *Fortune* magazine described Wal-Mart stock as being hot again and noted that the reason stemmed from earnings. The article described Wal-Mart as having applied its "Main Street marketing skills" to its interactions with Wall Street analysts. Discuss what it means to apply Main Street marketing skills.

4. On August 19, 2004, the Internet search firm Google went public, at an offer price of $85 per share. The IPO was unconventional in that Google used an auction to determine its offer price and to sell shares to investors. In this respect, underwriters did not allocate shares to clients. Instead investors registered to participate in the auction and indicated the maximum price they were willing to pay, along with the number of shares they wished to purchase. If a registered investor's maximum price was at least the offer price, the investor paid the offer price, not their maximum price. Google had established its initial file range for the offer price to be $108 to $135 a share. However, based on the interest shown by investors in registering for the auction, the firm's executives reduced the range to between $85 and $95. On its first day, Google stock opened at $100 per share. Were investors who purchased Google shares at $100 irrational, in that they could have paid $85 the day before? Or might there be some other explanation for the 17 percent jump in price when the stock began to trade publicly? Discuss.

5. In 2004, 55 percent of firms provided guidance to analysts, down from 72 percent in the prior year.[21] Before Google's IPO, the firm's executives announced that they did not plan to issue earnings guidance to analysts. Discuss the pros and cons of such a decision.

Minicase

The IPO of Palm

Between January 1997 and August 1999, when the market rose sharply, 3Com's stock declined in value. In August 1999, about half of the analysts following 3Com were bearish on its stock and expressed widely divergent views about the firm's mixture of businesses.

At the time, 3Com had three businesses: modems and adaptor cards, networking equipment, and personal digital assistants (PDAs). CEO Eric Benhamou and CFO Chris Paisley considered whether their firm had become unfocused. In September 1999 3Com announced its intention to spin out its PDA Palm division, making it an independent publicly traded company, and refocusing on networking equipment.[22]

In March 2000, 3Com began to separate its handheld organizer division by selling 6 percent of Palm's outstanding shares, mostly in an initial public offering (IPO).[23] As part of the IPO, 3Com sold the shares to an investment banking syndicate, which in turn placed the shares with institutional investors at a price agreed upon by the investment banks and 3Com. (The lead underwriters were Goldman Sachs and Morgan Stanley.)

Between August 1999 and March 10, 2000, the Nasdaq composite index virtually doubled, and peaked at 5132 on March 10. Palm went public on March 2, 2000.

Palm's offer price was $38 per share. At the pricing meeting that established the offer price, 3Com executives realized that there would be severe initial underpricing. However, an offer price higher than $38 would have required refiling with the Securities and Exchange Commission and that would have resulted in a delay.

On March 2, Palm stock opened at $165 and closed the day at $95. When Palm went public, it had fewer than 700 employees. At $165 per share, Palm's valuation was $92.7 billion, placing it in the company of some of the largest firms in the United States, such as Disney and Boeing whose market capitalizations that day were $71.4 billion and $33.5 billion, respectively.

At the close of its first day of trading, Palm was worth $53.4 billion, more than 3Com's value of $28 billion. And 3Com still held 94 percent of Palm.[24] Why did the market permit Palm's stock to trade as high as it did early on, especially in March of 2000? Was there not a clear profit opportunity there? Indeed there was. However, investors who thought that Palm was highly overvalued at that time could not find shares to borrow in order to short the stock. Therefore the beliefs of excessively optimistic investors set the price of Palm.

In October 2000, *The Wall Street Journal* ran an article describing growing consumer demand for Palm PDAs. At the time, Palm's shares were trading at a forward P/E ratio of 350 and a price-to-sales ratio of about 20. Paul Sagawa, a wireless telecommunications analyst at Sanford Bernstein, rated Palm's shares as "outperform," called it his favorite stock, and described it as cheap because of its enormous upside potential. *The Wall Street Journal* article mentioned that Sagawa's enthusiasm for the stock increased after he purchased a Palm for his wife and watched her use it to keep track of her phone numbers and social appointments.

Eleven months after Palm's IPO, its stock was trading at $21. At that time, 3Com executives concluded that Palm was overvalued. For their part, Palm's executives acknowledged being uncertain how to compute Palm's fair value. And they did rely on P/E and price-to-sales in order to assess Palm's intrinsic value, comparing Palm's ratios to the ratios for other comparable firms. However, they were well aware about hot and cold issue markets. Eleven months after Palm's IPO, the firm's CFO indicated that Palm would not have wanted to raise equity in the conditions prevailing at the time, with Palm's stock down 45 percent from its offer price and the Nasdaq composite down by about the same amount.

The price of Palm's stock went from its all-time high of $165 on March 2, 2000, to $0.60 in August 2002.

The general evidence in respect to fundamental value is that the executives of many Internet firms did not believe their firms were overvalued at the time of their IPOs.[25] Some years after Palm's IPO, former 3Com executives were asked whether in retrospect 3Com had sold overvalued shares to the public.[26] They responded saying that they viewed Palm's shares as being overvalued relative to fundamentals, but undervalued at a $38 offer price relative to what the market was willing to pay in the aftermarket.

As to being overvalued relative to fundamentals, 3Com executives stated that they had the responsibility of maximizing value for their current shareholders at the time, and that it would be irresponsible not to do so, despite the likelihood that the return on Palm stock would be low in the long term.

Case Analysis Questions

1. Discuss whether any of the three IPO phenomena apply in regard to the Palm IPO.
2. Is the Palm IPO an extreme case?
3. Discuss whether Palm and 3Com were efficiently priced on Palm's first day of trading.
4. Analyze the assessment of Palm made by analyst Paul Sagawa.

Chapter **Six**

Capital Structure

The main objective of this chapter is for students to demonstrate that they can identify the manner in which biases impact the decisions that managers make about capital structure, amount of financing, and capital budgeting.

After completing this chapter students will be able to:

1. Describe the evidence that the primary factors that drive managers' decisions about capital structure are dilution, market timing, and financial flexibility, while traditional considerations such as taxes, costs of financial distress, and information asymmetries are secondary factors.
2. Compute adjusted present value to assess how the managers of a financially constrained firm with undervalued equity should choose between repurchasing shares and undertaking new profitable projects.
3. Explain why concerns about dilution and market timing lead investment policy to be sensitive to cash flows, causing excessively optimistic, overconfident managers of cash rich firms to adopt some negative net present value projects, and excessively optimistic, overconfident managers of cash poor firms to reject some positive net present value projects.
4. Identify excessive optimism and overconfidence in the psychological profile of executives.

6.1 TRADITIONAL APPROACH TO CAPITAL STRUCTURE

There are two main approaches to capital structure: **(1)** Modigliani-Miller tradeoff theory and **(2)** Myers-Majluf pecking-order theory. Tradeoff theory focuses on the tradeoff between debt tax shields and financial distress. Because interest paid is tax deductible, capital structure affects the after-tax cash flows to the firm's investors. In this respect, taxes confer a tax shield on the firm's investors, typically valued as the product of the corporate tax rate and the amount of debt.

Bankruptcy results in additional direct legal expenses. Moreover, bankruptcy involves the appointment of a court-ordered trustee with the charge of protecting the interests of debt-holders rather than shareholders. As such, a firm operating under bankruptcy incurs indirect costs of financial distress, as the trustee imposes constraints on the decisions of managers.

Taking on additional debt typically involves a tradeoff: increased tax shields on the positive side, and increased personal taxes and expected costs of financial distress on the negative side. A firm that chooses its debt-to-equity ratio in order to equate the two effects at the margin is said to choose an optimal capital structure.

Pecking-order theory suggests that a firm does not have an optimal debt-to-equity ratio. Instead, the firm follows a pecking order. If it needs additional financing, the firm first uses internally generated equity (cash). Once it exhausts its cash, it resorts to debt financing. If it exhausts its debt capacity, then it moves to new equity as a last resort.

What is the rationale behind the use of a pecking order? The answer is asymmetric information. Potential new shareholders might bid down the price of new equity, out of concern that managers know more than they themselves do and issue new equity when it is overvalued. For their part, managers do not wish to issue new equity when they perceive it to be undervalued and therefore might only do so once they have exhausted other sources of financing.

6.2 HOW DO MANAGERS CHOOSE CAPITAL STRUCTURE IN PRACTICE?

In practice, behavioral considerations combine with traditional considerations to drive the capital structure decisions made by executives. The main behavioral consideration is market timing, meaning buying low and selling high to take advantage of perceived inefficient prices. Executives sell high when they issue equity that they perceive to be overvalued. They buy low when they repurchase equity that they perceive to be undervalued. In this connection, perceptions are key, being unbiased in some circumstances and biased in others.

A good indication that capital structure decisions reflect both traditional considerations and market timing comes from the cover story of the September 2003 issue of *Financial Executive,* the main publication of Financial Executive International (FEI). That story was devoted to capital structure and was based on a series of wide-ranging interviews conducted with chief financial officers, corporate treasurers, consulting experts, and financiers.[1]

Those interviewed for the cover story explicitly state that the theoretical models taught in traditional finance classes are too static to provide them with the framework they need to make decisions about capital structure. Instead the interviewees focused on volatility associated with the future cash flows of their firms, uncertainty about subsequent investment opportunities, and conditions in capital markets. Many indicated that flexibility is key so that their firms can take advantage of opportunities involving investments, acquisitions, or market mispricing.

New Equity: Market Timing

Financial executives explicitly state that market timing is an important consideration in their capital structure decisions. General evidence about the views of financial managers on capital structure comes from a survey of CFOs conducted jointly by FEI and Duke University. Of the executives in 4,400 firms surveyed, 392 responded.

The FEI survey posed the following question to financial executives: "Has your firm seriously considered issuing common stock? If 'yes', what factors affect your firm's decision about issuing common stock?" The survey offered a series of factors from which executives could choose. Executives were asked to respond on a scale from 0 (not important) to 4 (very important).

In responding to this question, executives rated as the second most important consideration "the amount by which our stock is undervalued or overvalued in the market." Notably, 63 percent of CFOs attach a 3 or 4 to the following factor: "If our stock price has recently risen, the price at which we can sell is high." The mean response for this factor was 2.69. That is to say, market timing is a prominent consideration driving capital structure decisions, at least in the short-term.

Empirical evidence suggests that firms tend to issue new equity, and therefore achieve lower debt-to-equity ratios, when their market-to-book ratios are high.[2] This finding suggests that managers issue equity when that equity is most likely to be overvalued. Supporting evidence for this statement comes from a finding that when managers issue new shares, they also tend to engage in insider selling in respect to their personal portfolios.[3] As was discussed in Section 4.5 of Chapter 4, this aspect of managers' behavior appears to be driven by gambler's fallacy. Strictly speaking, managers might not perceive their stocks as being overvalued, but instead perceive their stock prices as high. Some researchers have concluded that issuing equity when the market-to-book ratio is high is no short-run phenomenon, meaning that fluctuations in market value can have very long-run impacts on capital structure.[4]

Number One Consideration, Earnings Dilution

The highest-rated consideration in respect to equity issuance was "earnings dilution." Sixty-nine percent rated this factor as either a 3 or 4, and its mean rating was 2.84. What does this mean? In the traditional approach, expected earnings per share (EPS) is directly related to the debt-to-equity ratio. Therefore, an equity issue would lower the debt-to-equity ratio, thereby driving down expected EPS. And executives might interpret lower EPS as dilution. In the behavioral approach, dilution is associated with market timing, a point taken up later in the chapter.

New Debt: Financial Flexibility

Consider next the factors that drive financial executives' decisions about new debt. The FEI survey tells us that the top factor is financial flexibility: having enough internal funds available to pursue new projects when they come along. This item had a mean survey rating of 2.59: sixty percent rated it as either a 3 or 4. Not surprisingly, flexibility was also a key theme in the comments of those interviewed for the *Financial Executive* cover story mentioned earlier.

Convertible Debt

The survey finds that more than 55 percent of CFOs who issue convertible debt assign either a 3 or 4 to the statement that convertible debt is an inexpensive way to issue "delayed" common stock. Indeed, 50 percent assign a 3 or 4 to the statement that they issue convertible debt because their stock is currently undervalued.

Convertible debt exhibits at least two behavioral features that make it appear attractive to financial executives.[5] First, the interest rate on convertible debt tends to be less than the interest rate on fixed debt, so convertible debt appears to be a cheap form of debt financing. Second, because convertible debt converts to equity only when the future stock price rises, it appears to be a cheap form of equity as well. These framing features by no means imply that convertible debt is necessarily a cheap form of financing. That depends on how the debt is priced in the market. Indeed there is evidence that hedge funds trade convertible debt in order to exploit mispricing. In some instances, this trading activity injects considerable volatility into the firm's stock price.[6]

Target Debt-to-Equity Ratio

The FEI survey indicates that executive decisions about capital structure reflect traditional tradeoff considerations as well as market timing. At the same time, the survey evidence indicates that executives assign tradeoff considerations a lower priority than other competing concerns.

The main survey question that elicited executives' responses asked: "What factors affect how you choose the appropriate amount of debt for your firm?" Among the factor choices that the survey offered CFOs was "maintaining a target debt-to-equity ratio," this being the central issue in tradeoff theory. Just over 50 percent of CFOs assigned either a 3 or 4 (very important) to this factor. In other words, 50 percent indicate that a major feature of tradeoff theory is important. At the same time, this factor is rated fifth.[7]

In answering the question, 57 percent of CFOs attach a 3 or 4 to the firm's "credit rating (as assigned by rating agencies)," and 45 percent mention "the tax advantage of interest deductibility." These were the second- and fifth-highest rated items, respectively. Interestingly, less than 5 percent of CFOs attach a 3 or 4 to the "personal tax cost our investors face when they receive interest income."

Some empirical studies conclude that executives do establish target debt-to-equity ratios and attempt to close half the gap between current ratios and target ratios in less than two years.[8] These studies suggest that market timing is a minor consideration. However, other empirical studies conclude that market timing is a major consideration, so the issue is not settled.[9]

The tax benefit of debt has been estimated to be about 9 to 10 percent of firm value, before taking into account the effect of personal taxes. Personal taxes bring the estimate down to 7 percent.[10] Although traditional theory predicts that firms with lower costs of debt will choose to hold more debt than firms with higher costs of debt, the evidence suggests that the opposite is true. Chapter 1 provided a behavioral loss aversion-based explanation for why this is the case.

Firms with low expected costs of financial distress use debt conservatively. Large liquid firms in noncyclical industries use debt conservatively. During the early 1990s, the magnitude of unexploited tax shield by U.S. firms was about the same as the overall tax shields. During the early 1980s, the unexploited tax shield was almost three times higher.

Traditional Pecking Order

The traditional pecking-order theory predicts that investors' concerns about being informationally disadvantaged relative to managers will lead managers to prefer internal equity to debt financing, and debt financing to external equity financing. Notably, when large firms engage in substantial investments, they tend to rely on debt financing. However, they do not appear to exhaust their cash reserves before undertaking debt.[11] Therefore, managers do not behave in strict accordance with the predictions of pecking-order theory.

The FEI survey reports little support for the asymmetric-information basis underlying traditional pecking-order theory. To be sure, CFOs are reluctant to issue equity when they believe that their firms' stocks are undervalued. However, the FEI survey finds little evidence to suggest that executives believe that the source of the undervaluation is perceived information asymmetry.

6.3   BEHAVIORAL APV

The behavioral approach to capital structure involves the same general framework as the traditional approach but incorporates the impact of biases. In the traditional approach, managers make financing and investment decisions by maximizing adjusted present value (APV), the sum of net present value (NPV) and the value of associated financing side effects. Traditional financing side effects include tax shields and the flotation costs associated with new issues. However, financing side effects can also include terms that reflect perceived market mispricing. In this respect, the **behavioral APV** framework can accommodate behavioral elements as well as traditional elements.

behavioral APV
The inclusion of behavioral elements in adjusted present value to reflect either mispricing or managerial biases.

Perception of Overvalued Equity: New Issues

The first chief executive officer of the biotechnology firm Amgen quipped that managers should issue new equity whenever markets are receptive, whether or not they need to finance projects at the time. Hypothetically, suppose that Amgen could issue $1 billion worth of stock, with flotation costs amounting to $30 million. Suppose that it has no projects to fund at the time, but judges that the intrinsic value of the equity is only $750 million. In this case, the APV associated with the new issue would be $220 million (= $1 billion − $750 million − $30 million).

In this example, Amgen's executives would do its current shareholders a service by incurring a $30 million fee in order to transfer $250 million of wealth from new shareholders to them. APV measures the net benefit to current shareholders.

Perception of Undervalued Equity: Repurchases

Financial executives who perceive the equity of their firms to be underpriced can repurchase shares. For example, imagine that Amgen's market value is underpriced by 25 percent. Then if Amgen spends $1 billion in cash to repurchase shares, it receives $1.25 billion in value. The APV associated with the decision is $250 million and represents a wealth transfer from shareholders who tender their shares to shareholders who retain their shares.

In 2003, the firm AutoNation was the largest seller of used and new cars in the United States. In June 2003 AutoNation held more than $200 million in cash. Its CFO at the time was Craig Monaghan. Suppose that Monaghan correctly judged that AutoNation's stock was undervalued. What action could Monaghan take to exploit this situation, buy low or sell high? In this case, he would buy low, meaning that AutoNation would engage in a share repurchase.

Although AutoNation could use some of its cash to repurchase shares, should it? The answer depends on the opportunity cost of that cash. At issue is how else that cash could be spent. What projects might not get funded if AutoNation uses cash to repurchase shares?

Between January 2002 and June 2003, AutoNation implemented an $836 million stock repurchase program and repurchased 20 percent of its outstanding shares. Notably the firm makes its decisions about repurchasing shares in conjunction with its operational goal of earning a 15 percent return on its investments. In this respect, the repurchasing decision to exploit market mispricing is treated like an investment project in respect to opportunity costs.

Craig Monaghan states that when he was in business school, he learned the traditional approach to capital structure and capital budgeting. Notably, the traditional approach is premised on market efficiency. However, in practice Monaghan bases his capital structure decisions on market timing, as he describes here:

> Right now we can move from acquisitions to share repurchases to spending on infrastructure. So if we see an opportunity to spend $100 million on an auto dealership, we can do it. Or we can do a stock buyback if the stock goes down . . . My professors at Wharton will tell you that a stock buyback is a wash. But when companies buy back their stock, they are sending a message loud and clear that management and the board have a strong belief that the company has more value and a brighter future than the market is recognizing. . . .

Source: Paul Sweeney "Capital Structure: Credibility and Flexibility," *Financial Executive International,* September 2003, pp. 33–36.

The results from the FEI survey indicate that 75 percent of firms make the decision about repurchase policy after having determined their investment plans. Many financial executives are willing to reduce repurchases in order to fund new projects.[12] Moreover, only about 25 percent believe that there are negative consequences attached to a reduction in repurchase activity.

In the traditional approach, market timing is not a traditional factor underlying the decision either to issue or repurchase shares. However, as the discussion about AutoNation in the Behavioral Pitfalls box above demonstrates, in practice financial executives come to learn that market timing is an important consideration in their decisions about capital structure.

Underreaction

In some instances, managers actually announce that they are repurchasing shares because they believe that their firms are undervalued. The evidence supports the idea that managers who repurchase shares are sending the market a clear signal. The average market response to the announcement of an open market repurchase is 3.5 percent.

Notably, investors appear to underreact to repurchases, in that stock prices drift upward when firms repurchase shares.[13] This drift effect comprises the flip side to the drift effect associated with new issues. (As was mentioned in Chapter 5, the market appears slow to adjust to new issues: The stocks of firms with new issues underperform for several years after the offering.)

As to long-run performance, the stocks of firms who repurchase shares and have high book-to-market equity earn abnormal returns of 45.3 percent over four years. When averaged over all firms, the average abnormal return after the initial announcement is 12.1 percent.

6.4 FINANCIAL FLEXIBILITY AND PROJECT HURDLE RATES

Undervalued Equity: Cash-Poor Firms Reject Some Positive NPV Projects

Suppose that AutoNation had a project whose NPV managers perceived to be $100 million. Imagine that undertaking the project required that AutoNation raise external financing in the amount $150 million at a time when its managers perceived the market value of their equity to be one-third of the intrinsic value of their equity. Suppose further that AutoNation had no debt capacity and almost no cash. In this case, AutoNation's managers would perceive the intrinsic value of a $150 million equity issue to be $450 million, thereby resulting in a $300 million wealth transfer from old shareholders to new shareholders ($300 = $450 − $150).

According to the FEI survey, the top factor that financial executives consider in their decision to issue new equity is dilution. In this example, the $300 million dilution cost outweighs the NPV of $100 million, leading the net effect on APV to be −$200 million. As a result, the managers of cash-poor AutoNation would be wise to avoid issuing equity and to reject the project.

Undervalued Equity for Cash-Limited Firms: Invest or Repurchase?

According to the FEI survey, the top factor that financial executives consider in their decisions about debt is financial flexibility. Inadequate financial flexibility means that the firm's managers might have to make their decisions about capital structure and investment jointly instead of separately. Just as the traditional approach adjusts project hurdle rates using an after-tax weighted average cost of capital to reflect tax shields, the behavioral approach adjusts hurdle rates to reflect mispricing.

In the traditional approach, a firm like AutoNation computes the NPV of its average project by discounting future expected cash flows at its cost of capital. If AutoNation's cost of capital is 15 percent, then it uses a hurdle rate of 15 percent to compute the NPV component of APV. As long as the firm has adequate cash or access to external capital markets, it can finance all projects that feature nonnegative perceived APV and can draw on cash holdings or debt capacity to repurchase shares.

A firm with limited cash and debt capacity might have to choose between repurchasing shares and financing investment projects. In this situation, managers should view a share repurchase as akin to an investment project. Those shareholders who do not tender would view a repurchase favorably, as long as engaging in the repurchase does not siphon away funds that would otherwise have been used to finance more valuable projects.

Suppose that AutoNation had limited cash, had no debt capacity, and is undervalued in the market. How would its managers choose between using the firm's cash to repurchase shares and using the firm's cash to finance a new project? The answer is that they base their choice on APV.

Consider an example. Imagine that the firm's shares are undervalued by 25 percent. Suppose that the project requires an initial investment of $500 million and has an NPV of $100 million. Which decision would create more value for investors, spending $500 million to repurchase shares or spending $500 million to fund the project? The value received from the share repurchase is $625 million (= 1.25 × $500 million), whereas the value received from the investment project is $600 million (= $500 million + $100 million). Transaction costs aside, repurchasing creates more value.

The point of this example is that repurchasing increases the opportunity cost of the firm's investment projects. Two key variables determine the appropriate adjustment to project hurdle rate: the firm's financing constraints and the impact of the firm's repurchase activity on the price of its shares. Suppose a firm has enough debt capacity to fund half the project with debt and uses its cash to fund the other half. In this case, the project will have a lower hurdle rate than if it is entirely financed with cash. Second, suppose that the firm's repurchasing activities cause its share price to rise dramatically. In this case, its managers might engage in limited repurchase activity, even if they only had mediocre projects available. Hence, the associated hurdle rate would be lower than if the repurchase activity had a lower impact on the market price.[14]

6.5   SENSITIVITY OF INVESTMENT TO CASH FLOW

sensitivity of investment to cash flow
Investment depends on how much cash a firm holds.

The authors of the report describing the FEI survey results conclude that executives make decisions about capital structure by relying heavily on practical, informal rules or heuristics. Managers who rely on rules might adjust their capital structure as a by-product of their investment policy, particularly if they follow a pecking order where they finance first from cash.

The tendency for investment policy to depend on how much cash a firm holds is known as the **sensitivity of investment to cash flow.** The evidence is strong that when firms receive more cash or take on less debt, they invest more.[15] Consider the example presented in the Behavioral Pitfalls box that appears on the next page.

In 2001, Adaptec CFO David Young also served as national chairman of FEI, the source of the survey data described previously. In this regard, FEI's chairman approached decisions about capital structure at his firm in much the same way as FEI's general membership. Notably, there are three important issues about Adaptec's approach to capital structure.[16]

First, Young tells us that before his tenure as CFO, Adaptec made unwise investments when it was cash-rich and its stock price was high. In this respect, Adaptec is typical when it comes to the sensitivity of investment to cash flow. The evidence is strong that when firms receive more cash or take on less debt, they invest more. Other instances of cash flow sensitivity that have been documented are as follows:

- Firms' acquisition activity increases when they are the recipients of large cash windfalls coming from legal settlements unrelated to their ongoing lines of business.[17]

Adaptec is a Silicon Valley firm headquartered in Milpitas, California, that produces and sells networking and storage devices. Adaptec was founded in 1981 and went public in 1986.

In 1991, Adaptec's debt-to-equity ratio, measured using book values, was close to zero. However, in 1996 Adaptec increased that ratio to 33 percent, and it stayed between 25 percent and 30 percent for the next five years.

David Young was chief financial officer at Adaptec between 2000 and 2003. In a presentation made in December 2001, Young was asked about the factors he takes into consideration in determining Adaptec's capital structure. In response, Young mentioned a variety of issues.

The first factor was cash. Young indicated that financial executives spend less time thinking about the debt-to-equity ratios of their firms when they have cash than when they do not. In this respect, he stated: "Cash is king and we live by that motto." At the conclusion of its fiscal year 2001, Adaptec had over $600 million in cash, and therefore did not have to go to the capital markets to raise funds.

The second factor was the current stock price. Adaptec's stock price had steadily climbed during 1999 and rose from about $10 per share, peaking above $50 per share in early 2000. See Exhibit 6.1.

However, as technology stocks fell during the remainder of 2000 and 2001, Adaptec's stock fell below $10. At the time of the discussion with Young, in November 2001, Adaptec's stock price stood at about $14. Young indicated that he did not view the market at the time as appropriate for Adaptec to be issuing new equity. He indicated that the issue of new equity would lead to a "dilution effect" for its existing shareholders because the price of its stock was "so low."

Young mentioned that Adaptec had last gone to the debt market in 1998, with a $200 million convertible issue bearing a $4\frac{3}{4}$ percent coupon rate. He stated that if Adaptec did need to raise $200 million at the time of his presentation, then it would do so in the debt market rather than the equity market. However, were the firm's stock price to be in the $30 to $40 range, then he would be willing to raise funds in the equity market, rather than the debt market.

Young described investments that his firm had made prior to his taking over as CFO. He pointed out that Adaptec had generated a lot of cash during the bull market of the 1990s. He stated: "Adaptec built a large Milpitas campus and a factory in Singapore when they had lots of cash coming in, that's what companies do." He then noted that the company had overinvested in both.

Source: Presentation made by Adaptec's chief financial officer at the time, David Young, on November 9, 2001, at Santa Clara University.

- Reinsurance companies reduce the supply of earthquake insurance after their capital positions have been impaired by large hurricanes.[18]
- When cash flow increases or leverage decreases in one division of a firm, investments in other divisions of the firm increase significantly.[19]

Second, in line with the FEI survey, market timing was an important consideration for Adaptec in its approach to capital structure. Had the firm a need for external financing in 2001, Young would not have chosen to issue what he perceived to be undervalued equity. Instead, he would have chosen to issue convertible debt.

Third, in line with the FEI survey, Young made no reference to a target debt-to-equity ratio. Instead, he approached capital structure with a pecking order in mind: cash, followed by convertible debt, followed by external equity as a last resort. However, the basis for the pecking order did not appear to be asymmetric information, but rather his perception that Adaptec's stock was undervalued in the market.

EXHIBIT 6.1

**(a) Adaptec Stock Price
January 1990–
October 2001
(b) Adaptec Net Income
(Loss) 1990–2001**

Source: Center for Research in
Security Prices, Compustat.

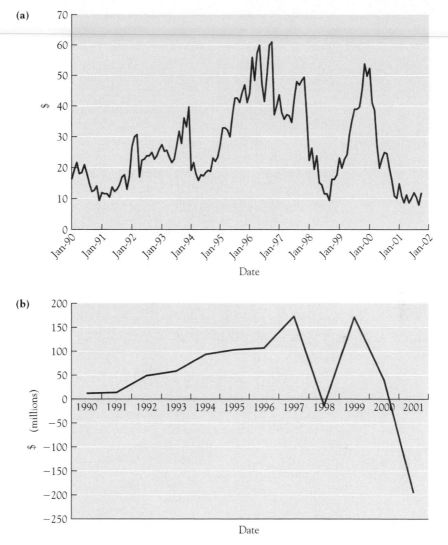

6.6　EXCESSIVE OPTIMISM, OVERCONFIDENCE, AND CASH

The discussion in this chapter about market timing is couched in terms of perceived mispricing. In some instances, managers' perceptions are correct, and in other instances they are not. The behavioral approach is concerned with both.

The most pervasive behavioral biases afflicting managers are excessive optimism and overconfidence. As discussed in the following, the combination of excessive optimism and overconfidence leads the managers of cash-rich firms to undertake negative NPV projects. The discussion of Adaptec serves to illustrate this point. However, as in Section 6.4, excessive optimism and overconfidence might also lead the managers of cash-poor firms to reject some positive NPV projects. Taken together, this implies that the investment policy in firms whose executives are excessively optimistic and overconfident will tend to display cash flow sensitivity. The evidence indicates that on balance, these firms overinvest.[20]

It is easy to see why the managers of cash-rich firms undertake negative NPV projects. Excessive optimism and overconfidence leads managers to overestimate future project cash flows and underestimate project risk. As a result, these managers overestimate project NPV. When their firms are fairly valued in the market, the same biases lead them to conclude that their firms are undervalued. However, because they are cash-rich, they have no need for external financing. As a result, they use their cash to fund projects that they perceive to feature positive (or zero) NPV, but which in reality feature negative NPV.

Excessively optimistic, overconfident managers of cash-poor firms also overestimate project NPV and are prone to conclude that their firms are undervalued in the market. However, these managers face a dilemma. In computing APV, they overestimate both project NPV and the associated financing side effects. In particular, their reluctance to avoid dilution can dominate their desire to fund a positive NPV project. The net result is that excessively optimistic, overconfident managers misjudge APV to be negative when it is, in reality, positive. As a result, they reject some positive NPV projects when they are cash-poor and have limited debt capacity.

Identifying Excessively Optimistic, Overconfident Executives

press coverage overconfidence indicator
The press uses the words *optimistic* and *confident* to describe an executive.

There are at least two indications that a CEO is excessively optimistic and overconfident. The first indicator is press coverage. When press descriptions of a CEO tend to use words such as *optimistic* and *confident,* there is good reason to suspect that the executive is actually excessively optimistic and overconfident. Call this the **press coverage overconfidence indicator.** Concept Preview Question 6.1 sets the stage for the second indicator.

CONCEPT PREVIEW
Question 6.1

Imagine that you are the chief executive officer of a firm that has granted you one million stock options. These options were granted to you seven years ago and will expire in three years time. Your firm has done very well in the last seven years, your current outlook is bright, and your stock now trades at $35 per share. At the same time, your options are said to be deep "in-the-money" and allow you to purchase your firm's stock at a price of $10 per share. Suppose that you face a choice. You can do one of the following:

- Exercise the options today, sell the stock, take the $25 million profit, and purchase other assets for your portfolio.
- Delay exercising your options, hoping the stock price will go up even more.

What would you do if you were the CEO?

The second indication of CEO excessive optimism and overconfidence is that CEOs hold their executive stock options until they are close to expiration. Unlike outside investors, CEOs will be much more exposed to the unique risk associated with their firms, and therefore their portfolios will tend to be undiversified.

There are two main reasons for lack of diversification in CEO portfolios. First, CEO compensation contracts regularly contain large quantities of stock and option grants in lieu of cash compensation. To maximize the incentive effects of these holdings, boards prohibit their CEOs from perfectly hedging against the risk by selling company stock short. Second, the CEO's reputational capital is invested in the firm, so a bad outcome in her firm will not only negatively impact her personal portfolio but will also reduce her outside opportunities.

There are several psychological phenomena associated with the choice in Concept Preview Question 6.1. Because the worst outcome is that the options expire worthless, the two alternatives lie in the domain of gains. Remember from Chapter 1 that risk aversion in the domain of gains leads people who delay exercising their options to expect more than $25 million by accepting the risk of delay. Therefore, excessive optimism and overconfidence can trump loss aversion and induce people to delay exercising instead of accepting the sure $25 million.

The duration of a typical executive option is 10 years, and the option becomes fully vested after four years. How long should a CEO delay exercising his or her options, if those options are in-the-money? To answer this question, a CEO must trade the option-value of holding the stock options against the costs of being undiversified. In typical situations, the optimal exercise schedule involves exercising well before the final year.

longholders

Excessively optimistic, overconfident CEOs who hold their options into the final year.

Excessively optimistic, overconfident CEOs who hold their options into the final year are called **longholders.**[21]A study based on 477 large[22] publicly traded U.S. firms, for the period 1980 through 1994, found that 16 percent held an option at least once until the year of expiration. Further, these options were typically deep in-the-money, the median percentage by which the market price exceeds the exercise price having been 253 percent.

As was mentioned, the investment policies of firms with excessively optimistic, overconfident managers display excessive sensitivity to cash flows. The evidence indicates that firms with longholder CEOs are more likely to rely on internal cash to finance investment than other firms.[23] Longholding figures prominently as one of the key determinants of investment activity, along with cash flow, size of board of directors, and a measure of growth opportunities.[24]

Behaviorists do not say that people never learn, only that they learn slowly. Excessively optimistic, overconfident CEOs make the mistake of holding their executive options too long and end up losing money. Interestingly, a substantial number repeat the mistake. Notably, firms whose investment is especially sensitive to cash flow have CEOs who have repeated the mistake at least once and have lost money on their options at least once as a result. Moreover, for these firms, the sensitivity of investment to cash flow is stable over the tenure of the CEO. The next Behavioral Pitfalls box illustrates the two overconfidence indicators in respect to the CEO of Sun Microsystems Scott McNealy, whose

Chapter 1 mentions that the cover story in the July 26, 2004, issue of *BusinessWeek* is about Scott McNealy, the chief executive officer of high-technology firm Sun Microsystems. The *BusinessWeek* article uses the following adjectives to describe Scott McNealy: optimistic, smart, and cocky. Such coverage reflects the first indicator of excessive optimism and overconfidence.

Consider the second indicator. Is Scott McNealy a longholder? In 2004, McNealy received a salary of only $100,000 per year. The rest of his compensation was in the form of executive stock options.

In August 1997 Scott McNealy exercised options to buy 300,000 shares at $4.19. He sold them on the same day for over $46, receiving a gain of about $12.6 million. A spokesperson for Sun said that McNealy exercised the options because they were about to expire after 10 years.

In August 2001 McNealy exercised options to buy 929,088 shares for 74 cents apiece. He sold them for $17.03 each, for a net gain of more than $15.1 million. A spokesperson for Sun said that McNealy exercised the options because they were about to expire, but declined to comment further on the transactions. At the time, McNealy held more than 55 million shares of Sun.

In 2002 McNealy exercised existing stock options for a $25.2 million gain. A Sun spokesman said that most of the options McNealy exercised that year had lost most of their value and were about to expire. McNealy kept most of the shares.

In an interview published on April 1, 2002, McNealy told *BusinessWeek* that Sun's stock price was highly overvalued when it reached its peak of $64 two years before. In this respect, he sold about $100 million of Sun's stock in the fiscal year ending June 2000. However at that time he did not choose early exercise for the stock options that expired in 2002, which lost most of their value by the time he did exercise them.

Perhaps McNealy suffered from **hindsight bias** in 2002, the tendency to view events as obvious or almost certain when viewed in hindsight when those events were neither obvious nor almost certain when viewed in foresight.

In April 2003, McNealy exercised options to buy 1.6 million Sun shares for 86 cents a piece and sold those shares for about $3.30. A spokesperson for Sun said that the options were to expire in August.

As of May 2003, McNealy owned about 56 million shares of Sun, valued at about $227 million. As of September 2002, he also held 16.4 million exercisable options, according to the company's proxy statement filed with the Securities and Exchange Commission.

Sources: Dan Lee, "Sun Microsystems Chief Executive Gains $3.88 Million on Sale of Shares," *San Jose Mercury News*, May 26, 2003; Gary Strauss, "McNealy's Pay Value: $87M," *USA Today*, October 1, 2002; "Sun Microsystems CEO McNealy Exercises Stock Options," *Associated Press Newswires*, October 8, 2001; Duncan Martell, "Sun Executives Cash in on Options, Sell Shares as Stock Price Doubles," *Austin American-Statesman*, August 30, 1997; "A Talk with Scott McNealy: Sun's Chief on the Post-Enron Economy, HP, and More," *BusinessWeek*, April 1, 2002, p. 67.

hindsight bias
The tendency to view events as obvious or almost certain in hindsight when they are neither obvious nor almost certain when viewed in foresight.

experiences were discussed in Chapter 1. As you read the contents of the box, keep in mind that analysts had been critical of Sun Microsystems decision to invest heavily when it was cash rich but its sales and stock price were in rapid decline.

Assessing Value

Adaptec's CFO indicated that the firm's investment policy exhibited cash flow sensitivity. His comments also suggested that Adaptec followed a pecking order that was driven by market timing, in that he judged the stock to be undervalued. Was that judgment reasonable?

Consider the two panels in Exhibit 6.1. The top panel displays the stock price between 1990 and October 2001, just before Adaptec's CFO made his remarks. The bottom panel depicts Adaptec's earnings history between 1990 and 2001.

In December 2001, when Adaptec's CFO made his presentation, Adaptec's stock price stood at $14. Based on the information in Exhibit 6.1, how would you judge Adaptec's stock at this time?

1. Overpriced
2. Fairly priced
3. Underpriced

In respect to Concept Preview Question 6.2, subsequent events offer a little guidance. Adaptec's stock price and earnings both declined in 2002, as did the S&P 500. However, in 2003, when the S&P 500 returned 28.6 percent, Adaptec's stock price rose by 56.4 percent from $5.65 to $8.84. Still, this was a far cry from the $30 to $40 that in 2001 Adaptec's CFO considered to be fair.

Excessive optimism and overconfidence lead executives to conclude that the stocks of their firms are undervalued. The FEI survey documents that most financial executives view the stocks of their firms as being undervalued. Only about 25 percent of managers believe that their stocks are correctly valued.

The traditional DCF approach to valuation relies on the cost of equity. How do financial managers estimate the cost of equity in practice? The FEI survey posed this question to CFOs. The result? Seventy-four percent of the responding CFOs use the CAPM to estimate the cost of equity for their firms. Between 30 and 40 percent use the historical average arithmetic return. Between 30 and 40 percent also take other factors into account and use a multifactor approach.

Of special interest are the factors that CFOs focus upon. The most cited factor is interest rate risk, closely followed by foreign exchange risk, and then business cycle risk. After that come unexpected inflation, size, commodity prices, term structure, and distress.

At the bottom lie book-to-market equity and momentum. As was mentioned in Chapters 4 and 5, book-to-market equity and momentum play especially prominent roles in academic studies of the determinants of stock returns. Yet, most executives accord them little weight.

6.7 CONFLICT BETWEEN SHORT-TERM AND LONG-TERM HORIZONS

Proponents of behavioral finance suggest that stock returns tend to feature short-term momentum and long-term reversals. This pattern represents a challenge for financial managers. For example, suppose that investors are irrationally exuberant about a firm's prospects and would bid up a firm's stock price if its managers undertook a particular project. If managers believe that the project features negative NPV, should they undertake the project?

Consider the case of a firm whose book-to-market equity ratio is low and whose stock price has increased rapidly. From a behavioral perspective, such a firm is

Debiasing for Better Decisions

Errors or biases: Managers of cash-rich firms undertake negative NPV projects and hold too little debt, while managers of cash-poor firms avoid issuing external equity and reject positive NPV projects.

Why does it happen? Excessive optimism and overconfidence.

How does it happen? Excessively optimistic, overconfident managers misjudge APV. They overestimate the NPV of their potential projects as well as the intrinsic value of their firms.

What can be done about it? Executives can check *two* indicators for excessive optimism and overconfidence. The first is the financial press to ascertain whether they have been characterized as optimistic and confident. The second is their own exercise policy in respect to stock options. Executives who have been granted executive stock options can ask themselves whether their exercise behavior qualifies them as longholders. One technique to mitigate excessive optimism and overconfidence is to employ the two-step outside approach. In the first step of the outside approach, a firm's managers assess how successful managers at other comparable firms have been in making the same types of decisions. In the second step, managers ask themselves if they can honestly identify reasons why they should expect to be more successful than their peers.

likely to earn low returns long-term, not because it is relatively safe, but because its stock is overpriced and its price will revert toward intrinsic value. Therefore, managers who adopt projects for short-term gain effectively act as if they use low discount rates in their capital budgeting analysis.

In theory, managers have to decide whose interests they serve, investors who hold the stock for a short period and sell, or investors who plan to hold the stock long-term. There is no easy prescription to offer. In general, managers need to balance the two competing interests.[25]

In practice, managers place little weight on momentum and book-to-market equity when estimating the cost of equity. Therefore, relatively few managers might explicitly consider the tradeoff between serving the interests of investors who plan to hold the stock for a short period and those who plan to hold the stock long-term. From a capital budgeting perspective, the means by which managers estimate the cost of equity might lead them to downplay the gains from exploiting short-term mispricing.

Summary

Survey evidence indicates that dilution and market timing are the top factors that influence financial executives' decisions about issuing new equity. The top factor influencing financial executives' decisions about new debt is financial flexibility. As a group, financial executives also report that they attempt to target values for their firms' debt-to-equity ratios.

The behavioral APV approach to capital structure features errors and biases by managers, the market, or both. Managers who perceive that the securities of their firm are mispriced will be prone to engage in market timing. Such activity will be tempered by the extent to which the firm is financially constrained, its growth opportunities, and the sensitivity of its market price to new issues or repurchases.

Excessively optimistic, overconfident managers of cash-poor firms are prone to reject positive NPV projects because they overvalue the equity of their firms. Excessively optimistic, overconfident managers of cash-rich firms are prone to adopt negative NPV projects because they overvalue the cash flows from those projects.

Two indicators of CEO overconfidence involve press coverage and options exercise behavior. The behavioral approach to capital structure suggests that firms with excessively optimistic, overconfident managers feature investment policies that exhibit excess sensitivity to cash flows. Empirical work shows that firms with long-holder CEOs have investment policies that are excessively sensitive to cash flows.

Additional Behavioral Readings

Baker, M. and J. Wurgler, "Market Timing and Capital Structure," *Journal of Finance,* vol. 57, 2002, pp. 1–32.

Graham, J., "How Big Are the Tax Benefits of Debt?" *Journal of Finance* vol. 55, 2000, pp. 1901–1941.

Malmendier, U. and G. Tate, "CEO Overconfidence and Corporate Investment," Forthcoming in the *Journal of Finance.* 2004.

Stein, J., "Rational Capital Budgeting in an Irrational World," *Journal of Business,* vol. 69, no. 4, 1996.

Key Terms

behavioral APV, *96*	press coverage	sensitivity of investment to
hindsight bias, *104*	overconfidence	cash flow, *99*
longholders, *103*	indicator, *102*	

Explore the Web

www.adaptec.com
The Web site for Adaptec describes products and provides financial information about the firm.

www.autonation.com
The Web site for AutoNation provides a customer interface for customers to purchase vehicles.

www.psineteurope.de and **www.multimap.com**
Web sites for PSINet Europe. PSINet is the subject of the minicase.

www.cfosurvey.org
This site contains the results from the ongoing survey conducted by Duke University and Financial Executives International. In addition to the current survey results, see the tabs Past Results and Special Surveys.

Chapter Questions

1. In August 2004, Google went public at a price of $85 per share. One year later, its stock price reached $285, as the firm's earnings consistently exceeded analysts' consensus forecasts. At that time, its forward P/E ratio was 37.5 and its ratio book-to-market equity was 0.052. In August 2005, Google announced that it planned to issue 14,159,265 new shares in a seasoned equity offering. At the price prevailing at the time, the amount of the new offering would have been about $4 billion. In its SEC filing, Google managers stated that the proceeds for the offering were for general corporate purposes but the firm had no current agreements or commitments concerning material acquisitions. Analysts reacted with a series of speculative comments about what Google's managers might be planning to do

with the proceeds of the new issue. Discuss Google's seasoned equity offering in the context of the ideas described in the chapter. In addition, comment on the choice of the precise number Google managers selected in respect to the number of shares in its offering.

2. From January 1990 through March 1993, the stock of Cypress Semiconductor Corp. underperformed the S&P 500 by 26.5 percent on a cumulative basis. Then in April, the firm announced that its board authorized the repurchase of an additional one million common shares of the 37.6 million shares that were outstanding. In making the announcement, Cypress's management stated that they believed their firm's stock to be undervalued. In response to the announcement, Cypress shares rose 25 cents, closing at $10.125. Over the next year, Cypress's stock outperformed the S&P 500 by 66.4 percent. Over the next four years, Cypress's stock outperformed the S&P 500 by 16 percent on an annualized basis. Is the experience of Cypress Semiconductor typical or atypical of firms that repurchase shares?

3. On December 19, 2000, an article appeared in *The Wall Street Journal* discussing stock price declines that followed share repurchases made by AT&T, Intel, Microsoft, and Hewlett-Packard.[26] The article mentions that Warren Buffett, chairman of Berkshire Hathaway, criticized firms that engaged in share repurchases. In a letter to shareholders, he noted that share repurchases made sense during the mid-1970s, when many stocks traded below their intrinsic value. However, he argued that conditions changed during the bull market of the 1990s, even though share repurchases had become much more frequent. He also suggested that the motivation for share repurchases had also changed and that during the 1990s firms bought back their shares in order to pump up their stock prices. Discuss Warren Buffett's views in the context of the chapter text.

4. The March 11, 2004, issue of *BusinessWeek* magazine reported that Standard & Poor's had reduced Sun Microsystem's debt rating to junk status. Over the course of the next two days, Sun's stock price fell by 11 percent. Both S&P and the financial analysts covering Sun had been expressing concerns about the firm's profitability and urging the firm to cut costs. In response, Sun's executives stated that the concerns expressed were overblown. They pointed out that the firm had more than $5.1 billion in cash and short-term investments and was hardly on the verge of ruin. Discuss the response of Sun's executives within the context of the chapter material.

5. Imagine that AutoNation is contemplating a project that requires a $350 million initial outlay and features an NPV of $48 million. The firm is all-equity financed and has $150 million in cash that it plans to invest in the project. AutoNation's current market value of equity is $3.4 billion. AutoNation's investment bankers have advised the firm's financial managers that they could raise $200 million of external financing either by issuing new debt at 5 percent or by issuing new equity. If the firm issues new equity, then the new shareholders would come to hold 5 percent of the firm, whose total value, conditional on adopting the project they estimate to be worth about $4 billion. Suppose that AutoNation's managers have concluded that their firm is overvalued in the market. Specifically, they have concluded that the minimum which new shareholders should demand for the $200 million is 5.3 percent of the firm. In this respect, the managers estimate that the intrinsic value of the firm would be about $3.8 billion if they adopt the project. Assume that flotation costs are zero. Suppose that the corporate tax rate is 35 percent, the risk of financial distress is low enough to be ignored, and that the firm can borrow at an interest rate of 5 percent. Compare the APV of the project if financed with debt to the APV of the project if financed with equity. Which is the better way to finance the project, with debt or with equity?

6. Imagine that Adaptec is contemplating a project that requires a $3.75 billion initial outlay and features an NPV of $466 million. The firm is all-equity financed and has $1 billion in cash that it plans to invest in the project. Adaptec's current market value of equity is

$6.68 billion. Adaptec's investment bankers have advised the firm's financial managers that they could raise the $2.75 billion by issuing new equity. However, Adaptec has no capacity for debt. If the firm issues new equity, then the new shareholders would come to hold 28.5 percent of the firm, which is conditional on adopting the project they estimate to be worth $9.569 billion. The investment bankers have computed the NPV of the project to be about $227 million, not the $466 million computed by Adaptec's managers. Adaptec's managers have concluded that their firm is undervalued in the market and that its intrinsic value would be about $13 billion if it adopts the project. In addition, the managers have concluded that the new shareholders merit 21.2 percent of the firm for their $2.75 billion investment. Nevertheless, the investment bankers have made it clear that unless Adaptec's managers agree to give up 28.5 percent of their firm, they will not be able to raise the $2.75 billion. Assume that flotation costs are zero. Suppose that Adaptec has no debt capacity and has to rely on external equity. What value of APV would the managers of Adaptec compute if they adopted the project and financed it with equity?

Minicase

PSINet

The fiber-optic communications firm PSINet went public in 1995 and raised $46 million. Shortly thereafter, PSINet began to serve business customers as well, establishing 100,000 business accounts in 27 countries. They undertook a strategy to run one of the world's largest networks, linked to a massive number of PSINet-owned Web-hosting centers.

During this time, PSINet's debt load increased 36-fold, from $112 million to $4 billion. Its annual interest obligations went from being $5 million in 1997 to being $400 million in 2000. In April 1998, for the first time in its history, PSINet issued debt that was below investment grade (junk), selling $600 million in bonds paying 10 percent.

The firm then made a series of large investments: It spent $34 million for new headquarters, purchased a corporate jet, and agreed to pay $90 million in order to have the new Baltimore Ravens football stadium bear its name.

The cover story in the May 28, 2001, issue of *Forbes* magazine describes how PSINet's CEO, William Schrader, and its board of directors assessed the firm's financing strategy.

"We knew we were going to be heavy on the debt side, light on the equity side," says William Baumer, a board member and an economist who heads the University of Buffalo's philosophy department. "The assessment was that the debt markets are wide open, the equity markets not as good, and if we are successful here, we won't have any trouble retiring this debt." Schrader insists Wall Street would have been cool to additional stock offerings, despite PSINet's lofty price. "Wall Street says when you can raise equity," he claims.

In the two years leading to the peak of the technology bubble in March 2000, PSINet's stock price rose from $7 to $60. Between 1997 and 2000, PSINet made 76 acquisitions.

After a period of very rapid growth in the second half of the 1990s, the telecommunications sector began a sharp decline in the autumn of 2000. On May 1, 2001, PSInet began to default on its $400 billion debt. It missed a $20 million interest payment and announced that it would likely seek bankruptcy protection. Its stock fell to 18 cents a share and was delisted.

PSINet's CEO and founder, William Schrader, resigned in May 2001. The *Forbes* story contains an interesting description of Schrader, stating that "implacable self-confidence helped Bill Schrader transform a few leased phone lines into a sprawling global network."

Case Analysis Questions

1. Was the main factor driving PSINet's capital structure (a) the tradeoff between tax shields and costs of financial distress, (b) asymmetric information, (c) its cash position, or (d) perceived mispricing?
2. Did PSINet's managers use a financing pecking order?
3. Did PSINet's cash position affect its investment policy?
4. Was PSINet's chief executive officer overconfident, and did he believe that PSINet's equity was undervalued?

Chapter **Seven**

Dividend Policy

The main objective of this chapter is for students to demonstrate that they can identify the manner in which biases and framing impact the behavior of managers, investors, and market prices in respect to dividend policy.

After completing this chapter students will be able to:

1. Explain why framing effects lead some investors to find cash dividends attractive.
2. Identify conditions under which managers cater to investors' preference for cash dividends.
3. Describe heuristics that managers use to set the dividend policies of their firms.
4. Describe the manner in which managers view dividends differently from share repurchases.

7.1 TRADITIONAL APPROACH TO PAYOUTS

The traditional framework for analyzing dividend policy was developed by Merton Miller and Franco Modigliani and is known as MM.[1] The basic premise of the MM framework is that investors are immune to framing effects, so that value is based on cash flows no matter how these flows are framed.

MM suggests that when taxes and transaction costs are set aside, dividend policy is irrelevant. According to this theory, if there are tax disadvantages to dividends, firms should choose low or zero payout rates. The MM argument for dividend irrelevancy assumes that investors are immune from framing effects. MM points out that if investors desired dividends, and firms were not paying dividends, then investors could create homemade dividends by selling shares.

There is no single traditional view about what constitutes appropriate dividend policy. Some follow MM and advocate minimizing dividend payouts. Others advocate dividend payouts because of issues that MM does not take into account, such as agency conflicts. In this respect, zero dividend payouts might make sense if investors could trust managers to avoid adopting projects that benefit the managers but carry negative NPV from the perspective of shareholders.

There are other reasons why firms might pay out dividends: Managers often know more than investors. For example, think about what happens when managers, as insiders, have good projects, with high NPV, but regular investors lack the inside information to assess the value of these projects properly. In that case, managers with high-NPV projects might choose to pay a dividend, in order to signal that they can afford the tax-related penalty.

Notably, there is a tax penalty attached to cash dividends. Dividends are taxed immediately as ordinary income; however, capital gains can be deferred until they are realized. Of course, if firms plow back all their earnings instead of paying dividends, then investors receive their wealth in the form of capital gains instead of dividends and only pay tax when they sell the stock. The benefits of deferred taxation discourage dividend payouts.

Is there an alternative to paying the cash out to shareholders, an alternative that avoids double taxation? Indeed yes, namely share repurchase: The firm can simply repurchase shares on an intermittent, irregular basis. However, repurchases need to be intermittent and irregular. Otherwise they will be treated as dividends and subject to tax.

In the absence of transaction costs, a share repurchase offsets a new issue of the same magnitude. Setting aside tax considerations, the argument developed by MM makes clear that the same relationship holds in respect to dividends and new issues. In this respect, share repurchases have identical cash flow implications as dividends, meaning that the two can be considered as a substitute means for distributing cash to shareholders.

7.2 CHANGES IN TAX POLICY

In May 2003 the individual tax rate for both dividends and capital gains was reduced to 15 percent. Before that, dividends had been taxed as ordinary income, at a top rate of 38.6 percent, and capital gains had been taxed at 20 percent. The previous tax differential had imposed a penalty on investors who favor cash dividends over capital gains.

With the differential eliminated, firms increased their payouts, thereby indicating that dividend policy is important and responsive to economic conditions. In May 2004 *The Wall Street Journal* reported that firms in the S&P 500 paid out record-level dividends. Indeed, 75 percent of firms in the index, 376 in total, were paying dividends, up from 351 in 2002. The firms that paid out the most in dividends were Citigroup, General Electric, and Exxon Mobil. Notably, 119 firms in the index raised their payouts, among those being Wal-Mart, Coca-Cola, and Harley-Davidson. Only three reduced their payouts.[2] Among those, Winn-Dixie Stores was the only firm to suspend its dividend.

Changing Attitudes and Perceptions about Risk

catering
Choosing a dividend policy with the purpose of responding to investors' psychological needs, be those needs associated with preferences or with investor sentiment.

The attitudes of investors and analysts toward dividends were dramatically different in 2003 than they had been in the 1990s. Therefore, both tax considerations and attitude toward risk provide reasons why managers might reconsider the manner in which their dividend policies are **catering** to investors. An article that appeared in *Barron's Online* on July 17, 2003, pointed out that investors no longer viewed dividends as negative and passé, as they did during the 1990s dot-com bubble.[3]

Example: Microsoft

In January 2003, Microsoft Corporation announced that after a two-for-one stock split it would pay an annual dividend of 8 cents per share, beginning in March. The March dividend was the first in Microsoft's history and amounted to a total payout of $870.6 million at a time when Microsoft held $43.4 billion in cash and cash equivalents. Eight months later, it announced that it would double its dividend payout.

On July 20, 2004, Microsoft announced that it would pay a special dividend of $32 billion in December 2004, would double its regular dividend to $3.5 billion, and would repurchase $30 billion in stock over the subsequent four years. The $32 billion payout would be a record. In response to the announcement, the price of Microsoft stock rose 5.7 percent in after-hours trading. Notably, Microsoft had the largest cash holdings of any firm, $56.4 billion.

In a front page story, the July 21 issue of *The Wall Street Journal* stated that Microsoft was seeking to broaden its investor base and was moving in the direction of the old AT&T model, that is, a *widows-and-orphans* stock in respect to regular dividend income and low risk. A widows-and-orphans stock, whatever does that mean? The answer turns out to be psychological, as we shall now see.

7.3   DIVIDENDS AND INDIVIDUAL INVESTORS: PSYCHOLOGY

Do individual investors realize that dividend policy would be irrelevant in a world with zero taxes and transaction costs? Do they find the cash flow framing effects described by MM to be transparent? These questions lie at the heart of the behavioral approach to dividend policy.

CONCEPT PREVIEW

Question 7.1

Imagine that you are retired and use three sources to fund your monthly expenses. You use

- Social Security to fund 20 percent of your expenses.
- A defined benefit pension plan that funds 45 percent of your expenses.
- Dividends from the one stock you own, a utility stock, to fund the remaining 35 percent.

Suppose that because of new investment opportunities, the managers of the utility have decided to omit the next quarterly dividend. You have a choice. Either you can let your consumption expenditures decline by 35 percent over the next 3 months, or you can sell some of your stock and spend the proceeds on consumption. If you had to choose between the following two courses of action, what would you do?

1. Cut consumption by 35 percent.

2. Sell some stock, and cut consumption by less than 35 percent.

Concept Preview Question 7.1 presents people with a dilemma. For people immune to framing effects who regard wealth as fungible, there is no reason to think that consumption should drop by the same amount as the omitted dividend. After all, investors can also use their equity wealth to fund consumption by selling some of their shares. Yet, it is typical for 90 percent answering Concept Preview Question 7.1 to say that they would cut consumption by the amount of the omitted dividend.[4]

In 1974, the shareholders of utility firm Consolidated Edison actually faced the dilemma described in Concept Preview Question 7.1.[5] However, the precipitating circumstances did not involve new investment opportunities but the sudden quadrupling of oil prices that occurred as part of the energy crisis of 1974. The higher associated costs led Consolidated Edison to omit a dividend for the first time in 89 years. The comments made by shareholders during its 1974 shareholder meeting focused on the demographic character of Con Ed's shareholder base. Shareholders were older, retired, and in many cases widowed, who placed their dividend income in the same category as their Social Security income. They relied on both their dividends and their Social Security checks to fund consumer expenses.

Next you will read excerpts from Con Ed's 1974 shareholder meeting that convey the attitudes of its individual shareholders. As you read these excerpts, keep Concept Preview Question 7.1 in mind. It reflects the situation that these investors faced.

In 1974, Con Ed's chairman was Charles Luce. Luce replied to a statement of concern from Wilma Soss, president of the Federation of Women's Shareholders in American Business, a proxy holder of about 1600 shares. She claimed to be representing "those who are retired and living on their pensions, as which are their dividends, and they have no other pensions except dividends." In his reply, Luce stated:

> I know, too, that your most immediate concern, which Miss Soss has just said, is the dividend on your Common Stock: Why did we pass the June dividend, and when will we recommence paying dividends?
>
> Investors buy Con Edison stock for assured income. A typical stockholder lives in or near New York City, and we certainly see evidence of that here today, owns about 100 shares—of course, many own more, but some own less—is retired or nearing retirement. Most of our stockholders are women, many are widowed, all are feeling the squeeze of inflation. When the dividend check doesn't come, there is real hardship for many people.

During the subsequent question-and-answer session, individual Con Ed shareholders continually reiterated Chairman Luce's comment about hardship. Here are two examples:

1. A lady came over to me a minute ago and she said to me, "Please say a word for the senior citizens." And she had tears in her eyes. And I really know what she means by that. She simply means now she will get only one check a month, and that will be her Social Security, and she's not going to make it, because you have denied her that dividend.
2. I recommend that you shall hold an executive meeting again, a special meeting by the board of directors, to bring to them the order of this meeting, ordering, not asking, ordering the restoration of the dividend, and to—(applause) and restore the good name of Con Edison that has been known for 89 years as a widow's stock, and no risk involved of ever eliminating the dividend.

Self-Control and Behavioral Life Cycle Hypothesis

How can we understand the preceding remarks made by Con Ed investors? In the traditional MM argument, investors can always create homemade dividends to fund consumer expenses by selling a portion of their stock holdings. In practice, older retired investors are reluctant to do so. The behavioral explanation for this reluctance is known as the **behavioral life cycle hypothesis.**

behavioral life cycle hypothesis
Over the course of their lives, people use mental accounts to cope with potential self-control problems that cause inadequate savings.

In the aggregate, people are challenged by the task of saving adequately for retirement.[6] Many fail to save adequately because the allure of current consumption overpowers their desire to delay gratification. People often use psychological techniques to help themselves face this challenge. One of the most important techniques involves **mental accounting,** the separation of information into manageable pieces, through the maintenance of separate accounts.

mental accounting
Mentally separating information into manageable pieces, by maintaining separate accounts.

People who behave in accordance with the behavioral life cycle hypothesis establish mental accounts for their wealth and adopt spending rules that are tied to their associated account balances. Broadly speaking, the mental accounts correspond to (1) current income, (2) liquid assets, (3) home equity, and (4) future income.

Consider an example to illustrate the general idea behind mental accounting–based spending rules. Suppose that a person, call her Jane, has learned that she will receive a special bonus over and above her regular compensation. This special bonus will be paid during the ordinary cycle, it will be paid monthly over the course of a year, and it will increase her (after tax) take-home pay by $500 a month for the next 12 months. By how much would Jane plan to increase her household monthly consumption during the next year? The typical answer is $200.

Suppose that instead of receiving a $6,000 bonus at work, Jane learned that one of her distant relatives died and left her a small inheritance with an after-tax value of $6,000. However, she was told that she would not receive the money for five years. During that time the money would be held in a unit investment trust where it would be invested in conservative interest-bearing securities. At the end of five years, she would definitely receive the $6,000 plus the interest that accrued. By how much would you expect Jane's household's consumption to increase over the next 12 months as a result of this gift? The typical response is $0.

When people are surveyed as to how they would behave if they found themselves in both of the situations described, many say that they would spend a substantial portion of the $6,000 if the money arrived as part of their monthly paycheck but save the entire $6,000 if it arrived in the future. Notably, even people holding large amounts of liquid assets, who could borrow if they wished, would not increase spending in anticipation of receiving the $6,000 plus accumulated interest.[7]

The bottom line is that people appear to organize their wealth into different mental accounts. The $500 monthly bonus amount went into the current income mental account. The $6,000 inheritance plus accumulated interest went into the future income mental account. People appear to follow rules whereby money in the current income account is used to fund current expenses. Money in the future income account is off-limits when it comes to funding current expenses.

If dividend income is allocated to current income, then people tend to treat that income as "spendable." In this respect, retired individual investors use dividends to mimic pension income, Social Security checks, and the paychecks of yesteryear. That is why dividends are labeled as "income."[8] However, equity is typically held in an asset account. Retired investors who adopt the rule "don't dip into capital" essentially prohibit themselves from spending out of their asset accounts.

self-control
The act of exercising control over one's impulses, usually to delay gratification.

Many older, retired stockholders will not dip into capital in order to exert **self-control.** They seem to worry that if they allow themselves to sell stock in order to finance consumer purchases on a regular basis, they will be raiding their nest egg and killing the goose that lays their golden eggs.[9]

Dividends and Risk

The behavioral life cycle hypothesis explains why older, retired investors often find dividends attractive. They use dividends to mimic foregone income from wages and salaries. Younger, employed investors are another matter. They are still receiving wages and salaries. Although younger employed investors might use mental accounting–based spending rules, dividends are not likely to play an important role in funding consumption. Might dividends play another role for younger investors?

CONCEPT PREVIEW
Question 7.2

1. Imagine that you face the following choice. You can accept a guaranteed $1,500 or take a risk. If you take the risk, the outcome will be determined by the toss of a fair coin. If heads comes up, you win $1,950. If tails comes up, you win $1,050. Would you accept the guaranteed $1,500 or take the risk?

2. Imagine that you took a risky decision that resulted in a gain of $1,500 for you, and you pocket the money. Now you have the opportunity to take a second risk. If you take the second risk, the outcome will be determined by the toss of a fair coin. If heads comes up, you win $450. If tails comes up, you lose $450. Would you accept the second risk?

Typically more people say they are willing to accept the second risk in part 2 of Concept Preview Question 7.2 than to accept the risk in part 1. Yet, in terms of incremental cash flows, the two risks are identical. Therefore, people who respond differently to the two parts of the question exhibit frame dependence. Apparently, people prefer to experience gains separately rather than together. This is part of a general phenomenon known as **hedonic editing.**

hedonic editing
People prefer to experience gains separately rather than together, but integrate small losses into larger gains.

The main point is that people are more willing to accept risk when the payoff is decomposed into a certain prior gain and an uncertain outcome than when the payoff is not decomposed. In this respect, the total return on a stock can be decomposed into a dividend yield and a capital gain (or loss). In the traditional framework, investors only care about after-tax total return: the decomposition is irrelevant. This is not so in the behavioral framework.

In the case of dividend-paying stocks, cash dividends play the role of the certain prior gain. Some people are more willing to accept risk when their payoffs are framed as packages of a safe component, such as a dividend, and a risky component, such as an uncertain capital gain. That is why a dividend is sometimes described as "a bird in the hand," as contrasted with "two in the bush."

Question

My wife and I are past 65 and retired. Ten years before retirement, we invested in electric utility stocks. The dividends from this investment now supplement our pensions. What are your thoughts on our method of investment?

Answer

Your results show your method is excellent. In general, utility stocks are conservative investments whose dividends and share prices rise moderately, but not spectacularly, over the years. And utility stocks seldom take big plunges in price.

Question

Some stocks used to be described as suitable for widows and orphans. Are there any such stocks left?

Answer

Thousands of income-starved investors—largely retirees, if not actually widows and orphans—still pine for low-risk stocks with high and predictable dividends. A classic example is the old AT&T, which paid its shareholders exactly $1.50 per share each year from 1922 to 1958, and then raised its payout consistently until 1983, after which the company was forced to break up.

In recent years, however, companies have turned away from paying dividends. And with the deregulation of once-predictable industries such as utilities, old-style widows-and-orphans stocks have become extremely rare. Bonds aren't an ideal alternative: Although companies can raise stock dividends, a bond comes with a fixed-interest coupon.

However, if you're willing to bend the rules to include stocks that pay high and stable dividends but whose prices bounce around more than the old AT&T, you can turn up several dozen candidates, mostly banks, basic industries, oil and gas suppliers, and conservative utilities. Each of the following firms has an annualized total return of 7% or better over the past 10 years and a dividend yield of at least 2%: Southern Co. (symbol SO), an electric utility; banks Wilmington Trust (WL) and National City (NCC); manufacturer Emerson Electric (EMR); and oil companies ExxonMobil (XOM) and ChevronTexaco (CVX).

Sources: William Doyle, "Your Money: Well-chosen Utility Stocks Can Be a Good Investment," *Atlanta Journal and Constitution,* May 30, 1991; "Answers to Your Money Questions," *Kiplinger's Personal Finance,* June 1, 2003.

Insights from Financial Columnists

Individual investors often turn to financial columnists for advice, and often ask about dividends. The excerpts featured in the Behavioral Pitfalls box above, provide some insight into the questions investors have asked over the years and the advice they have been given at various points (1991 and 2003).[10,11] As you read through the questions and answers, see if you can relate the discussion to the two behavioral phenomena described earlier, the behavioral life-cycle hypothesis and the decomposition of returns into a safe component and a risky component.

7.4   EMPIRICAL EVIDENCE

Analysis of individual investor accounts provides support for the anecdotal evidence discussed in the previous section.[12] The data involve the accounts of almost 78,000 investors trading at a large discount brokerage firm between 1991 and 1996. Depending on their personal circumstances, some individual investors find cash dividends especially attractive.

In particular, investors over the age of 65 concentrate their stock holdings in firms that pay high dividends, especially if the investors are retired. These investors hold over 80 percent of their stock portfolio in dividend-paying stocks. In contrast, investors under the age of 45 hold 65 percent of their portfolios in dividend-paying stocks.

Older investors exhibit a strong preference for dividends regardless of their income. They not only hold dividend-paying stocks, but assign considerably greater weight to stocks featuring high dividend yields. For example, older investors place 31 percent of their portfolio into the 20 percent of stocks that feature the highest dividend yield. However, only 16 percent allocate a portion of their wealth to the 20 percent of stocks that feature the lowest dividend yield. In addition, they actively purchase dividend-paying stocks during the week before ex-dividend days, but are not net buyers in the week following ex-dividend days. Moreover in the weeks after a firm has announced that it intends to omit a dividend, older investors reduce their holdings of its stock.

Notably, among young investors, those with lower incomes also assign a greater portion of their portfolios to high-dividend-yielding stocks. The tax penalty on dividends during this period might explain part of this pattern. The size of the penalty would have been smaller for individuals whose incomes were lower and who therefore faced lower income tax rates.

Older investors comprise 15 percent of the study sample. On average, older investors held a portfolio consisting of six stocks with a value of $55,685. In contrast, younger investors held a portfolio consisting of four stocks with a value of $24,402. Older investors also traded less frequently than younger investors.

Individual investors who prefer dividends might do so for at least three reasons: (1) to finance consumption in their later years, (2) to mitigate the experience of risk, and (3) because of tax effects. Evidence suggests that there are clienteles of investors, with each clientele motivated by at least one of these three reasons. Notably, the clientele associated with age appears to be dominant. In addition, there is evidence to suggest that individual investors reinvest less than 10 percent of their dividend income within two weeks of receiving that income. This finding supports the notion that investors tend to use dividends to finance consumption.[13]

Contrast with Institutional Investors

Individual investors have a larger average ownership in non-dividend-paying stocks than in dividend-paying stocks. However, the reverse is true for institutional investors, whose ownership in dividend-paying stocks is about twice as large as in non-dividend-paying stocks.

Nevertheless, institutional investors have a much different perspective on the attractiveness of dividends than do individual investors. Among institutional investors, pension funds and banks find dividends attractive mainly because of stricter "prudent-man" rules, rather than because of a sizeable payout. However, the evidence suggests that institutional investors favor repurchases over dividend payouts.[14] When a firm increases its dividend payouts, institutions tend to decrease their holdings. The following Behavioral Pitfalls box illustrates the differences between individual and institutional investors.[15]

In November 2002 the shareholders of Cisco Systems voted on a proposal that Cisco initiate a cash dividend and rejected the proposal by a margin of 10-to-1. At the time, Cisco held $21 billion in cash, and it had been generating cash flow from operations at the rate of $4 billion per year. Cisco's board of directors had authorized share repurchases up to $8 billion, and Cisco had repurchased about $3 billion during the prior 14-month period.

Cisco's board and managers opposed the proposal to initiate a cash dividend. Institutional investors also objected, stating instead their preference for share repurchases. At the same time, individual investors had been pressing for dividends at Cisco's annual shareholder meeting.

Consider the comments made by Lionel Stevens, a 71-year-old retired airplane-maintenance worker, who owned roughly 1,000 Cisco shares. Mr. Stevens' views about cash dividends were quoted in *The Wall Street Journal*. He said: "You know you're getting something. Growth is fine, but at the moment, it's not doing me much good."

The article in *The Wall Street Journal* quoting Mr. Stevens went on to make an interesting observation.

Analysts, investors and executives said decisions about paying dividends involve judgments about investor psychology and who can put the cash to better use. Paying a dividend would make Cisco more attractive to value investors; managers of some mutual funds are limited to investing in stocks that pay dividends. At the same time, some investors might view a dividend as a statement that managers expect slower growth.

To what psychological phenomena is this quotation referring? Does the issue involve agency conflicts as well as behavioral phenomena? If so, Cisco's managers apparently resented the implication. And the vote cast by Cisco's institutional investors indicated that they trusted the firm's management.

Source: Scott Thurm, "Companies: Cisco Systems' Shareholders Reject Proposal for Dividend," *The Wall Street Journal*, November 20, 2002. Copyright 2002 by Dow Jones & Co Inc. Reproduced with permission of Dow Jones & Co Inc in the format textbook via Copyright Clearance Center.

7.5   HOW MANAGERS THINK ABOUT DIVIDENDS

Consider the factors that drive managers' decisions about dividends. The discussion begins with a historical perspective.

Changing Payout Policies: Some History

Companies pay out cash to shareholders in three distinct ways: (1) cash dividends, (2) share repurchases, and (3) liquidating dividends to the shareholders of a target firm that has been acquired.[16] Large corporations typically pay out a substantial percentage of their earnings in the form of dividends and repurchases. During 1999, U.S. corporations paid out more than $350 billion in dividends and repurchases and over $400 billion in liquidating dividends. In the early 1970s, dividends dominated repurchases as a form of payout. Corporations paid out more than $10 in dividends for every $1 spent repurchasing shares.

During the 1980s this situation began to change, as corporations increased the frequency with which they repurchased shares. See Exhibit 7.1, which displays the historical yield series for both dividends and total payouts (the sum of dividends and repurchases). In 1990, dividend payouts were only twice as large as share repurchases. For corporations with positive earnings, dividends amounted to roughly 25 percent of earnings. Starting in the early 1980s, most corporations initiated their

EXHIBIT 7.1
Dividend Yield and
Payout Yield 1971–2003

Sources: Franklin Allen and Roni Michaely, "Payout Policy." In George Constantinides, Milton Harris, and René Stulz (eds.), *North-Holland Handbooks of Economics;* Jacob Boudoukh, Roni Michaely, Matthew Richardson, and Michael Roberts, "On the Importance of Measuring Payout Yield: Implications for Empirical Asset Pricing," Working Paper, New York University, 2003.

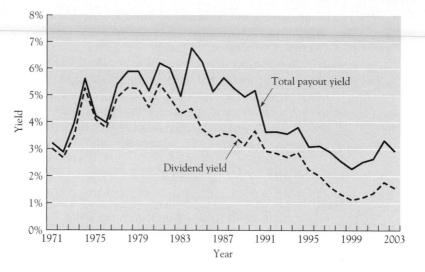

cash payments to shareholders in the form of repurchases rather than dividends. The percentage of firms doing so went from 27 percent in 1974 to 81 percent in 1998.

Between 1973 and 1996, individuals received more than half of the dividends that corporations paid out. Moreover, these individuals were in high tax brackets (40 percent) and therefore paid substantial taxes on these dividends.

Corporations smooth dividends relative to earnings. Between 1972 and 1998, aggregate earnings fell five times. However, aggregate dividends fell only twice, once in 1992 and again in 1998, and the decline was much smaller than for earnings. However, repurchases are more intermittent and irregular in their timing. Therefore, repurchases are more volatile than dividends. Between 1972 and 1998, aggregate repurchases fell seven times.

Dividend increases occur much more frequently than dividend decreases. During 1999 there were 1,703 dividend increases or initiations. In contrast, there were only 135 decreases or omissions during the same period. At the same time, it appears that corporations might have become less reluctant to omit dividends. Between 1989 and 1992, the average number of omissions was 302. Between 1993 and 1998, the average had grown to 1,087.

Notably, the market reacts positively to announcements of repurchases and dividend increases and negatively to announcements of dividend decreases. The effect is asymmetric: The price impact associated with a decrease in dividends is considerably stronger than the impact associated with an increase in dividends.

Survey Evidence

What are the factors that in practice determine corporate dividend policy and investors' differential attitudes toward payouts? In a classic 1956 article, John Lintner sought to understand how managers think about dividends by asking them directly, in interviews.[17] In doing so, he discovered that they establish long-run target payout ratios, yet smooth dividends in the short-run. He reports that managers are particularly concerned about having to rescind a dividend increase.

Lintner conducted his survey over a half century ago. Do CFOs still follow the heuristics identified by Lintner? The answer to this question is the subject of a recent survey of financial managers.[18] Apparently, little has changed in respect to what CFOs regard as the important factors in a company's dividend decisions. The factor most frequently cited is maintaining consistency with the firm's historic dividend policy, which was mentioned by over 80 percent of respondents. This was closely followed by stability of future earnings, and a sustainable change in earnings.

CFOs and Dividend Policy

CFOs are explicit, indicating strong agreement with the following statements[19]:

- We try to avoid reducing dividends per share.
- We try to maintain a smooth dividend stream from year to year.
- We consider the level of dividends per share that we have paid in recent quarters.
- We are reluctant to make dividend changes that might have to be reversed in the future.
- We consider the change or growth in dividends per share.

The authors of the survey updating Lintner's study conclude by stating that

> Weak support for the modern theories of payout policy points to the third dimension revealed by our surveying and interviewing hundreds of financial executives. Due to the complexity and high dimensionality of the optimal decision-making process, executives tend to employ decision rules (rules of thumb) that are fairly straightforward, in response to a handful of widely held beliefs about how outsiders and stakeholders will react.[20]

Dividend Heuristics

What are the rules of thumb, or heuristics, that executives follow when setting dividend policy? The authors of the study state the following:

> There is a severe penalty for cutting dividends, meet investors' expectations about the magnitude and form of payout (these expectations are set according to the firm's tradition and the stability of earnings), do not deviate far from competitors, maintain a good credit rating, it is good to have a broad and diverse investor base, maintain flexibility, and an important portion of investors price stocks using earnings multiples, so do not take actions that reduce earnings. These rules of the game are consistent with the informal rules[21] that . . . most affect debt policy, such as the desire for flexibility and a good credit rating, and equity policy, such as earnings per share and stock price appreciation.

Dividend Targets

Consider the findings that lead the study authors to these conclusions. One of the survey questions poses the following question to CFOs whose firms have paid dividends for the prior three years: "What do you target when you make your dividend decisions?" The most frequent target is dividends per share, a response that drew just under 50 percent. This was followed by the dividend payout ratio (about 25 percent), and growth in dividends per share (also about 25 percent).

Dividends as a Conveyor of Information

Consider whether CFOs consciously use dividends to convey information. Do they use dividends to affect investors' perceptions about the riskiness of their firm? The survey results are illuminating. Over 75 percent of respondents believe that dividends convey information about their firm to investors, and over 80 percent state that there are negative consequences to reducing dividends. About a third believe that paying dividends, instead of plowing back earnings, makes a firm's stock less risky. Given the strength with which these views are held, it is no surprise that just over 60 percent would rather raise funds to finance new investment projects than reduce dividends to finance those projects.

Attracting Investors

Presumably, CFOs set dividend policy with investors in mind. In the survey results, just under 50 percent mention that they set their policy in order to attract institutional investors to hold their stock, or to influence institutional investors. Is this because CFOs believe that paying dividends serves as a disciplinary device to reduce agency cost, by reducing managers' ability to choose negative net-present-value projects? About 30 percent cite "attracting institutional investors because they monitor management decisions." Yet, fewer than 15 percent cite "paying out dividends to reduce cash, thereby disciplining our firm to make efficient decisions."

Just over 40 percent mention that they set policy in order to attract individual (retail) investors. In this last respect, fewer than 30 percent mention the tax penalty associated with dividends, which is very interesting indeed.

Signaling

Some academics suggest that firms could use dividends as signals. Signaling theory is similar to a ceremony associated with the Native American celebration known as a *potlatch*. In Native American communities, blankets were important commodities that took many hours to produce. Yet, in some ceremonies, the members of one tribe would sometimes make a display by burning their own blankets in front of the members of some other tribe. Why? They did this in order to signal their wealth, meaning they were wealthy enough to burn blankets and not suffer unduly.

In the signaling theory of dividends, cash payouts play the same role as burning blankets. Managers who can afford to pay the cash out as a dividend, despite the associated tax cost to investors, will do so because their firm has highly profitable projects.

Do CFOs see themselves as using dividends as a signal? In particular, do they see dividends as the analogue of potlatch, burning blankets to show that they can afford the loss? As it happens, very few claim to use dividends in this way. Fewer than 10 percent indicate that they pay dividends to show they can afford to bear the costs of external funding or of passing up profitable investments, in order to make their firms look better than competitors.

Fewer than 20 percent of CFOs indicate agreement with the following statements:

- We pay dividends to show that our firm is strong enough to raise costly external capital if needed.

- We pay dividends to show that our stock is valuable enough that investors buy it even though they have to pay relatively costly dividend taxes.
- We pay dividends to show that our firm is strong enough to pass up some profitable investments.

Dividend Initiation

Consider firms that do not yet pay dividends but might initiate payouts. What are the main factors that their CFOs see as important to the decision? The following items were cited by over 40 percent of respondents:

- Increasing earnings per share.
- The influence of our institutional shareholders.
- Our company having extra cash/marketable securities.
- Having fewer profitable investments available (e.g., as our industry matures).

Fewer than 30 percent cited the attraction of retail investors or the undervaluation of their stock. As for using dividends as a disciplining device, fewer than 10 percent cited this issue.

What Has Changed Since 1956?

Some things have changed since Lintner conducted his survey in 1956. The evidence indicates that relatively fewer firms currently target the dividend payout ratio. Instead, more target the current level of dividends or the dividend growth rate. Notably, executives indicate that these targets are quite flexible through time.

7.6   CATERING TO INVESTORS' TASTES FOR DIVIDENDS

Dividend policy is partly a marketing decision, involving market segmentation. Investors arrange themselves into dividend clienteles. Managers need to think about their shareholders in the same way that they think about their customers. Like customers, investors have needs that are psychologically based. Just as customers react favorably or unfavorably to a firm's product or service, investors react favorably or unfavorably to a firm's dividend policy.

Through experience, financial managers have developed a set of heuristics to guide their dividend decisions. In particular, they smooth dividends. Think about the marketing implications of smoothing. For older, retired investors, personal consumption expenses have a regular, predictable pattern. Therefore, investors relying on dividends to fund personal consumption expenses will want dividends to have a regular, predictable pattern. If a firm's shareholders hold its stock because they like dividends, then managers may find it in their interest to smooth dividends relative to earnings.

During a bear market, investors who engage in hedonic editing might also favor stable dividend payouts because they are more tolerant of risk when they can frame total return into a stable dividend and a risky capital gain. A stable dividend payout caters to these investors' needs. However, during a bull market, changes in investors' perceptions of risk and return lead investors to regard dividends as passé.

Managers cater to investors' needs when they choose their payout policies to reflect the degree to which investors favor dividends.

Citizens Utilities Company

Between 1956 and 1989, Citizens Utilities Company offered two classes of shares, one that paid cash dividends and one that paid stock dividends. By charter, the payouts from the two shares had to have the exact same pretax value. Because of special Internal Revenue Service exemptions, the regular stock dividends were not taxable as ordinary income. Therefore, on an after-tax basis, the class paying stock dividends was superior to the class paying cash dividends. Yet, the cash dividend class actually traded at a premium over the stock dividend class.[22] This phenomenon is consistent with the idea that investors view the attractiveness of cash dividends as something special.

The case of Citizens Utilities suggests that investors' preference for cash dividends can lead to pricing effects in the market. Therefore, managers who understand that investors have a special preference for cash dividends might cater to this preference through their payout policy.

Catering and Price Effects

One way to gauge whether or not the stocks of dividend-paying firms are priced differently from the stocks of non-dividend-paying firms is to compare their book-to-market ratios.[23] If investors favor cash dividends, then we would expect the stocks of dividend-paying firms to have higher market values and therefore lower book-to-market equity than those of non-dividend-paying firms. Moreover, we would also expect that the difference in these ratios would change over time, with the differential being wider during the bear market of the 1970s than during the bull market of the 1990s.

As it happens, this is the way things have worked. Indeed, the magnitude of the book-to-market equity differential turns out to be correlated with the price differential between the two classes of shares offered by Citizens Utilities. The evidence supports the idea that many managers initiate dividend payments in an effort to cater to investors' demand for cash dividends. Initiations rise when the book-to-market equity differential widens.

Dividend increases occur after past earnings have improved, and stock prices respond positively to announcements about dividend increases.[24] However, future earnings are at best weakly related to past dividend changes. The strongest link seems to be that firms that increase dividends are less likely to suffer future earnings decreases than firms that maintain dividend payouts. Changes in dividends signal the past rather than the future.[25] That is, managers engage in unwarranted trend extrapolation.

Consider how the market reacts to a dividend omission?[26] Most firms that omit dividends are prior losers. (Therefore, it is reasonable to hypothesize that the same features would be at work as in the winner–loser effect that was described in Chapter 5.[27]) It is reasonable to predict that the market would overreact to the news of a dividend omission, at least in the long-term. However, it turns out that markets actually underreact. Following the announcement, prices drift for at least a year. The reaction to dividend initiations, not surprisingly a price rise, also features drift. But the strength of the effect is half as large as it is for dividend omissions. In this respect, remember that psychologically losses loom at least twice as large as gains.

Debiasing for Better Decisions

Errors or biases: Individual investors do not treat money as fungible.
Why does it happen? Mental accounting.
How does it happen? People attach mental tags to dollars depending on their sources or uses, and use spending rules that are based on mental accounting.
What can be done about it? The choice of dividend policy should reflect the manner in which shareholders treat dividends. Managers of firms whose shareholders rely on dividends to fund consumption expenses need to understand that as a result, they too might need to treat money as if it is not fungible. For example, managers might need to rely on external financing to fund new projects instead of reducing the dividend.

Summary

Policies regarding dividends and repurchases, relate to framing. In the traditional MM approach, people are assumed to be impervious to framing effects. In the behavioral approach, mental accounting and hedonic editing feature framing effects that lead individual investors to find dividends especially attractive. Older, retired investors find dividends attractive because they view dividends as a replacement for wage and salary income. Young, employed investors find dividends attractive because regular dividends make it easier for them to tolerate risk.

Managers have developed heuristics to set dividend policies in order to meet investors' psychological needs. Those heuristics involve smoothing. Managers who set dividend policies with investors' needs in mind are said to cater to investors.

Share repurchases are not psychologically equivalent to dividends. In this respect, managers also think about share repurchases differently than they think about dividends. Share repurchases need not be regular, whereas dividend payouts entail much more of a commitment to regularity.

Prices are impacted by changes in dividend policy and share repurchases. Many of these impacts give rise to price inefficiencies, notably drift effects. Markets underreact to both dividend omissions and dividend initiations, and the strength of the price impact is twice as large in the case of omissions. Markets also underreact to share repurchases.

Additional Behavioral Readings

Allen, F. and R. Michaely, 2003. "Payout Policy." In G. Constantinides, M. Harris, and R. Stulz (eds.), *North-Holland Handbooks of Economics,* vol. 1A, 1B, 2001. North Holland, Amsterdam.

Baker, M. and J. Wurgler, "A Catering Theory of Dividends," *Journal of Finance,* vol. 59, 2004, pp. 271–288.

Graham, J. and A. Kumar, "Dividend Preference of Retail Investors: Do Dividend Clienteles Exist?" *Journal of Finance,* forthcoming.

Shefrin, H. and M. Statman, "Explaining Investor Preference for Cash Dividends," *Journal of Financial Economics,* vol. 13, June 1984, pp. 253–282.

Key Terms

behavioral life cycle
hypothesis, *114*

catering, *111*
hedonic editing, *115*

mental accounting, *114*
self-control, *115*

Explore the Web

www.conedison.com
The Web site for the utility firm Consolidated Edison discussed in this chapter.

www.czn.net
The Web site of Citizens Communications, formerly Citizens Utilities, a firm discussed in this chapter.

www.nipsco.nisource.com
The Web site for Nipsco, a firm discussed in this chapter.

Chapter Questions

1. On July 23, 2002, an article entitled "Investors Appreciate Dividends Again, See Them as Safer Bets in Bear Market" appeared on *Associated Press Newswires*.[28] The article described two reasons why financial planners have routinely recommended that investors hold dividend-paying stocks, especially in bear markets such as the period 2001–2002. First, retired investors who use quarterly dividends to augment their income find dividends to be more attractive during bear markets. Second, investors search for a bird in the hand, which dividends represent. In this respect, dividends provide investors with the ability to be patient and wait out the market decline. The article quotes Steve Wetzel, a professor of finance at New York University's School of Continuing Education and a certified financial planner, and Arnie Kaufman, editor of Standard & Poor's newsletter *The Outlook*. Discuss both reasons mentioned, in the context of the chapter text.

2. Ashland Inc. is an oil services and diversified chemical company that is located in Covington, Kentucky. In 2002 Ashland Inc. was paying an annual dividend of $1.10 per share and was planning to keep its dividend payout steady. However, the firm's chairman, Paul Chellgren, noted that he was receiving more inquiries about its dividend policy from investors than at any time in his 28 years with the firm. He also noted that during the bull market of the 1990s, investors had asked him why the firm did not eliminate its dividend, since it was no longer important. Discuss Ashland's experience with investor communications in the context of the chapter text.

3. An article that appeared in *The Wall Street Journal* in February 2001 described the experiences of several investors who held dividend-paying stocks.[29] The article mentions two investors, Wayne Denny and George Gleghorn. Wayne Denny was 72 years old at the time of the article and had been living off $35,000 a year of annual dividends. His portfolio included AT&T, Edison International, and J.C. Penney Co. The point of the article was that all three firms had omitted their dividends during the past year. George Gleghorn was 73 at the time and had long preferred safe stocks that pay regular dividends. He too had invested in the California utility Edison International, as well as Pacific Gas and Electric. However, in the wake of deregulation in the electricity-generating industry, both stocks had fallen by more than 50 percent in the previous six months, and the two firms had omitted their dividends. Discuss the experiences of investors like Wayne Denny and George Gleghorn in the context of the chapter text.

4. In 1996, Kodak paid a cash dividend of $1.60 per share. At year-end 1996, Kodak shares were trading at about $80 per share. Between 1997 and 2001, Kodak paid $1.76, and in 2002 raised its dividend to $1.80. Yet, despite the stable dividend payout, the price of Kodak stock steadily fell, reaching $27 in 2003. At that time, the firm announced its

intention to reduce its dividend to about $0.50 per share, in order to invest $3 billion in digital technology purchases. Investors reacted to the announcement by bidding down Kodak shares by 14 percent. On October 21, 2003, *The Wall Street Journal* reported that some of Kodak's larger shareholders attempted to persuade Kodak executives to abandon their plan.[30] Discuss this issue in the context of the chapter text.

5. On January 31, 2005, an article appeared in *The Wall Street Journal* comparing the relative performance of stocks in the S&P 500 that pay dividends with stocks in the S&P 500 that do not pay dividends.[31] Between the end of the bear market in October 2002 and the date of the article, January 2005, nondividend payers rose by 63 percent, whereas dividend payers rose by 52 percent. Notably, dividend payers have tended to outperform nondividend payers when the market is soft, but not when the market is strong.[32] Based on these patterns, the article contends that the change in the tax treatment of dividends that was made in 2003 did not change investors' preferences for dividend-paying stocks. Discuss this contention.

Minicase

Nipsco

Nipsco Industries Inc. (Northern Indiana Public Service Company) is a utility-based holding company involved in providing natural gas and electricity in northern Indiana, water in central Indiana, and interstate natural gas pipeline services.

In December 1997, Nipsco's board announced that it planned to split its stock two-for-one, and also to raise the quarterly common dividend payment from 45 cents to 48 cents per presplit share. The press release stated that the dividend increase was in keeping with the firm's goals of maintaining a 60 percent payout ratio tied to growing earnings each year. The firm claimed that the increase reflected continued improvement in the firm's operating and financial performance.

Despite having beaten analysts' earnings forecasts in three of the four quarters prior to splitting, Nipsco's stock had underperformed the S&P 500. At the time, Nipsco's ratio of book-to-market equity was 0.33. Nipsco's chairman and chief executive officer, Gary L. Neale, stated: "The two-for-one split is a strong expression that we continue to believe our stock is undervalued. The split will make it easier for retail shareholders to more fully participate in the company's growth."

During 1997, Nipsco had beaten analysts' consensus earnings per share expectations in January (by 2 cents), April (by 12 cents), and July (by 3 cents). It missed in October (by a penny). Despite having beaten expectations, in 1997 Nipsco stock underperformed the S&P 500 through November by 5.6 percent. In fact through July of 1997 Nipsco had underperformed by 19 percent. After splitting its stock, Nipsco outperformed the S&P 500 by 32 percent for the next nine months. At the end of December 1998, Nipsco returned 27.5 percent for the year, while the S&P 500 returned 26.6 percent. At the end of December 1999, Nipsco's cumulative return since the stock split was −22 percent, while the S&P 500's cumulative return was 51.4 percent.

Case Analysis Questions

1. Discuss Nipsco's dividend policy in the context of the chapter text.

2. For those students who have read Chapter 5, discuss the extent to which Nipsco's stock split fits the general pattern of firms who split their stocks.

Chapter Eight

Agency Conflicts and Corporate Governance

The main objective of this chapter is for students to demonstrate that they can identify key psychological phenomena that serve to obstruct good corporate governance.

After completing this chapter students will be able to:

1. Explain how overconfidence prevents corporate boards from putting compensation systems in place that align the interests of managers and shareholders.
2. Explain the role of prospect theory casino effects in aligning the interests of shareholders and managers.
3. Describe how aversion to a sure loss can interfere with the alignment of the interests of investors and the interests of auditors engaged to monitor managers.
4. Analyze how, because of aversion to a sure loss and overconfidence, stock option–based compensation can exacerbate agency conflicts.

8.1 TRADITIONAL APPROACH TO AGENCY CONFLICTS

Agency theory is used to study the structure of compensation contracts that principals offer to agents engaged to act on their behalf. In the corporate governance setting, shareholders are the principals, the board of directors is charged with representing the interests of shareholders, and the firm's managers are the agents.

In order to identify the main issues in agency theory, consider the film, and later well-known successful musical, *The Producers*. The plot of *The Producers* features Broadway producer Max Bialystock developing a scheme to defraud investors. Bialystock raises a large amount of money from investors by selling more than 100 percent of a new show—25,000 percent actually—and enlists a meek accountant named Leo Bloom to produce a flop that will enable him to hide his actions. In Bialystock's plan, the show fails, enabling him to apologize to investors for having lost their money, which he then proceeds to keep.

The plot of *The Producers* has three key features. First, there is a principal–agent relationship involved, where principals (the investors) entrust their money to an agent (the producer), who is supposed to take an action on their behalf. Second, there is an inherent conflict of interest between the principals and the agent. Third, the agent is better informed than the principals. Only a successful show would reveal the producer's true action. Of course, in the film and musical, Bialystock's show turns out to be a hit despite his best efforts.[1] But as they say, that's show business.

The plot of the producers serves to highlight the conflicts of interest and information asymmetries between corporate executives and investors. The executives are supposed to act as agents of the shareholders, with a fiduciary interest to act in their best interests. But executives know more than shareholders know. The combination of information asymmetries and inherent conflicts of interest give rise to agency conflicts.

participation constraint

The principal offers attractive enough terms to the agent to induce the agent to participate.

incentive compatibility constraint

The principal chooses the carrot-and-stick differential, in terms of pay for performance, so as to induce the agent to represent the interests of the principal.

nonoverpayment constraint

The principal does not overpay the agent.

Rational principals offer contracts to rational agents that combine positive rewards and penalties, so-called carrots and sticks, with three goals in mind. The principal's first goal is to offer the agent a contract that is at least as attractive as the agent's next best alternative, in order to induce the agent to participate. This goal is known as the **participation constraint.** The second goal is to set the differential between the carrot-and-stick components so as to induce the agent to represent the interests of the principal. This goal, the alignment of managers' interests and investors' interests, is known as the **incentive compatibility constraint.** The third goal is for the contract not to be unduly generous to the agent. This goal is known as the **nonoverpayment constraint.**

In the traditional approach, incentive compatibility typically prevents managers from diversifying away all the unique risk of their firms, especially career risk. Managers who bear such risk might react by behaving in too risk averse a fashion, to the detriment of investors. In theory, managerial risk aversion can be countered by using stock options. This is because options reward managers for favorable outcomes but do not penalize them for unfavorable outcomes.

8.2   PAYING FOR PERFORMANCE IN PRACTICE

The evidence about how well the traditional approach to agency conflicts applies in practice is mixed. The most influential academic studies on executive compensation conclude that CEO pay varies far too little to be consistent with traditional theory.[2] These studies, published in 1990, indicate that most corporate boards do not structure salaries, bonuses, and stock options so as to provide either large rewards for superior performance or large penalties for poor performance. Executive pay has featured too narrow a carrot-and-stick differential, resulting in low variability in respect to corporate performance. The frequency with which CEOs are dismissed for poor results is low. And corporate stock options do not appear to play a major role in aligning the interests of executives and investors. Some evidence points to the relative strength of shareholder rights as being key.

Low Variability

For the median CEO in the 250 largest companies, a $1,000 change in corporate value corresponded to a change of just 6.7 cents in salary and bonuses over two years. Accounting for all monetary sources of CEO incentives—salary and bonuses, stock options, shares owned, and the changing likelihood of dismissal—a $1,000 change in corporate value corresponded to a change in CEO compensation of just $2.59. In this regard, the value of shares owned by the median CEO changed by 66 cents for every $1,000 increase in corporate value. At the median, stock options added another 58 cents worth of incentives.

What does the $2.59 mean when it comes to bad decisions? Consider a CEO who makes a wasteful investment, such as purchasing a new aircraft for the firm's executive fleet, which benefits him but diminishes the market value of the company by $10 million. The total wealth of this CEO, if he is representative, would decline by only $25,900 as a result of the misguided investment. Is this a large penalty or a small penalty? Given that the average compensation of CEOs was $20,000 a week, the penalty is small.

Dismissal

As to dismissal, the CEOs of poor-performing firms are only 6 percent more likely to leave their jobs than CEOs of companies with average returns. In respect to the $2.59 mentioned, by affecting dismissal prospects, a $1,000 change in corporate value translates into an estimated median change of 5 cents in CEO wealth.

Stock Options

During the 1990s, corporations in both the United States and Europe increased their use of executive stock options and employee stock options. Shares allocated to employee incentive plans in the 200 largest U.S. firms increased from 6.9 percent in 1989 to 13.2 percent in 1997. In 2001, 29 percent of CEOs received option grants that had a face value at least eight times their annual cash compensation.

There is some evidence that firms offering stock options to their employees perform better than those that do not.[3] A study of 200 firms whose stocks trade on the Nasdaq suggests that executive and employee stock options do lead to increased firm value, principally because they aid in employee retention and serve as a substitute for cash compensation in cash-strapped firms. Less clear is whether stock options serve to align the incentives of executives and employees with those of shareholders.

Despite their increased popularity, the use of stock options has been controversial. Investment legend Warren Buffet has been a long-time critic of the manner in which firms use stock options. He suggests that although options can be appropriate in theory, in practice their use has been capricious, inefficient as motivators, and very expensive for shareholders. The manner in which options are recorded in financial statements has been a long-running subject of debate, whether as footnotes or expensed. The issue came to be politicized. Federal legislation along with the rulings of accounting standards boards has increasingly favored the expensing position.

Shareholder Rights

An important aspect of corporate governance is shareholder rights. Provisions that move away from one share, one vote and put antitakeover provisions in place contribute to weak shareholder rights. The evidence indicates that firms with stronger shareholder rights are associated with higher firm value, higher profits, higher sales growth, lower capital expenditures, and fewer corporate acquisitions. In this regard, an index known as the Gompers-Ishii-Metrick index rates firms on corporate governance.[4] In the same vein, the California Public Employees' Retirement System (CalPERS) has taken an activist position in respect to corporate governance, maintaining a focus list of firms with poor investment records and poor corporate governance.

Behavioral Phenomena

The point of this section is to indicate that the arrangements between principals and agents often fall short in respect to paying properly for performance and avoiding overpayment. The point of the chapter is to explain the psychological factors that lead to this state of affairs. The remainder of the chapter focuses on two key psychological phenomena: overconfidence and prospect theory. Overconfidence affects directors and executives. Prospect theory affects executives and the auditors monitoring firms upon whose opinions investors depend.

8.3   OVERCONFIDENCE AMONG DIRECTORS AND EXECUTIVES

Overconfidence on the part of directors will lead them to underestimate the extent of both traditional agency conflicts and behavioral biases on the part of executives that contribute to those conflicts. At the same time, overconfident directors will be inclined to think that they do a better job of addressing agency conflicts than they do. In consequence, overconfident directors will be prone to approve compensation policies that exhibit insufficient pay for performance and that overpay executives.

In 2001, *Fortune* magazine interviewed a group of high-ranking corporate directors in respect to executive compensation.[5] In exchange for remaining anonymous, most offered candid comments suggesting serious difficulties with executive compensation. Anonymity produced insightful anecdotes of directors' behavior. Interestingly, it also produced colorful language that in some cases required some editing.

Overconfident Directors

A director who has served on several large boards and is the well-paid CEO of a Fortune 500 company identified overconfidence as a major reason why boards fail to address agency conflicts appropriately.[6] He stated:

> Compensation committee members are not malevolent. I've seen situations that are messed up, and yet the directors think they're doing a hell of a job. They delude themselves. They think things are being done right and fairly—they don't think they're being had—when actually the excesses they're approving are just mind-boggling. . . .
>
> It's really "amateurs vs. pros." I'm classing the directors, in most cases, as amateurs, and management, together with the compensation consultants they hire, as pros. You can have a very sophisticated board—and it'll still be amateurs vs. pros. . . .

Insufficient Variability in Pay for Performance

Why do overconfident directors approve compensation packages that feature insufficient variability in pay for performance? One reason is that they fail to take proper account of the behavioral biases that afflict managers. Managers also tend to be

[T]here was a case at [a] company about five years ago in which I took a strong stand regarding a guy who ran a major division. He was the architect of some terrible deals for the company. . . . All of his projections for his division were wrong. He underestimated what capital expenditures needed to be. He was way off on growth.

So the comp committee has a meeting to talk about bonuses—and if there was ever a person who didn't deserve one, it was this fellow I'm talking about.

Nevertheless, the CEO came into the meeting and recommended that this guy get a pretty good-sized bonus. And I said, "How can you do this? This guy's poor decisions have cost the company billions of dollars. If you're going to pay for performance, you have to have both a carrot and a stick. Basically, this guy should be kicked out of the company. But if he's going to be around, you've got to send a message not only to him but even more importantly to the organization that if someone screws up, they don't get a bonus."

Well, I think the committee sort of agreed with me. But ultimately the others said, "We've got to let the CEO have the authority to run his organization," which I actually think is a bunch of crap. So what happened—and I think this was mainly because of my bitching and complaining—is that the CEO cut this fellow's bonus by half. That meant he ended up getting a reasonable amount for costing the shareholders billions.

Source: Carol J. Loomis, "Executive Pay: This Stuff Is Wrong," *Fortune,* Monday, June 11, 2001. © 2001 Time Inc. Reprinted by permission.

self-attribution error
The tendency for people to take credit for positive outcomes and to blame others or bad luck for negative outcomes.

overconfident. An important facet of overconfidence is **self-attribution error,** the tendency for people to take credit for positive outcomes and to blame others or bad luck for negative outcomes.[7]

Directors need to understand that managers are prone to self-attribution bias. The combination of self-attribution bias and self-interest will lead managers to resist a low reward for poor performance, but seek a high reward for good performance that stems from external factors rather than their own efforts. The following two comments by directors illustrate the issue. The first comment pertains to poor performance, and the second comment pertains to good performance.

> So my view of incentive comp of any kind is that it's fine if it isn't just a giveaway program. The pendulum has to swing both ways—and usually it doesn't. A comp committee also hears a lot about external factors, things that couldn't have been anticipated when the budget was being made. People say, "We worked our butts off"—da-da-da-da. And you have to answer, "Look, that was the deal. You agreed to work here for a year under that deal, and if the shareholders get dung, then you get dung."

> CEOs will claim it's all deserved, saying, "Look at the way I made my stock go up." That's bunk in a lot of cases, egregiously so at companies that don't pay dividends. Let me refer you to a Treasury zero bond: If you buy one today and hold on for 10 years, it will rise by 74 percent. And you won't even have had to give President Bush an option on the bond.

Better-Than-Average Effect in the Boardroom: Overpayment

Another important facet of overconfidence is the *better-than-average effect.* The better-than-average effect involves more people viewing themselves as above the median in ability than below the median. The following quotation illustrates why overconfident directors are prone to overpay executives.

How in the world do you stop that when every self-respecting compensation committee—I just read this once again today in a proxy—says, "We want our CEO's compensation to be between the 50th and 75th percentile in our peer group." If everybody does that, it's Lake Wobegon, where every kid is above average.

8.4 STOCK OPTION–BASED COMPENSATION

There are three important behavioral phenomena associated with stock options being used to compensate employees, especially executives. First, excessively optimistic, overconfident employees will overvalue their firms, thereby overvaluing the stock options they are granted. Second, many employees have a preference for the small probability of a large payoff, what some call a **casino effect.** Third, stock option compensation increases the propensity to engage in accounting fraud, a point taken up in Section 8.7.

casino effect
Preference for the small probability of a large payoff.

Overvaluing Options

The evidence suggests that firms pay their employees in options whenever employees are irrationally exuberant about the prospects of their firms.[8] In this regard employees are especially apt to purchase company stock for their 401(k) and ESOP plans at market prices, after their company stock has performed well. Moreover, when upper-level executives believe that their firm's stock is overvalued, they appear to grant more options to rank-and-file employees.

Casino Effect

A comment made by one of the directors quoted in the *Fortune* magazine article introduces the concept of *casino effect.*

> What's going to happen this year about compensation, generally? I think bonuses will go down—sharply. Companies may award more options to make up the downdraft. They'll say, "I gave good ol' George $2 million in options last year. This year the stock is down 75%, so I'll give him four times as many options." That'll fit what most people want. They say, "You can fiddle with my bonus, but don't cut out my options"—because they know there's the big casino waiting out there.

CONCEPT PREVIEW *Question 8.1*	Indicate which of the following two risky alternatives you would prefer to choose, **A** or **B.** (You can also indicate indifference, if you wish.)

A: Winning $2,000 with a 90 percent probability.
    Winning $0 with a 10 percent probability.
B: Winning $4,000 with a 45 percent probability.
    Winning $0 with a 55 percent probability.

Next, imagine that you are registering to participate in a lottery, where the probability of winning is 0.002 (actually 2/900). If you win the lottery, your prize is the opportunity to face either alternative A or alternative B. The person who is registering you explains the rules of the lottery and indicates that you need to commit, in advance, whether you would prefer to play alternative A or alternative B should you win the opportunity to do so. Please indicate which you would prefer to play should you win the lottery, alternative A, alternative B, or indifference.

In answering Concept Preview Question 8.1, the majority of people choose A over B in both parts. Now consider a related question.

CONCEPT PREVIEW

Question 8.2

Of the two given alternatives below, please indicate which one you find preferable, alternative **C** or alternative **D**. (You can also indicate indifference, if you wish.)

C: Winning $2,000 with probability .002.
Winning $0 with probability .998.

D: Winning $4,000 with probability .001.
Winning $0 with probability .999.

---

overweighting of small probabilities
People tend to overweight low probabilities attached to extreme events.

Overweighting of Small Probabilities

In developing prospect theory, psychologists Daniel Kahneman and Amos Tversky documented that people tend to overweight low probabilities attached to extreme events and to underweight high probabilities associated with moderate events. In this respect, consider Concept Preview Question 8.1. In responding to the first part of this question, most people choose alternative A over alternative B. In responding to Concept Preview Question 8.2, most people choose alternative D over alternative C.

There is a general lesson in the choice pattern described in the preceding discussion. The second part of Concept Preview Question 8.1, where the probability of winning the lottery is 2/900, effectively asks people to choose between C and D. In other words, Concept Preview Question 8.2 is a reframing of the second part of Concept Preview Question 8.1. To see why, just multiply the probability of winning the lottery (2/900) by the probability of winning $2,000 in A (.9) to obtain .002 − 2/900 × .9.

The point is that when people focus directly on the low probabilities, they act as if they overweight lower probabilities relative to higher probabilities. In choosing alternative D over alternative C, they act as if they are risk seeking rather than risk averse. However, in Concept Preview Question 8.1, where they focus on probabilities that are much higher, they act as if they are risk averse.

According to prospect theory, people often act as if they are risk averse when facing the possibility of only gains, and risk seeking when facing the prospect of only losses. Kahneman and Tversky suggest that the overweighting of low probabilities reverses this behavior pattern: People purchase lottery tickets thereby seeking risk in respect to gains (casino effect), and purchase insurance policies to reduce risk in respect to losses.

8.5   AUDITING: AGENCY CONFLICTS AND PROSPECT THEORY

According to prospect theory, people behave as if they seek risk when facing the prospect of what they perceive to be a sure loss. Aversion to a sure loss can wreak havoc with the traditional incentives normally relied upon to resolve agency conflicts. To see how this can happen, consider the issues associated with the auditing services upon which corporate boards and investors depend.

Managers, as agents, release financial statements in order to report the financial results of their firms to the owners, or principals. How do the principals monitor managers to verify that these results are accurate? The conventional way is for managers to hire the services of a professional external auditor to perform an audit and then provide an opinion about whether the financial statements are in conformity with generally accepted accounting principles.

Traditional Perspective

In theory, auditing firms serve the interests of investors. Auditors examine the financial statements of firms and decide whether or not they can offer clean opinions on the integrity of those statements. However, auditors receive their fees from the firms they audit, not investors. As a result, auditors face a potential conflict of interest in serving the needs of investors. They are vulnerable to being "bribed" by unscrupulous firms in order to issue clean opinions.

Notably, auditing firms are partnerships, not corporations. Hence, auditing partners are personally liable for the actions of their firms, a feature that allows for a large stick to be wielded in the carrot-and-stick framework. The traditional view holds that auditing firms have reputations for integrity to protect. According to the conventional wisdom, this reputation is sufficiently valuable so as to deter dishonest behavior on the part of auditors. In other words, the conventional wisdom holds that it is in the auditors' best interests to issue honest assessments rather than issue clean opinions in cases that do not merit them.

Another aspect of the firm's choice of auditor involves signaling. A firm that seeks to communicate that its financial statements are indeed clean might engage the services of an auditor with a high reputation who also charges high fees. The theory stipulates that firms who face accounting problems would not have an incentive to use such an auditor, and therefore the choice of auditor in and of itself sends a strong signal to investors. Now read the Behavioral Pitfalls box on the following page to illustrate signaling.

Think about policy 2X in the context of prospect theory. Did 2X amount to a shift in reference point? Given the departure of the consulting division, did 2X shift Andersen's auditors from perceiving themselves to be in the domain of gains to perceiving themselves to be in the domain of losses? Does attitude toward risk depend upon whether a person perceives him- or herself to be in the domain of losses as opposed to the domain of gains?

These are important questions. If the answer to all of them is yes, then prospect theory suggests that policy 2X placed Andersen's auditors into the domain of losses. As a result, aversion to a sure loss induced them to take actions that were bad bets on average but offered the possibility of large payoffs.

Conflicts of Interest

At the time Arthur Andersen decided to take on the roles of both internal and external auditor, Arthur Levitt chaired the Securities and Exchange Commission (SEC). He raised concerns that practices of this sort would jeopardize the quality of audits, because it introduced a potential conflict of interest. In retrospect, that concern was justified. In respect to Enron, Andersen hired the firm's entire team of 40 internal

During the twentieth century, the accounting firm Arthur Andersen was one of the largest and most respected auditing firms in the world. However, a series of events took place in the 1980s and 1990s that led to the firm's demise in 2002.

For years, accounting firms also performed consulting services. By developing expertise in the effect of technology on business strategy, the consulting group at Arthur Andersen, known as Andersen Consulting, became especially profitable during the 1980s. Notably, the consulting division had become much more profitable than the auditing division, a fact that created considerable resentment on the part of the consultants. The resentment stemmed from the fact that Andersen pooled the profits from its two divisions before sharing them, thereby leading the consultants to subsidize the auditors. Indeed, in 1989, the consultants managed to alter the profit-sharing rule, in their favor.

The change in sharing rule left the auditors facing a different economic environment. Because of competition, growth in the demand for auditing services was slowing. Audit fees were declining. The salaries accountants earned were lagging behind those of attorneys, investment bankers, and especially consultants.

The auditing division at Andersen responded to the changing circumstances in a number of ways. They began a separate consulting group of their own, Arthur Andersen Consulting, to compete directly with sister division Andersen Consulting. In this respect, the firm began to urge accounting partners to sell consulting and other services, in addition to traditional auditing.

Their colleagues at Andersen Consulting were not amused. In 1997, the partners at Andersen Consulting voted to split off completely from Arthur Andersen to become Accenture. In the wake of their departure Arthur Andersen instituted a policy known as "2X." Under 2X, for every dollar of auditing work, partners were required to bring in twice the revenue in nonauditing work.

Most firms hire accountants as employees to perform internal audits that complement the activities conducted by external auditors. One of Andersen's initiatives was to encourage clients to engage Andersen for both internal and external auditing services. Among the list of Arthur Andersen's audit clients were Boston Market, Sunbeam, Waste Management Inc., WorldCom, and Enron. At each of these firms, a major scandal ensued.

After Enron's difficulties became public, Andersen employees tampered with documents. On June 14, 2002, the firm was found guilty of obstructing justice and was subsequently dissolved. In June 2005, the conviction was overturned, but the company did not rise from the ashes.

auditors and subsequently engaged in a series of aggressive reporting practices that created friction between the Andersen group responsible for Enron and Andersen's own Professional Standards Group. Ironically on October 15, 2001, the evening before Enron was due to announce its third-quarter earnings, Andersen accountants indicated that they could not approve the financial statements that Enron wished to release. Several weeks later, Enron declared bankruptcy.

8.6 SARBANES-OXLEY

Fraud is an extreme example of agency conflict, where behavior crosses from being unethical to being illegal. Since 2000, a succession of corporate scandals with varying degrees of fraud made clear that compensation in the form of stock and stock options could not be counted upon to align the interests of investors and managers. Among the firms involved in fraudulent activities were Coca-Cola, IBM, Sunbeam, Cendant, Xerox, Lernout & Hauspie, Parmalat, Enron, WorldCom, and HealthSouth.

In the wake of these financial scandals, Congress passed the Sarbanes-Oxley Act of 2002, directing the SEC to require that the chief executive officer and chief financial officer of every publicly traded firm certify, under oath, the veracity of their firm's financial statements. The first test of the rule came on August 14, 2002, when many firms were scheduled to file their quarterly financial statements with the SEC. An unusual number of firms chose to restate earlier results in connection with their filings.[9]

Sarbanes-Oxley increased the number of independent directors on corporate boards. Independent directors neither work for nor do business with a corporation or its executives. Board audit committees are required to include at least one financial expert. Every quarter, after the CEO and CFO have certified the firm's financial statements, the full panel must review those statements. Sarbanes-Oxley also encouraged independent directors to meet separately from management on a regular basis.

In making executives legally liable for the veracity of their firm's financial statements, Sarbanes-Oxley altered the "stick" component associated with the incentives that executives face. Recall that a key theme that emerged in the earlier discussion of incentives was the reluctance of boards to enforce low pay for poor performance.

How much of a difference has Sarbanes-Oxley made? According to *The Wall Street Journal,* in the first year after its enactment, several firms were in violation. The list included HealthSouth, Qwest Communications, Gemstar-TV Guide, and Footstar Inc. However, the SEC sanctioned only one firm, HealthSouth, for violating Sarbanes-Oxley.[10]

Because of staffing shortages at the SEC, the agency indicated when Sarbanes-Oxley was passed that it would check for certification violations on a spot-check basis. At the same time, the SEC affirmed that its staffers had been focusing their attention on the financial statement certifications by executives and affirmed its belief that in the main Sarbanes-Oxley had refocused executives' attention on the disclosure documents.

Without question, Sarbanes-Oxley has focused executives' attention on avoiding errors in financial statements and resulted in higher costs associated with accounting. At the same time, it remains to be seen whether the act turns out to be an overreaction on the part of legislators. During 2003, many executives wondered whether having to restate their financial statements because of a misunderstanding or error would expose them to criminal prosecution.

8.7 FRAUD AND STOCK OPTIONS: ILLUSTRATIVE EXAMPLE

In theory, granting stock to executives serves to align their interests with those of shareholders. In theory, executive stock options serve to counteract executives' reluctance to accept risky projects that would benefit shareholders. An implicit assumption in traditional theory is that market prices are efficient. In practice, prices might be inefficient, and the use of stocks and stock options can provide managers with perverse incentives.

Excessive optimism and overconfidence already counteract managers' undue caution. Indeed, the granting of stock options might serve to induce managers to accept risky projects that feature negative net present value. Moreover, excessively

HealthSouth was founded in 1984. At year-end 2001, HealthSouth was the largest U.S. provider of outpatient surgery, diagnostic imaging, and rehabilitation services. A Fortune 500 firm, its stock belonged to the S&P 500 Index. Based in Birmingham, Alabama, HealthSouth had almost 1,700 facilities and 51,000 employees in all 50 states and abroad.

In 2002 HealthSouth was investigated for an accounting fraud that prosecutors suspect began as early as 1986. According to the complaint filed by the SEC, between 1999 and the second quarter of 2002, HealthSouth overstated its income by $1.4 billion. It did so by making false journal entries that overestimated the amount of third-party insurance reimbursement and underestimating expenses.

The SEC accused HealthSouth executives of having engaged in insider trading by selling substantial amounts of HealthSouth stock while they knew that the firm's financial statements grossly misstated its earnings and assets. As part of their compensation, HealthSouth's executives received options on 3.6 million shares of HealthSouth stock. Five former HealthSouth chief financial officers pled guilty to the SEC charges.

The SEC charges included securities fraud and insider trading. HealthSouth's founder and CEO was Richard Scrushy. Specifically, the SEC alleged that Scrushy induced HealthSouth executives to manipulate the firm's stock price until he could sell off large blocks of stock worth $25 million. The SEC claimed that since 1991 Scrushy sold "at least 13.8 million shares for proceeds in excess of $170 million," based on knowledge of HealthSouth's "actual financial results and the impact that disclosure of those results would have."

CEO Scrushy also enjoyed numerous perquisites such as a fleet of 12 corporate jets facetiously referred to as "Air Birmingham," and a helicopter that was used to transport Scrushy from HealthSouth headquarters to the nearby Birmingham airport, to take Scrushy and his family to his luxury family compound, or to take Scrushy's wife shopping in Atlanta.

HealthSouth's auditor, Ernst & Young LLP, was a top-tier accounting firm. HealthSouth appears to have engaged in numerous practices that were intended to deceive its auditors.

In 2001 HealthSouth paid Ernst & Young $1.16 million in auditing fees. It also paid an additional $2.39 million in "audit-related fees" for what HealthSouth called "pristine audits," where Ernst & Young junior-level accountants visited HealthSouth facilities in order to check whether magazines in waiting rooms were orderly, toilets and ceilings were free of stains, and trash receptacles had liners.

Sources: Jonathan Weil, "What Ernst Did for HealthSouth—Proxy Document Says Company Performed Janitorial Inspections Misclassified as Audit-Related," *The Wall Street Journal*, June 11, 2003; Liz Vaughan-Adams, "HealthSouth Paid Ernst & Young More to Check Its Toilets Than to Audit Its Accounts," *The Independent—London*, June 12, 2003; Kris Frieswick, "How Audits Must Change: Auditors Face More Pressure to Find Fraud," *CFO Magazine*, July 1, 2003; Julie Piotrowski, "Noose Tightens: Link to Scrushy Alleged in Criminal Case," *Modern Healthcare*, April 28, 2003.

optimistic, overconfident managers who are unethical will be prone to underestimate the chances that fraudulent behavior on their parts will be discovered. Indeed, stock and stock option compensation can actually amplify agency conflicts when managers find they can manipulate the market value of their firms. The general evidence indicates that firms that were found to have engaged in fraud are more prone to use stock option-based compensation than firms that were not found to have engaged in fraud. The propensity to commit fraud appears to be related to corporate governance. The propensity is higher in firms featuring high institutional holdings and large blockholders, where CEOs are more likely to be dismissed for poor performance. The propensity is reduced if the board features a high proportion of independent outside directors.[11]

Consider the example presented in the above Behavioral Pitfalls box. Far from aligning the interests of managers and investors, stock options provided HealthSouth's

EXHIBIT 8.1   (a) HealthSouth versus S&P 500, Cumulative Returns, Sept. 1986–Dec. 2002; (b) HealthSouth Return on Equity, 1986–2001

Sources: Center for Research in Security Prices, Compustat.

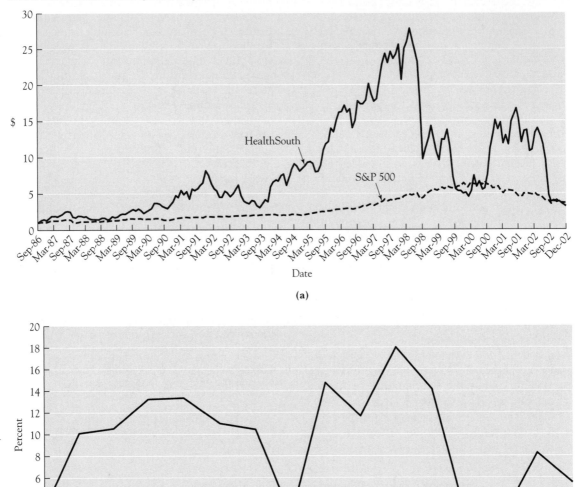

(a)

(b)

executives with a motive to exploit shareholders. They did so by using fraudulent financial statements, despite having engaged a top-tier auditing firm, Ernst & Young LLP.[12]

The fraud committed by executives with large holdings of HealthSouth stock enabled them to sell their shares at grossly inflated prices. Exhibit 8.1a displays how

HealthSouth's stock performed between 1986 and 2002, relative to the S&P 500. Exhibit 8.1b displays the time path of HealthSouth's return on equity for this period, derived from its accounting statements. A comparison of the two graphs suggests that the firm's stock price was largely driven by its financials.

Auditors

HealthSouth appears to have engaged in numerous practices that were intended to deceive its auditors. For example, HealthSouth was aware that Ernst & Young did not question fixed asset additions below a particular threshold. HealthSouth's managers exploited this knowledge by making random entries in their balance-sheet accounts for fictitious assets that were worth less than the threshold amount.

As was mentioned, the relationship between HealthSouth and Ernst & Young involved two fees, $1.16 million in auditing fees and an additional $2.39 million for "pristine audit" consulting where accountants checked sanitary facilities. Interestingly, the accountants were specifically trained at HealthSouth facilities for the purpose of conducting the pristine-audit program. Ernst & Young's motto is Quality in Everything We Do. Notably, Richard Scrushy conceived of the pristine-audit program.

Signs of Disease?

Were there any signs that HealthSouth was not especially healthy? There were certainly some major dips in Exhibit 8.1. However, the stock outperformed the S&P 500 on a cumulative basis for most of the period. Until recently, it had not been fashionable for analysts and managers to look at free cash flows. Exhibit 8.2 displays HealthSouth's free cash flows during the period. It portrays a less healthy picture than Exhibit 8.1.

Much of HealthSouth's negative free cash flow in Exhibit 8.2 stems from continued borrowing. High leverage does not necessarily force fraudulent firms to fail in short order. Only on April 1, 2003, did the firm announce that it would default on

EXHIBIT 8.2
HealthSouth Free Cash Flows, 1986–2001

Source: Compustat.

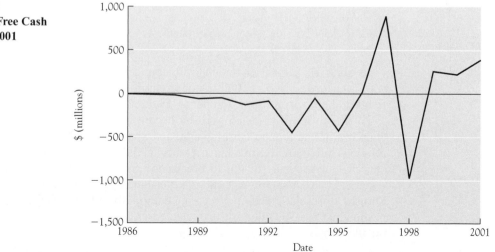

Debiasing for Better Decisions

Errors or biases: Managers behave unethically.
Why does it happen? High ambitions coupled with aversion to a sure loss.
How does it happen? Ambitious managers set high goals for themselves, thereby perceiving situations in which they miss their goals as being in the domain of losses. Losses are painful, and managers lack the willpower to exercise self-control.
What can be done about it? Reset reference point or make use of an explicit rule that mandates that losses be recognized beyond a prespecified level. Also, remember that most people do not beat the odds. The executives at Enron, World-Com, Arthur Andersen, and HealthSouth did not meet their ambitious goals, but instead lost their honor, their good names, and the respect of their communities. Many served prison terms.

a $350 million bond payment and was dismissing its CEO Richard Scrushy. In December 1998, HealthSouth's market value of equity was about $12 billion. Its long-term debt was about $3 billion, and it paid $143 million in net interest. By the end of 2001, its net interest paid rose to about $215 million. The firm had increased its debt sharply in 1993 and continued to maintain a debt-to-asset ratio in the range of 40 to 60 percent for the latter half of the 1990s. Apparently there was enough cash flow to enable HealthSouth to perpetuate its fraud for many years without failing.

In a conversation that was secretly taped on March 18, 2003, by one of Health-South's chief financial officers, Scrushy comments on the role of bank debt in respect to the firm's fraudulent financial statements. The CFO had indicated a concern about going to prison for "signing these phony financial statements." In his reply to the CFO, Scrushy stated[13]:

> When they get you is when you go into bankruptcy. That's when they come in on you. They don't come in on a company that's paying their bank debt down. They don't come in on a company that's doing good. They come in on a company that's screwed up. And we're, we're seeing a healthy day right now in stock. We're seeing that. I just hate to go down there and just give the keys to them.

In his trial, Scrushy maintained his innocence and insisted that the executives who over time served as HealthSouth's chief financial officers had perpetrated the fraud of their own volition, and not at his direction as they had alleged.

At the outset of his trial, Scrushy began to preach regularly at fundamentalist churches in and around Birmingham, and appeared daily on a morning television religious program. Before his trial began, he also joined an African-American church, but was careful not to preach in churches attended by the six African-Americans who sat on his jury. Nevertheless, the prosecution suggested that Scrushy's preaching activities were an attempt to influence jurors indirectly, a suggestion that Scrushy's defense team denied. In June 2005, the jury acquitted Scrushy on all charges.

Summary

Incentive-based compensation lies at the heart of good corporate governance. A corporation's board of directors needs to ensure that executive compensation is enough to attract and retain talented managers, that compensation packages serve to align the interests of managers with shareholders, and that managers are not overpaid.

The empirical evidence indicates that in practice, executive compensation displays too little variability in respect to pay for performance, insufficient dismissal, and excessive payment for executives. Directors' own comments reveal that the members of corporate boards have been overconfident in their ability to structure incentives appropriately without overpaying executives. Directors also suggest that their tasks are made that much more difficult by overconfidence on the part of executives.

In traditional theory, employee stock options are used to align the risk attitudes of managers and shareholders. In the traditional approach, the inability of managers to diversify their portfolios as well as shareholders leads managers to be more risk averse than shareholders. However, managers who behave in accordance with prospect theory might find the risk characteristics of stock options attractive because of its casino effect. In this respect, stock options might also induce risk-seeking behavior because of the tendency to overweight low probabilities. Moreover, firms appear to pay their employees in options when the latter are inclined to overvalue those options.

The combination of aversion to a sure loss and overconfidence can also induce ambitious, unethical managers to manipulate accounting information in order to exercise their stock options when the stock is overpriced. In this respect, a combination of behavioral phenomena and agency conflicts affected some accounting firms. Those events were the catalyst for the passage of the Sarbanes-Oxley Act.

Additional Behavioral Readings

Gompers, P., J. Ishii and A. Metrick, "Corporate Governance and Equity Prices," *Quarterly Journal of Economics*, vol. 118, no. 1, February 2003, pp. 107–155.

Jensen, M. and K. Murphy, "CEO Incentives—It's Not How Much You Pay, But How," *Harvard Business Review*, no. 3, May–June 1990, pp. 138–153.

Jensen, M. and K. Murphy, "Performance Pay and Top Management Incentives." *Journal of Political Economy*, vol. 98, 1990, pp. 225–264.

Key Terms

casino effect, *132*

incentive compatibility constraint, *128*

nonoverpayment constraint, *128*

overweighting of small probabilities, *133*

participation constraint, *128*

self-attribution error, *131*

Explore the Web

www.healthsouth.com
Web site for the firm HealthSouth, updating its experiences from events in 2003.

www.ey.com
Web site for Ernst & Young.

www.ey.com/global/download.nsf/US/Restoring_Investor_Confidence:_The_Boards_ Role/$file/RestoringInvestorConfidenceFortuneTurleyColvin.pdf
Ernst & Young chairman and CEO, Jim Turley, discussed the critical role of boards of directors in restoring investor confidence.

Chapter Questions

1. The following quotation appeared in the *Fortune* magazine issue discussed in the chapter.

   The consultants are hired by management. They're going to be rehired by management. There's some thought given by conscientious compensation committees to hiring their own consultants. But the consultants don't want to be hired that way, because then they cut themselves off from management.

   Discuss any agency conflicts associated with this quotation.

2. The following quotation appeared in the *Fortune* magazine issue discussed in the chapter.

   They now use performance formulas—based, say, on return on equity—that determine the size of the bonus pool. Most of the formulas are b.s. When you've got a formula, you've got to have goals—and it's the people who are the recipients of the money who are setting these. It's in their interests to keep the goals low so that they will succeed in meeting them. You've got the fox in the chicken coop. . . . Anyone who is greedy, anyone who is on the make, anyone who is aggressive about what they're being paid will get rid of formulas they don't like. . . .

   Discuss any agency conflicts associated with this quotation.

3. The following quotation appeared in the *Fortune* magazine issue discussed in the chapter.

   I have never asked to serve on a corporate board, never even hinted at wanting to be on one. And I have never asked to be on a compensation committee. I suspect that the reason I've been put on so many is that word gets around that I believe in paying people very, very well. . . . I cannot sit and say to you what the right compensation number is. That's the judgment call, the business judgment call. That's what a board of directors does. . . . What I know most of all is that when I see extraordinary effort and results out of a CEO, you can't pay him enough.

   Evaluate the comments made by this particular director.

4. In July 2003 Samuel Waksal, the founder of ImClone Systems Inc., began a seven-year prison term. In December 2001 Waksal received word that the Federal Drug Administration (FDA) was about to issue a negative report on ImClone's cancer drug Erbitux. Although this knowledge was material information, and Waksal was an insider, he sold some of his ImClone shares and disclosed the information to his daughter, advising her to sell her ImClone shares. Martha Stewart, celebrity and chief executive of Martha Stewart Living Omnimedia, had once been a stockbroker and served on the board of directors of the New York Stock Exchange. She was also a friend of Samuel Waksal. A day before the FDA made its negative announcement about Erbitux, Martha Stewart sold 3,928 shares of ImClone stock at a price of about $60. In an interview with *The New Yorker* author Jeffrey Toobin, she indicated that the sale constituted about 0.03 percent of her assets.[14] On June 4, 2002, Martha Stewart was indicted and charged with nine counts of fraud, perjury, and obstruction of justice. In her defense she claimed that she had an informal stock loss order arrangement with her broker, at a price of $60. In March 2004 a jury found her guilty on all counts, and she served a prison term as a result. By design, the products and services sold by Martha Stewart Living Omnimedia are strongly identified with Martha Stewart the person. In this respect the personal actions of Martha Stewart affected the financial performance of Martha Stewart Living Omnimedia. On August 11, 2003, Martha Stewart Living Omnimedia announced that its quarterly earnings per share had fallen to 2 cents, from 14 cents the year before. An article that appeared in the June 16, 2003, issue of the *Chicago Sun-Times* asked the following question: "Why did this woman who already possesses enormous wealth and the devotion of countless numbers of fans put it all at risk to avoid taking a piddling loss on a single stock?" Martha Stewart was not actually charged with insider trading but with having lied to prosecutors about it when interviewed by them. Therefore, instead of being culpable for a civil offense (her trade) and a fine, she left herself open to being

found guilty of a criminal offense, which brought with it the risk of prison time. Discuss any behavioral phenomena that might have played a role in the behavior of Samuel Waksal and Martha Stewart.

5. On May 20, 2004, *The Wall Street Journal* ran a front page story entitled "Biotech's Dismal Bottom Line: More Than $40 Billion in Losses." The article makes several points. First, the majority of biotechnology firms have produced losses, with the result that the return to investments in the biotechnology sector between 1981 and 2004 lies below the return from holding Treasury bills. At the same time, a few biotechnology firms, such as Amgen and Genentech have been spectacularly successful. The article quotes one investor who likens biotechnology stocks to a lottery. Despite its track record, in 2003 U.S. biotechnology firms succeeded in issuing almost $4 billion in new equity. The article mentions that venture capitalists also provided funding to biotechnology start-ups hoping to earn a profit when these firms go public. Discuss whether there are any behavioral phenomena involved in the issues raised in the article.

6. Discuss any agency conflicts associated with HealthSouth's pristine-audit program.

Additional Resources and Materials for Chapter 8 Are available at www.mhhe.com/shefrin

---

Minicase

Tyco

Until 2002, Dennis Kozlowski, the chief executive of Tyco, International, had been one of the most celebrated CEOs in the United States. Although he was well known for his public pronouncements claiming devotion to high standards of corporate governance, in private he was charged with having diverted more than $135 million in Tyco funds for his own personal benefit. In addition, Kozlowski was charged with misrepresenting Tyco's financial condition to investors in order to boost its stock price as he sold $575 million in the firm's stock.

According to *The Wall Street Journal*, diverted funds were used to purchase an art collection and lavish real estate in Florida, New York, and New Hampshire. Kozlowski and Tyco's chief financial officer Mark Swartz were charged and tried for diverting these funds. During one of their trials, evidence was presented that Kozlowski had spent $2 million on a party for his wife on the

Mediterranean island of Sardinia and that he had purchased a $15,000 umbrella holder and a $6,000 shower curtain for an $18 million apartment that they used but that Tyco owned.

At their trials, the attorneys prosecuting Dennis Kozlowski presented evidence that Tyco's board of directors did not approve these extraordinary payments. In his defense, Kozlowski argued that the board was well aware of the payments, that they constituted normal compensation, and that the board did approve them. Jurors were not persuaded by this argument, and in June 2005, both Kozlowski and Swartz were found guilty of grand larceny and conspiracy, falsifying business records and violating general business law.

Tyco used PricewaterhouseCoopers LLP (PWC) as their auditing firm. Their annual auditing fees were in the vicinity of $16 million, and nonauditing services were another $32 million. Richard Scalzo was PWC's lead auditor on the Tyco account. In August 2003, the SEC barred Richard Scalzo from auditing publicly listed companies, describing his auditing work at Tyco as "reckless." The SEC criticized Scalzo for failing to examine Tyco's executive compensation payments such as forgiven loans totaling $96 million, and other related-party dealings that were not disclosed to Tyco's shareholders.[15]

The SEC expressed concern that in 1998, Mr. Scalzo's auditing team discovered these issues just before Tyco was to announce its year-end earnings. Correcting the accounting treatment would have led Tyco's quarterly earnings to fall by $40 million, causing the firm to miss analysts' earnings forecasts. However, rather than insist that Tyco comply with proper accounting conventions, Mr. Scalzo helped Tyco to manipulate its accruals in order to mask the problem. That is, the lead auditor cooperated with the firm's management in keeping the firm's audit committee and its investors uninformed about executive compensation.

Case Analysis Question

1. Contrast events at Tyco with the events at HealthSouth described in the chapter. In what ways were the events similar and in what ways were they different?

Chapter **Nine**

Group Process

The main objective of this chapter is for students to demonstrate that they can identify the manner in which biases and framing adversely impact the behavior of managers or directors when they work together in groups.

After completing this chapter students will be able to:

1. Explain why groupthink, poor information sharing, and inadequate motivation underlie suboptimal decisions made by a group engaged in judgmental tasks.
2. Assess the contribution of poor group process in the governance of firms that experienced major financial crises.
3. Describe the manner in which group process can amplify the risk attitudes of individual group members.
4. Identify debiasing steps that corporate groups can take to improve group process.

9.1 TRADITIONAL APPROACH TO GROUP PROCESS

Traditional textbooks in corporate finance do not include material on group process. Yet group process is critical to the effectiveness of corporate financial decisions. The major decisions about corporate governance take place in board meetings. The major decisions made by managers take place in managerial meetings.

Effective groups exploit potential synergies from bringing together people with different skills, perspectives, and values. Effective groups are said to experience process gains. In theory, the key to process gains is the constructive use of individual differences among group members.

9.2 PROCESS LOSS

Despite the potential for process gain, many groups are unable to exploit potential synergies and instead experience process loss. The source of this loss is typically psychological, in that group psychology often leads people to make different decisions when they operate as part of a group than when they act as individuals.[1]

accuracy
Groups outperform individuals when it comes to intellectual tasks, but do worse than individuals when it comes to judgmental tasks.

polarization
Group processes tend to accentuate attitudes toward risk.

acceptance
Group discussion tends to induce group members to accept a decision too readily.

illusion of effectiveness
Unwarranted confidence in the decision.

Behavioral studies have identified three important features about group behavior.[2] The three features are known as accuracy, polarization, and acceptance. A brief description of each follows:

1. **Accuracy:** Groups tend to outperform individuals in particular types of tasks known as intellectual tasks. An intellectual task is a problem with a "correct" answer that once identified, group members would readily acknowledge as being correct. In this respect, an intellectual task is sometimes called a *eureka problem*. Although groups tend to outperform individuals on intellectual tasks, the same is not true for judgmental tasks that are more subjective in nature.

2. **Polarization:** Groups often become polarized in respect to risk tolerance. For example, if at the individual level the members of a group are slightly risk seeking, group discussion typically amplifies the degree of risk-seeking behavior.

3. **Unwarranted acceptance:** Group discussion leads the members of a group to accept a decision readily. However, such acceptance is often unwarranted, producing a phenomenon akin to collective overconfidence known as the **illusion of effectiveness**.

9.3   GENERAL REASONS FOR GROUP ERRORS

Three main factors underlie group inaccuracy and unwarranted acceptance: groupthink, poor information sharing, and inadequate motivation. This section describes these concepts in general terms, and Section 9.4 provides some corporate examples.

Groupthink

Think about the concept of confirmation bias described in Chapter 1. Confirmation bias is the tendency to overweight evidence that confirms a hypothesis or view but underweight evidence that disconfirms that view. The discussion of confirmation bias in Chapter 1 pertained to individuals. However, a collective form of confirmation bias also affects groups, leading to the phenomenon known as **groupthink**.[3]

groupthink
The drive for achieving group consensus overrides the realistic appraisal of alternative courses of action.

A group exhibits groupthink when the drive for achieving group consensus overrides the realistic appraisal of alternative courses of action. The following conditions are especially conducive to the emergence of groupthink:

• The group dynamics feature amiability and esprit de corps.
• A powerful, opinionated leader leads the group.
• Group members operate under stress.
• Group members are strongly influenced by a desire for social conformity.
• There is no explicit decision-making procedure.

Poor Information Sharing

poor information sharing
Group members fail to share enough information with other group members.

People are often ineffective when it comes to sharing information within groups, a phenomenon known as **poor information sharing**.[4] One behavioral study analyzed information sharing about job candidates. Relevant information was distributed across group members to see if they would find a way to share the relevant information. The key finding in the study is that people refrain from sharing relevant information with others in their groups, even when the members of the group share a common goal.

In the study, groups made different choices according to how the information was distributed across members of the group. The group task involved ranking job candidates, although the same principles apply to ranking project proposals during capital budgeting. There were two versions of the task. In the first version, all group members received identical information about all candidates. This information strongly suggested that one particular candidate, call him Mr. A, dominated the other candidates. In this situation, most groups chose Mr. A.

In the second version of the task, information about candidates was distributed across members of the group, rather than shared. Collectively, the group had the same information that was available in the first version of the task. However, in order that the individual members come to possess full information, the group had to find a way to share the distributed pieces among themselves.

The information was initially distributed so that most group members perceived that some other candidate, Ms. B, was the dominant choice. When the group came together to discuss candidates, they soon focused on the fact that Ms. B appeared to be the best candidate. They did exchange information. However, the information that members offered was information that supported the choice of Ms. B. That is, the group experienced confirmation bias.

In order to arrive at the correct choice, Mr. A, the group would have needed to find a way to put forward disconfirming evidence in respect to the choice of Ms. B. However, doing so is counterintuitive for most people.

A pertinent example of poor information sharing involves the manner in which knowledge about terrorist threats to the United States was shared within the FBI and between the FBI and the CIA, prior to September 11, 2001. In the spring of 2002, poignant examples were provided during testimony in hearings conducted by the Senate Intelligence Committee and the Senate Judiciary Committee.

Inadequate Motivation

social loafing
Group members reduce their contributions, instead relying on others to exert the requisite effort.

Inadequate motivation leads to a free-rider agency conflict known as **social loafing.** In this regard, some members of the group might choose to reduce their level of effort, relying on the efforts of others to generate group benefits. In other words, individuals who work in groups might not work as hard as individuals who work alone. Setting incentives to deal appropriately with social loafing is difficult when the link between effort and outcome is weak and when responsibility within the group is diffused.

9.4 GROUPTHINK AND POOR INFORMATION SHARING: ILLUSTRATIVE EXAMPLES

In 2000 and 2001, corporate fiascos at Enron, WorldCom, and PSINet demonstrated that in practice corporate governance does not typically feature rational principals interacting with rational agents. This section considers the extent to which the boards of these firms used effective processes.

Effective groups exploit potential synergies from bringing together people with varying skills, perspectives, and values. The members of effective boards also need to be knowledgeable enough to challenge management and independent enough to be willing to do so. Yet even boards that look good on paper may fail in practice because of groupthink. Why? The comments made by one director quoted in *Fortune* magazine provide the answer.[5]

> I then said to the chairman of the committee, "This stuff is wrong." And he said, "I agree, but we've got to do it." Basically, what people understand they have to do is go along with management, because if they don't they won't be part of the club.

As the next part of the discussion demonstrates, groupthink turned out to be a prominent feature in the board deliberations of Enron, WorldCom, and PSINet.

Enron

On December 2, 2001, Houston-based energy firm Enron, the seventh largest firm in the United States, filed for bankruptcy protection. The history of its stock price return is displayed in Exhibit 9.1, and its return on equity is displayed in Exhibit 9.2. Enron management, apparently overconfident from its success in the natural gas business in the early 1990s, sought to repeat that success in markets where it lacked expertise, such as broadband, retail energy, electric power generation, water, and steel mills.[6] Enron invested more than $10 billion in ventures that produced a near-zero return. Ironically, the firm's managers discussed acquiring either WorldCom or PSINet as a replacement for its failed broadband business.[7]

Enron's board had approved the use of special-purpose entities, partnerships, to obscure the failure of its investments by means of off–balance sheet items.[8] Enron's

EXHIBIT 9.1
Enron versus S&P 500, Cumulative Return, 1987–2002

Source: Center for Research in Security Prices.

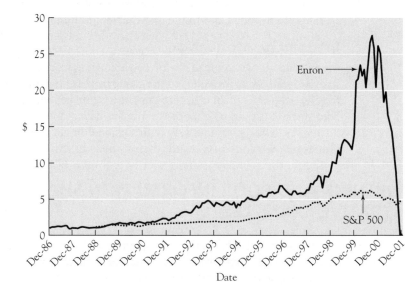

EXHIBIT 9.2
Enron Return on Equity, 1987–2002

Source: Compustat.

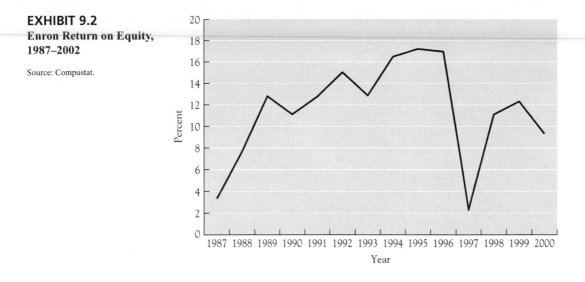

chief financial officer Andrew Fastow had set up one of these and named it LJM2, with the initials corresponding to the first names of his wife and two sons.

Fastow and his aide Michael Kopper ran LJM2, using it to enrich themselves at the expense of Enron's shareholders. In August 2002 Kopper agreed to plead guilty to two felony charges and to cooperate fully with government investigators. Fastow pled guilty to a lengthy indictment of charges and was sentenced to a 10-year prison term.

Why did Enron's board approve the partnerships? One possibility is that the partnerships were framed opaquely. An editorial that appeared in *The Wall Street Journal*[9] used a parable to render the framing more transparent.

Imagine a man named Andy, who paid $20,000 for a car that turned out to be a "lemon." Andy's wife complained bitterly about becoming annoyed every time that she saw the car in the garage. As a result, Andy sold the car to his friend Mike for $30,000. However, he loaned Mike the money for the purchase, with the stipulation that the money will be repaid a year later. To get the money for the loan, Andy pawned some of his wife's jewelry for $30,000.

Andy told his wife that he sold the car and made $4,000! Of course Andy's wife has less information than Andy. Because of this information asymmetry, Andy has been able to frame the issue opaquely, but in a way that has made his wife happy. She does not know that Andy lent his friend the money to buy the car at an inflated price and pawned her jewelry for $30,000 to do it. She does not know that Andy and Mike have kept $6,000 for themselves (6,000 = 30,000 − 20,000 − 4,000).

Just as Andy sold his lemon to Mike and reported the gain to his wife, CFO Andrew Fastow sold losing Enron projects to Merrill Lynch, and to LJM2, run by Michael Kopper. With Merrill Lynch, Enron agreed to repurchase the losing project (a Nigerian barge) at a future date.

With LJM2 Enron purchased put option insurance for its successful investments. That is, the partnership agreed to compensate Enron if the insured investment fell in value below a specified amount. Although LJM2's partners invested some money of their own to cover the insurance, Enron itself actually made most of the investment in the form of its own stock. In other words, Enron's investors were effectively self-insured, which is to say that they had no insurance.

Just as Andy's wife was duped into thinking that Andy had made money on his lemon car, Enron's investors were duped into thinking that Enron's projects were doing well. Just as Andy and Mike were able to pocket $6,000 from their lemon deal, Fastow and Kopper[10] earned millions in asset sales and management fees for running LJM2. Fastow alone earned $60.6 million.[11] As for handling the conflict of interest he faced as general partner of LJM2 and CFO of Enron, Fastow was explicit. While briefing prospective limited partners about joining LJM2, Fastow stated that he would use his informational advantage as Enron CFO to benefit the partnership.

Enron's Board

Enron's directors approved the creation of the partnerships that destroyed value for Enron's shareholders. They approved the waiving of Enron's code of ethics for CFO Fastow, in order that he might gain financially from leading the partnership. Why?

A large part of the answer is that Enron's management presented the partnerships to the board as a tool for improving Enron's earnings. Just as Andy reported a gain to his wife when he sold his lemon to Mike, Enron reported gains from its transactions with the partnerships. The directors asked few questions, readily accepted the answers they received, and cast no dissenting votes. They established no mechanisms to monitor for conflicts of interest on the part of Enron's CFO and did not ask to see the partnership prospectus material that identified the conflict.

Why did Enron's directors fail to exercise diligence in carrying out their fiduciary responsibilities? Were there not enough independent directors, meaning directors without formal business ties to the firm? Actually, Enron's board complied with conventional corporate governance standards. The majority of its board was indeed made up of independent directors. In addition, the board had an independent nominating committee.

In an article for *The New Yorker,* James Surowiecki suggested that the real problem with Enron's board was groupthink:[12] He pointed out that in general, virtually every board vote at Enron was unanimous. A notable exception involved the decision to acquire a water business, which two board members voted against.

Moreover, a financial expert, Robert Jaedicke, chaired the audit committee: Jaedicke was a professor of accounting and former Dean of the Stanford Business School. Despite Jaedicke's expertise, Enron's board and managers appeared to be totally focused on earnings rather than cash flow. In this regard, examine Exhibit 9.3, which displays the time path of Enron's free cash flows. Do you perceive any problems in the last half of the 1990s?

EXHIBIT 9.3
**Enron Free Cash Flows,
1987–2000**

Source: Compustat.

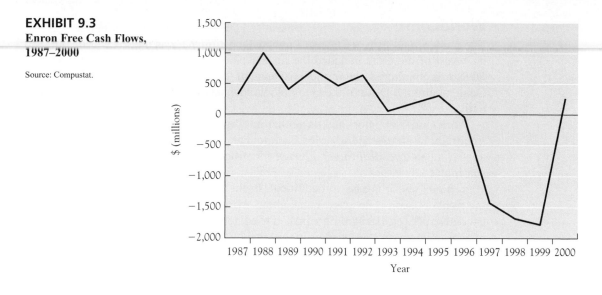

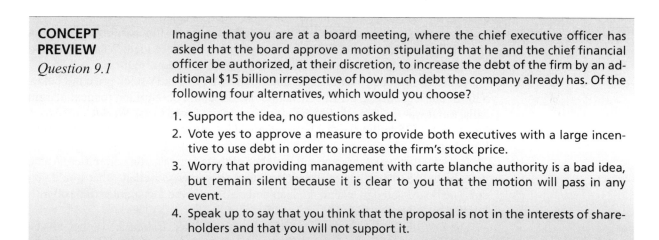

Imagine Yourself in the Boardroom

Concept Preview Question 9.1 is based on an article that appeared in the *Washington Post* on June 18, 2003.[13] The question asks you to imagine yourself to be the member of a corporate board.

CONCEPT PREVIEW *Question 9.1*	Imagine that you are at a board meeting, where the chief executive officer has asked that the board approve a motion stipulating that he and the chief financial officer be authorized, at their discretion, to increase the debt of the firm by an additional $15 billion irrespective of how much debt the company already has. Of the following four alternatives, which would you choose?

1. Support the idea, no questions asked.
2. Vote yes to approve a measure to provide both executives with a large incentive to use debt in order to increase the firm's stock price.
3. Worry that providing management with carte blanche authority is a bad idea, but remain silent because it is clear to you that the motion will pass in any event.
4. Speak up to say that you think that the proposal is not in the interests of shareholders and that you will not support it.

The situation described in the *Washington Post* article did take place and was described by former U.S. attorney general Richard Thornburgh, the judge charged with overseeing WorldCom's bankruptcy reorganization.

WorldCom

The unidentified firm in Concept Preview Question 9.1 was indeed WorldCom, and its board of directors included the former chief executive of MCI, the founder of UUNet Technologies, the former chairman of the National Association of Securities Dealers, and the Dean of the Georgetown law school. None chose the fourth alternative.

WorldCom's directors lacked neither intelligence nor experience. Therefore, it is important to understand what led them to make the decisions that they did. Articles appearing in *The Wall Street Journal* identified groupthink and poor information sharing as key issues.[14]

In hindsight, it is easy to be critical. In the atmosphere of the moment, making the right decision is not easy. Think about WorldCom. In a few short years, its chief executive officer, Bernard Ebbers, had used debt to make the firm one of the largest telecommunications companies in the world.

There is another story about debt at WorldCom, one that also involved its board.[15] In addition to leveraging the firm, Ebbers had taken out personal loans amounting to $253 million from Bank of America in order to purchase land, yachts, and boatyards. As collateral he posted 12.3 million of his shares in WorldCom. However, in September 2000 the price of WorldCom stock fell to $33.50 a share, from its all time high of $64.50. In consequence, the bank issued a margin call for the loan.

At the time of the margin call, Ebbers' holdings of WorldCom stock amounted to about $450 million. Ebbers could have met the margin call by selling some of his stock. In this respect, he approached the board to explain the situation. All parties believed that selling stock to meet the margin call would cause the stock price to drop further, thereby setting in motion further margin calls.

Ebbers asked the board for a $50 million loan to meet the margin call. It is not easy to be a board member in the kind of situation just described. What would you do if you were a board member? The board agreed to Ebbers' request.

As events unfolded over the next three weeks, WorldCom's stock price fell below $30. In consequence, CEO Ebbers had to use the entire $50 million to meet margin calls, but it was not enough. Ebbers went back to the board to ask WorldCom to loan him another $25 million so that he could avoid having to sell 3 million of his 20 million shares.

Stiles Kellett was a director and member of the compensation committee. At the time, he held $100 million of WorldCom stock. If you were Kellett, what would you do? The board voted to extend the loan and also approved a guarantee of $100 million for his other loans.

The end of the story came less than two years later. Ebbers had other assets, especially real estate, that he could have sold to meet margin calls. However, many of the properties he had bought declined in value below the price he had paid for them. In consequence, he was reluctant to sell them. In April 2002, largely because of the situation involving his personal loans, WorldCom's board fired Ebbers. In 2005, he was found guilty for his role in the accounting fraud that preceded WorldCom's bankruptcy, accused of directing the fraud to support WorldCom's stock price.

PSINet gorged itself on a diet of junk-bond debt, never learning to say no to a loan. It raised $4 billion and spent most of it "without the financial controls that should have been there," says board member Ian Sharp.

The company was running so hard that Schrader and his number two, Harold (Pete) Wills, separately pursued acquisitions willy-nilly, from Lebanese Internet service providers to Chicago-based consultancies, at times without telling the board. . . . Through it all, no one on the board, in the executive suite or on Wall Street stopped to caution that PSINet's addiction to debt threatened its existence.

At one meeting Schrader assessed the planned $1.4 billion acquisition of Metamor, an e-commerce consulting firm, thusly: "How do I know this is a good idea? Because Pete [Wills] says it is," according to an executive in the room. Another time Wills got interested in DSL technology and began making telecom deals without Schrader's prior approval.

"There wasn't a level of professional questioning that there should be between a CEO and a COO," says one former executive. "They both had a management style of 'We can do anything as a company.' The two of them would decide that a particular area was hot and dive into it without either one of them checking with the other one."

Source: Scott Woolley, "Digital Hubris PSINet Could Become the Biggest High-Tech Bankruptcy in a Decade. The Story behind the Fall," *Forbes,* May 28, 2001. Reprinted by permission of Forbes magazine. © 2001 Forbes, Inc.

PSINet

PSINet is a networking firm whose situation was described as a minicase at the end of Chapter 6. Like WorldCom, PSINet had grown quickly by using debt-financed acquisitions. Between 1997 and 2000, PSINet made 76 acquisitions. However, on May 1, 2001, PSInet began to default on its $400 billion debt, and its stock was delisted.

Its founder and chief executive officer was William Schrader, and its chief financial officer was Pete Wills. Ian Sharp, a member of PSINet's board, later replaced Schrader as CEO. Sharp offered some interesting comments about PSINet's board, in respect to overseeing the decisions of executives. He stated: "There were certain things going on in the company that I think both Bill and Pete share responsibility for, which were what you might call a little cavalier. Things were not approved at the board level which should have been—acquisitions and the spending of money one way or another."[16]

Sharp's comment raises an important behavioral point. Board members need to understand the psychological phenomena that lead managers to behave in a cavalier fashion. Otherwise, they too can be guilty of being cavalier.

Poor information sharing and the reluctance to question decisions go hand in hand. The cover story of the May 27, 2001, issue of *Forbes* magazine described the nature of decision making at PSINet. Consider the following excerpt from the article featured in the above Behavioral Pitfalls box.

Events at PSINet illustrate how groups can amplify judgmental errors rather than mitigate them. PSINet is hardly unique. An article that appeared in *Fortune* magazine describes some key reasons why CEOs fail.[17] The authors of the article ask why CEOs fail; they conclude that the answer is bad execution.

Debiasing for Better Decisions

Errors or biases: Groupthink.
Why does it happen? Desire for conformity leads to collective confirmation bias.
How does it happen? Members of groups become reluctant to share information or offer arguments to counter proposals made by other members of the group.
What can be done about it?

1. Ask group members to refrain from stating personal preferences at the outset of the discussion.
2. Explicitly cultivate debate, disagreement, and the sharing of information, as opposed to discouraging these behaviors as representing dissent and unnecessary criticism.
3. Designate one member of the group to play devil's advocate for each major proposal.
4. Regularly invite outside experts to attend meetings, with the charge that they challenge the group not to behave like meek conformists who, in the drive for consensus, value unity over truth.

The *Fortune* article describes groupthink at General Motors during the failed tenure of CEOs Roger Smith and Robert Stempel. The article notes that committees and policy groups essentially became time-consuming formalities where outcomes were rarely in doubt and serious deliberation was an infrequent occurrence. In contrast, Alfred P. Sloan, the legendary president and chief executive officer of General Motors from 1923 to 1946, articulated a different philosophy. Sloan charged his executives with the task of developing disagreement about major decisions, in order to gain a better understanding of the likely consequences.

9.5 POLARIZATION AND THE RELUCTANCE TO TERMINATE LOSING PROJECTS

Project termination illustrates polarization, the accentuation of attitude toward risk. As was discussed in Chapter 1, managers tend to become risk seeking when having to decide on whether or not to terminate losing projects. The point of this section is that the drive for consensus associated with groupthink also accentuates the risk-seeking tendencies of the individual group members, when faced with a sure loss.

Consider the findings of a major study that identified polarization. The investigators provided two descriptions of a particular project to study participants who played the roles of decision makers. Some participants acted alone; others acted as parts of groups.[18]

Although the future prospects for the project were not attractive, one description of the project featured a sunk cost, while the second featured no sunk cost. Notably, only 29 percent of the individual decision makers who received the description without mention of the sunk cost recommended that the project be funded. However, when the description included information about a sunk cost, 69 percent of individual decision makers recommended that the project be funded.

The interesting finding is what happens in groups. Only 26 percent of groups recommended funding in the case where no sunk cost was described. However, 86 percent of groups recommended funding when the description included a sunk cost. In other words, the behavioral error was actually amplified when the decision was made by a group rather than by an individual.

The results of the study illustrate the second of the three key issues described earlier, polarization of initial attitudes in respect to risk. Group dynamics accentuate the risk-seeking tendencies of the individual group members.

9.6   DEBIASING: ILLUSTRATIVE EXAMPLE

How can firms institute group processes that mitigate groupthink, poor information sharing, and inadequate motivation? As an illustrative example, consider processes that were developed at the firm Springfield Remanufacturing Corporation (SRC) and documented in a book written by its then CEO Jack Stack.[19]

While not foolproof, SRC's processes have achieved a measure of prominence and have been adopted by many firms, both large and small. Among adopting firms are SAIC (a Fortune 500 company, the largest employee-owned research and engineering company in the United States), Physicians Sales & Service (the leading distributors of supplies to physicians' offices in the United States), and R.R. Donnelley & Sons (the largest commercial printing firm in the United States which prints, among other items, *TV Guide, Reader's Digest, The New York Times Magazine,* and this book.)

SRC's processes are built around five components:

1. Standards
2. Planning
3. Compensation system
4. Information sharing
5. Equity stakes by employees

The following discussion describes each of these components, emphasizing how SRC's processes address groupthink, poor information sharing, and inadequate motivation.

Standards

The first characteristic of an effective group is having clear goals and well-defined roles and responsibilities. In this respect, *standards* refers to the use of financial statements in order to set realistic business goals. Stack calls these "critical numbers."

Stack emphasizes that in any given business environment, employees need to know what their critical drivers are, along with corresponding numbers that quantify those drivers. He describes these as the things most likely to keep managers up at night, the make-or-break variables. For some firms these might be cost of goods sold. For others it might be cash flow. The critical variables will vary from firm to firm and from business environment to business environment.

Standards are especially important in respect to information sharing and motivation. Effective groups efficiently share information that relates to standards. Moreover, the assignment to group members of well-defined roles and responsibilities in respect to standards, and the monitoring of underlying drivers, combine to mitigate social loafing.

Planning

Planning lies at the heart of the system that SRC has put in place. Stack makes the point that because a business plan has to be a tool, not a club, as many people as possible have to be involved in putting it together. In this respect, planning becomes the vehicle through which forecasts are developed, goals are set, incentives are put in place, and commitments are made.

At most firms, the planning process begins with a forecast of future sales. That is also the case at SRC, where the responsibility for developing the forecast is assigned to the sales force. In the spirit of avoiding groupthink, a task force is formed to challenge the assumptions underlying the sales forecast. Stack states: "It's in everybody's interests that we identify any problems, false assumptions, unrealistic expectations, and hidden risks."[20] Task force members are encouraged to ask all types of questions, from how vulnerable the firm is to competition to whether there is sufficient capacity to support projected sales.

Compensation

Because of agency conflicts, motivation requires an effective compensation system featuring pay for performance. At SRC, the workforce call their bonus plan "Skip the praise, give us the raise." Stack emphasizes the fundamental role of incentives in his firm, stating: "What a bonus plan does is communicate goals in the most effective way possible—by putting a bounty on them. . . . When you do that you'll get people's attention very fast. You'll send them a strong message. You provide them with a focus." Stack stresses the importance of a uniform compensation policy, meaning that people throughout the organization are rewarded in terms of the same criteria.

In order for a compensation policy to be effective, people need to understand how their actions can influence the rewards that they receive. Stack places a great deal of emphasis on the joint nature of incentives, training, and communication, stating: "No matter how clever you have been, no matter how carefully you have designed your payout system, your program simply won't motivate people if they don't get it, or if they can't follow what's happening. . . ."[21]

A good incentive system serves multiple functions. First, it provides an opportunity for education about the company's financial condition. Because it is in their self-interest, people throughout the firm focus their attention on understanding the firm's current financial statements. In developing a pro forma forecast during the planning phase, people are implicitly developing a forecast of their future compensation.

Second, the compensation policy encourages special attention on areas of vulnerability. Third, a uniform compensation policy serves to bring the organization together as one team. Fourth, a well-crafted compensation policy induces people to identify critical problems quickly.

Information Sharing

SRC calls their information-sharing process "huddling," and it is the heart of their communication system. SRC's huddle is a weekly meeting whereby selected representatives from across the company meet to exchange forecasts about how the actual financial statements will turn out at the end of the current month. These forecasts feature accountability. Managers take responsibility for developing the forecasts and then making decisions that result in their actual values. Forecasts are always made relative to reference points, the pro forma forecasts developed during the planning phase.

The exchange of information is accomplished sequentially, meaning that the line item forecasts are presented in sequence. After the forecasts have been made, the chief financial officer compiles them and presents the results to those in attendance.

A *variance* reflects the difference between the planned value of an item and its actual value. By convention, a positive variance is favorable, while a negative variance is unfavorable. Based on the variances arising from the CFO's presentation, those present then assess the firm's relative strengths and weaknesses and exchange views about the threats to coming in below plan or the possibility of coming in above plan.

In addition to information sharing, huddling features the opportunity to engage in monitoring and peer pressure. In this respect, the huddles at SRC provide for additional incentives to counter social loafing, above and beyond formal compensation. During huddles, managers take responsibility for particular line items in the financial statements.

At SRC, the time between huddles is used to engage in line-of-sight analysis, in order to drill down through the organizational layers to focus on the impact of decisions on future bonuses, and therefore value. Occasionally employees who are not normally part of high-level huddles, but who are responsible for either excellent decisions or poor decisions, will be invited to huddles. The purpose of such invitations is to explain the reason behind the forecasts being communicated. This serves as an incentive role as well as an informational role.

Stack indicates that the huddle keeps people focused on why what they do matters, draws the company together around common goals, and builds the organization through education. Most importantly, huddling provides a structured process to induce group members to share information.

Stock Ownership

The last component in an open-book system is stock ownership. By its nature, the compensation plan and attendant communication focuses on performance for the current fiscal year. However, value creation is a multiyear proposition. Hence, employee stock ownership serves to discourage the tendency to take decisions that improve short-term performance, but destroy value.

Summary

In theory, group process adds synergistic value to the efforts of the individual group participants. In practice, three factors lead this synergy to be less than maximal, and sometimes negative. First, although synergy is positive for tasks that are intellectual, it is typically negative for tasks that are judgmental. Second, group process often leads to polarization in respect to risk attitude. Third, group discussion typically leads its members to feel more effective than warranted, a form of group overconfidence known as the illusion of effectiveness.

There are three main reasons why judgmental tasks feature negative group synergy: groupthink, poor information sharing, and inadequate motivation. Groupthink appears to have been a major issue at several prominent corporate failures, for example, Enron, WorldCom, and PSINet. Groupthink affects group decision making at both the board and managerial levels.

Instituting effective group processes is not easy and requires continual investment on the part of the firm. Effective group processes within firms feature an integrated approach to strategic and financial planning, standards, compensation, monitoring, and stock ownership.

Additional Behavioral Readings

Russo, E. and P. Schoemaker, *Winning Decisions: Getting It Right the First Time,* New York: Doubleday, 2002.

Stack, J. with B. Burlingham, *The Great Game of Business,* New York: Currency Doubleday, 1992.

Surowiecki, J., *The Wisdom of Crowds: Why the Many Are Smarter Than the Few and How Collective Wisdom Shapes Business, Economies, Societies and Nations.* New York: Doubleday, 2004.

Whyte, G., "Escalating Commitment in Individuals and Group Decision Making: A Prospect Theory Approach," *Organizational Behavior and Human Decision Processes,* vol. 54, 1993, pp. 430–455.

Key Terms

acceptance, *146*

accuracy, *146*

groupthink, *146*

illusion of effectiveness, *146*

polarization, *146*

poor information sharing, *146*

social loafing, *147*

Explore the Web

www.greatgame.com
The Web site for The Great Game of Business, an organization devoted to firms using business processes developed by SRC.

www.saic.com
The Web site for the firm SAIC. This firm uses processes similar to those used at SRC.

www.sternstewart.com
The Web site for the consulting firm Stern-Stewart that advocates the use of compensation systems that tie managerial rewards to how much more than the cost of capital the firm earns.

Chapter Questions

1. In May 2002, Hewlett-Packard acquired Compaq Computer in a takeover that featured considerable drama. In deliberating the acquisition, H-P director Walter Hewlett, son of founder William Hewlett, suggested that the decision was not the right choice. He was concerned that the gap between the corporate cultures of the two firms was too wide to bridge, and he was troubled by the heightened focus on the PC business, a highly competitive business where H-P was not a low-cost leader. Hewlett opined that doubling down on PCs with Compaq would divert resources from H-P's enterprise business, thereby hurting the firm's ability to compete with IBM and Dell. He argued instead that H-P should essentially become a printer firm, focusing on its strongest business. Nevertheless, Walter Hewlett reluctantly voted for the acquisition of Compaq as a member of the H-P board. However, as chairman of the William and Flora Hewlett Foundation, he actively opposed the merger during a subsequent proxy battle. When Walter Hewlett's term on the board of H-P expired in 2002, he was not invited to rejoin. Discuss these events in light of the concepts described in the chapter.

2. In 2002 a Canadian study, the Report on Business, concluded that Canadian boards did not meet the new governance practices adopted by the New York Stock Exchange, in respect to the majority of their directors being independent and having fully independent audit, compensation, and nominating committees. The Report on Business found that almost 15 percent of companies listed in the S&P/TSX (Toronto Stock Exchange) index had directors who sit on three or more boards together, most of them on the boards of Canada's largest corporations. In particular, many directors of holding companies also serve on the boards of the subsidiaries of these companies. Some Canadians argued that the situation in Canada was different than in the United States, because Canada had more family-owned, smaller, and closely held companies than the United States. Proponents of the Canadian system pointed to the benefits of having directors of the holding company who are familiar with the associated subsidiaries so that directors have knowledge of how the whole operation works. Evaluate the arguments of those who oppose introducing the U.S. system into Canada.

3. Suppose that you were a member of Enron's board of directors from 1987 to 2000. Investors such as short-seller James Chanos of Kynikos Associates Ltd. estimated that Enron's cost of capital was between 9 and 12 percent, but its return on capital was closer to 7 percent. As a director, how would you use information about the cost of capital? As part of your answer, refer to Exhibits 9.1 to 9.3, and think about being a board member in two different time periods, 1987–1994, and 1995–2000.

   Next, put yourself in the position of Andy's spouse in the "lemon" parable that describes the nature of Enron CFO Andrew Fastow's use of off–balance sheet partnerships. Suppose that you asked Andy enough questions to ascertain that he had sold his lemon car to Mike at an inflated price and loaned him the money to do it. As someone concerned about your household's finances, what other questions would you have for Andy?

4. In 2001 the chief executive of AOL Time Warner, Gerald Levin, sought to acquire AT&T's cable business, the only cable business larger than the one already owned by AOL Time Warner. In doing so, he did not consult the firm's board, let alone its chairman Steve Case. Apparently, Case objected to Levin's approach, and Levin resigned in December 2001. Discuss Levin's approach to decision process in the context of judgmental tasks involving groups.

5. Firms whose boards are large (more than 12 members), and whose CEO also chairs the board, are less open to being acquired than other firms. Potential acquirers for these firms are more likely to engage in hostile takeovers rather than to negotiate a deal with the firm's board. In addition, potential acquirers find themselves having to make more attractive offers to firms whose boards are dominated by managers than firms whose boards are not dominated by managers.[22] Discuss whether any of the group issues brought up in the chapter can explain these patterns.

Minicase

Shugart

In the early 1980s Shugart was the leading maker of disk drives. One of its major divisions was producing products that, for the most part, had reached the mature stage. Eager once again to have a product that it perceived to be exciting and new, the firm invested heavily in what it perceived would be a high-volume, highly profitable project.

Unfortunately for Shugart's managers, the project, dubbed Project Golden, encountered serious technical difficulties. About a year and a half into the project, the controller and vice president for finance at Shugart proposed terminating the project. However, they were unsuccessful. Here is the controller's description of the situation.

> The V.P. of Finance and I presented an economic justification for eliminating this product in August of 1982. We felt very strongly about it. We presented the analysis at the Executive Staff Meeting. The V.P. of the Division immediately championed the product and signed up for lower costs. He also argued the asset recovery issue. I find that if any champion is willing to stick up for a project, then the financial analysis is rejected. Personalities are very important around here.

The vice president for another Shugart division described his view about losing projects.

> You can make a program look any way you want on paper for Business Plans. Another problem is that nobody wants to destroy the P&L. I really believe it's true that we are very risk taking with negative outcomes.

Project Golden was eventually terminated in August 1983, when costs were well over target and competitors had captured what market there was. The vice president for the division that ran Project Golden made the following comments:

> We lacked enforced milestones, reviews, and plans. Our business review meetings are not "meat and potatoes." You can't have a "meat and potatoes" meeting with thirty people. We should have progress reviews, and if need be force Marketing to stop taking orders and force Manufacturing to stop producing until the problems are resolved. One problem we have is frequent management turnover. Nobody ends up responsible for the problems at the project level.[23]

Case Analysis Questions

1. A Shugart vice president made a remark about being risk taking with negative outcomes. Discuss this remark in the context of the concepts described in the chapter.

2. Discuss the comments made by the vice president for the division that ran Project Golden in the context of group process.

Chapter Ten

Mergers and Acquisitions

The main objective of this chapter is for students to demonstrate that they can identify the manner in which biases and framing adversely impact the behavior of managers when they make decisions about mergers and acquisitions (M&A).

After completing this chapter students will be able to:

1. Explain why excessive optimism and overconfidence lead the managers of acquiring firms to overpay, thereby experiencing the winner's curse.

2. Use the press coverage measure and longholder measure to identify executives who are prone to engage in acquisitions.

3. Explain why the managers of target firms who are excessively optimistic, overconfident, and trust market prices can destroy value for their shareholders.

4. Identify the manner in which being in the domain of losses affects the decisions of executives and board members in respect to acquisition activity.

10.1 TRADITIONAL APPROACH TO M&A

In the traditional approach to M&A, prices are efficient. Therefore, the market prices of both the acquiring firm and the target firm coincide with their fundamental values, under the assumption that both remain stand-alone firms. However, a merger between the acquiring firm and the target firm holds the potential for synergy. In theory, the shareholders of the acquiring firm will capture this synergy through the acquisition of the target, by paying the current market value for the target. Therefore managers of the acquiring firm will only go forward with the acquisition if the value of the synergy is positive. Moreover, since wealth is fungible and all assets are priced correctly, the shareholders of both firms will be indifferent to the combination of cash and equity used to finance the acquisition.

10.2   THE WINNER'S CURSE

winner's curse
The winning bid in an auction results in the winner overpaying.

hubris hypothesis
Firms experience the winner's curse in mergers and acquisitions because of hubris.

When the winning bid in an auction leads the winner to overpay, the winner is said to experience the **winner's curse.** Because overconfident managers suffer from hubris, winner's curse in acquisitions stemming from overconfidence is known as the **hubris hypothesis.**[1]

The study of the winner's curse dates back to the early 1970s. In a 1971 article, three petroleum engineers raised the specter of the winner's curse.[2] They suggested that oil companies who had participated in government oil lease auctions for rights in the outer continental shelf had earned low returns in the 1960s. Thereafter academics began to study whether oil companies had failed to adjust their bids in order to anticipate the winner's curse.

The winner's curse extends to M&A activity. A study by KPMG International of the 700 largest acquisitions during the period 1996 through 1998 found that over half destroyed value. Acquisition activity peaked at $1.8 trillion in 2000, more than triple the level in the mid-1990s. Between 1995 and 2000, the average acquisition price in the United States rose 70 percent, to $470 million.

Between 1991 and 2001, the shareholders of acquiring firms lost $216 billion. Interestingly, a disproportionate share of these losses can be traced to very large losses by a few acquirers during the period 1998 through 2001. Many of the large-loss acquirers had been active acquirers prior to their large-loss acquisitions and the market values of their firms had been increasing.[3]

Consider the examples presented in the Behavioral Pitfalls box on page 163.

10.3   OPTIMISTIC, OVERCONFIDENT EXECUTIVES

The evidence suggests that excessively optimistic, overconfident CEOs are described as such in the press and wait too long before exercising their executive stock options.[4] Firms whose executives qualify as excessively optimistic and overconfident, in terms of both press coverage and the longholder measure, are 65 percent more likely to have completed an acquisition than firms whose executives do not so qualify. This tendency is compounded when the firm is generating positive cash flow, but mitigated when the board of directors has fewer than 12 members.

Excessively optimistic, overconfident executives press on with an acquisition, even when the reaction in financial markets is negative. A case in point is AT&T's acquisition of NCR mentioned in the Behavioral Pitfalls box on page 163. During a news conference to explain the rationale for the merger, a skeptical technology analyst asked AT&T executives if they could name a single high-technology merger between large firms that had turned out successfully. The question effectively prompted the executives to adopt an outside perspective rather than an inside perspective (as discussed in Chapter 3). One executive mumbled that he could not name a single successful merger among large high-technology firms, but the merger went ahead nonetheless.

The market appears to recognize when the executives of acquiring firms are optimistic and overconfident. The market discounts optimistic bids by roughly eight

In 1991, AT&T purchased computer firm NCR for $7.6 billion. Robert Allen was the CEO of AT&T from 1988 through 1995 and oversaw AT&T's acquisition of NCR. On announcing AT&T's intention to acquire NCR, Allen stated: "I am absolutely confident that together AT&T and NCR will achieve a level of growth and success that we could not achieve separately. Ours will be a future of promises fulfilled."

Despite Robert Allen's assertion of confidence, the market's reaction to AT&T's acquisition announcement was negative. AT&T completed the deal, and its computer operations subsequently lost $3 billion over the next three years.

In 1994 media firm Viacom agreed to purchase Paramount for $9.2 billion. By all accounts, Viacom overpaid for Paramount by $2 billion, despite strong signals from the market that this was the case.

What makes the overpayment especially interesting is the extent to which Viacom CEO Sumner Redstone's interests were aligned with shareholders. Redstone owned more than 75 percent of Viacom's cash flow and voting rights.

In 1999 Cisco Systems made its largest acquisition, paying $6.9 billion in stock for Cerent Corp., a small networking firm that had yet to show a profit, was expecting to raise about $100 million in an IPO, and had fewer than 300 employees. At the time, Cisco's market capitalization was about $225 billion, and it was the second largest firm trading on the Nasdaq. In other words, Cisco shareholders exchanged 3 percent of one of the world's most valuable firms for a small start-up that had yet to show a profit.

The telecommunications firm WorldCom engaged in 17 acquisitions using $30 billion of debt, and in 2002 became the largest firm to declare bankruptcy in U.S. history.

In 2002, the market concluded that $10 billion of investments in the personal computer business that Intel had made under its CEO Craig Barrett had generated little value. Indeed the firm's CFO Andy Bryant was quoted in *The Wall Street Journal* as saying: "I don't know of anything that we purchased that was worth what we paid for it."

Sources: Nikhil Deogun and Steven Lipin, "Deals & Deal Makers: Cautionary Tales: When Big Deals Turn Bad—Some Hot Mergers Can Come Undone for Many Reasons," *The Wall Street Journal*, December 8, 1999; Skip Wollenberg, "Viacom Head Confident of Handling Paramount," *Associated Press, Los Angeles Daily News,* February 22, 1994; Scott Thurm, "Joining the Fold: Under Cisco's System, Mergers Usually Work; That Defies the Odds—Ms. Gigoux's SWAT Teams Oversee the Integration of Newly Acquired Units—'The Borg' of Silicon Valley?" *The Wall Street Journal,* March 1, 2000; Don Clark, "Change of Pace—Big Bet Behind Intel Comeback: In Chips, Speed Isn't Everything—Semiconductor Giant Focuses on Products That Power Today's Wireless Gadgets—A Longer Life for Laptops," *The Wall Street Journal,* November 18, 2003; Pekka Hietala, Steve Kaplan, and David Robinson, 2003. "What is the Price of Hubris? Using Takeover Battles to Infer Overpayments and Synergies," *Financial Management* vol. 32, no. 3, 1–32.

basis points during a three-day window around the announcement of the acquiring firm's bid, beginning with the day before the bid and ending the day after the bid.[5]

Cash flow is important. When firms are financially constrained, excessively optimistic, overconfident executives choose not to go to the capital markets in order to secure the funds needed to conduct an acquisition. Instead they act as if the market undervalues the equity and/or risky debt issued by their firm. That is, the optimism-overconfidence effect is most pronounced for firms that have ample internal resources to finance acquisitions and for which the resulting acquisitions destroy value.

Most of the acquisitions conducted by excessively optimistic and overconfident CEOs stem from diversifying mergers, CEOs' attempts to acquire firms operating in different industries. In this regard, a study conducted by McKinsey & Co. found that

The financial press describes some CEOs as being excessively optimistic and overconfident, but not others. For example, *The Wall Street Journal* has used both *optimistic* and *confident* as adjectives to describe Wayne Huizenga, the founding CEO of Blockbuster Entertainment Group. At the same time, there are many CEOs for whom such attribution has not been made, such as J. Willard Marriott, the former CEO of Marriott International.

Excessively optimistic, overconfident CEOs are more prone to engage in acquisitions than CEOs who are not. During 14 years at the helm of Cook Data Services, Wayne Huizenga conducted six acquisitions. In contrast, during the 15 years Willard Marriott was at the helm of Marriott International, he did not conduct a single acquisition.

Viacom CEO Sumner Redstone has a history of communicating confidence in the face of declining value. In acquiring Paramount, for which he overpaid by $2 billion, Redstone took out several billion dollars in debt. He subsequently told the press that he was "confident" that the combined firm would generate sufficient cash to handle the debt. In this respect, Viacom paid $5.5 billion in cash.

Shortly after completing the Paramount deal, Redstone merged Viacom with Blockbuster. Redstone told the press that he was confident about the Blockbuster deal and stated that Huizenga, Blockbuster's chairman, is "as turned on as I am today by what we have wrought."

After the acquisition, Blockbuster turned out to be a major financial disappointment for Viacom. In January 2003, Redstone was commenting on Blockbusters' weak sales, telling investors he was confident that for global media and entertainment, the year would mark a "threshold to the next level of breakthrough financial performance." Later that year, in November, at an investor conference he explained why despite the fact that Paramount had had a mixed year, he was confident Viacom could bring in a "breakout year" in 2004.

As for Huizenga, after selling Blockbuster to Viacom, in 1995 he took control of Republic Industries (later AutoNation). Two years later, Republic's stock lost half its value, and Huizenga explained to stockholders why he was "confident that Republic stock would come back." And it did, from time to time, but with more than twice the volatility of the S&P 500.

Sources: "Viacom, Dis get bullish: Investors Hear Moguls Tout Gains," *Hollywood Reporter*, November 4, 2003; "Redstone Confident in B'buster: Viacom CEO Predicts Industry Is Poised for a Turnaround," *Hollywood Reporter*, January 9, 2003; Harlan S. Byrne, "Wheeler Dealer: Wayne Huizenga May Be the Ultimate Car Salesman, After All," *Barron's*, June 23, 1997; Skip Wollenberg, "Viacom Head Confident of Handling Paramount," *Associated Press, Los Angeles Daily News*, February 22, 1994; Pekka Hietala, Steve Kaplan, and David Robinson, 2003. "What is the Price of Hubris? Using Takeover Battles to Infer Overpayments and Synergies," *Financial Management* vol. 32, no. 3, 1–32.

executives of acquiring firms overestimate revenue synergies in 70 percent of cases, with the corresponding amount for cost synergies being 40 percent. The McKinsey report pointed out that upwardly biased estimates of synergies occur because executives underestimate customer-defection rates, make poor assumptions about market growth and competitive realities, and are excessively optimistic about the prospects for opportunities to engage in cross selling.[6]

As was mentioned in Chapter 1, the affect heuristic often induces executives to make acquisitions. The March 2005 issue of *CFO Magazine* points out that some executives base their acquisition decisions on intuitive judgment, intent on doing particular deals no matter what. These executives either fail to undertake formal valuations or else tweak the numbers to support the decision that they wish to make.[7] Consider the illustrations presented in the Behavioral Pitfalls box above.

10.4 THEORY

In order to understand the manner in which excessive optimism and overconfidence affect executives' decisions about merger and acquisitions activity, consider a theoretical example. The example sets the stage for the discussion of several acquisition cases later in the chapter. The example proceeds in segments, beginning with the case of rational managers and efficient prices. Later segments allow for excessively optimistic, overconfident managers and inefficient prices.

Symmetric Information, Rational Managers, and Efficient Prices

Suppose that an acquiring firm is considering the purchase of a target firm. For sake of illustration, assume that the market value of the acquiring firm is $2 million and the market value of the target firm is $1 million, where both are valued as stand-alone firms. However, let there be $850,000 in synergy from a merger of the two firms, so that the value of the combined firms is $3,850,000 (= $2,000,000 + $1,000,000 + $850,000).

Consider the case when prices are efficient, meaning that the market prices of the firms, both pre- and postmerger, coincide with fundamental values. Suppose too that information is symmetric, meaning that the managers of both the acquiring firm and the target firm are equally well informed.

CONCEPT PREVIEW *Question 10.1*	Put yourself in the position of the manager of the acquiring firm. 1. What is the maximum amount you should be willing to pay to acquire the target firm? 2. If your firm is the only bidder, what is the least amount you should expect to pay in order to acquire the target firm?

If the acquirer is the only firm bidding for the target firm and all managers are rational, then the acquirer can obtain the target by paying a hair more than the market value of $1 million. In this case, the acquirer's managers will do the shareholders of their firm a service by acquiring the target as long as the synergy value is greater than zero. In respect to Concept Preview Question 10.1, the maximum the managers of the acquiring firm should be willing to pay for the target firm is $1.85 million, the sum of the target's market value as a stand alone firm and the synergy. The least amount they should expect to pay is $1 million.

The acquirer might offer the shareholders of the target firm a combination of cash and shares in the combined entity. These shares represent some fraction of the value of the combined firm. For example, the acquirer might offer the target's shareholders $400,000 in cash together with $600,000 in shares of the combined firm. With a cash payout to the target's shareholders, rather than to the target itself, the value of the combined firm would fall by $400,000, the value of the cash payout. Therefore, the value of the combined firm would fall to $3,450,000.

In this case, the fraction of $3,450,000 that the acquirer offers the target's shareholders must equal $600,000. That is, the fraction offered must be 17.39 percent ($600,000/$3,450,000). In this case, the shareholders of the target firm end up with $1,000,000 in value, ($400,000 in cash and $600,000 in stock), while the shareholders of the acquiring firm end up with $2,850,000 (82.61 percent of $3,450,000). Not surprisingly, the shareholders of the acquiring firm end up with the original value of their firm plus the synergy from the combination.

Notice that in this scenario, the acquiring firm's shareholders end up with a value equal to the original value of the firm as a stand-alone, plus the value of the synergy, regardless of the cash portion of the payment to the target's shareholders. It is the magnitude of the value, not its form, that is critical.

Excessive Optimism and Overconfidence When Prices Are Efficient

Recall that people tend to be excessively optimistic when they believe they exert a lot of control over the outcome. Of course, managers do believe they exert a lot of control over corporate outcomes. Consider what happens when the acquiring firm's managers are excessively optimistic and overconfident, but the target firm's managers are rational. As previously, assume that prices are efficient.

An overconfident manager will typically overestimate the fundamental value of both the acquiring firm's shares and the amount of synergy in the merger. Therefore, an excessively optimistic, overconfident executive will typically overpay for an acquisition.

In the preceding example, suppose that the acquiring firm's managers believe that their firm is worth $1 million more than the market's judgment of $2 million. Suppose too that the acquiring firm's managers overestimate the amount of synergy by $100,000. How will the excessive optimism of the acquiring firm's managers impact the criterion they use to decide whether or not to proceed with the merger?

The acquiring firm's managers will have to balance two conflicting concerns. First, they will worry that because the target firm's shareholders do not appreciate what the acquiring firm's managers perceive to be the true value of the acquirer, the target firm's shareholders will demand too large a share of the combined entity. In this respect, there may be little the acquiring managers can do, except to accept that this will be part of the price that they pay for acquiring the target. Specifically, if the target firm's shareholders receive the fraction of 17.39 percent of the combined entity, then the acquiring firm's managers perceive them to be receiving an additional $173,900 that is unwarranted. Call this amount the **dilution cost.** Second, the acquiring firm's managers need to decide whether the amount of synergy that they perceive in the merger will justify the price to be paid.

In formal terms the acquiring firm's overconfident managers will go through the same kind of logic as their rational counterparts (described earlier). However, instead of pursuing the merger as long as the true synergy value is positive, they will

dilution cost
The value that acquirers believe that the target's shareholders receive because the acquiring firm's stock is undervalued in the market.

pursue the merger as long as the perceived synergy ($950,000) exceeds the dilution cost ($173,900).

As before, the acquiring firm's managers can offer to pay for the target through a combination of stock and shares. Recall that rational managers of an acquiring firm do not care about how payment is divided between cash and stock. However, over-confident managers who represent the interests of the acquiring firm's shareholders will care. Why? Because by paying in cash, the acquiring firm's managers perceive no dilution cost, whereas when they pay in stock they do perceive there to be a dilution cost.

What will the acquiring managers do as a result of the asymmetry between the two forms of payment? They will prefer to pay as much as possible in cash, in order to minimize the perceived dilution cost. That is, they will follow a pecking order.

When overconfident managers decide to pursue a merger, they believe that be-cause of the dilution cost, they will not be able to appropriate all the synergy for the acquiring firm's shareholders. There are at least three other reasons that may lead to the acquiring firm's shareholders not being able to capture the entire synergy. First, if the acquirer has a competitor who is also interested in acquiring the target, then the bidding pressure may force the acquirer to increase its bid. Second, if the man-agers of the target are themselves overconfident, they may demand more than the market value in order to agree to the takeover. Finally, other issues such as the impact on earnings per share (EPS) might lead the managers of the acquiring firm to agree to pay more than they would otherwise.

Inefficient Prices and Acquisition Premium

The preceding discussion concerns the actions of an overconfident management operating in an efficient market. How is the situation changed for a manager, over-confident or rational, who operates in an inefficient market?

Overvalued Acquirer

The heart of this issue is managers' perceptions of mispricing. In the preceding dis-cussion, managers of the acquiring firm perceive their firm to be undervalued, and it is this perception that drives their behavior. However, suppose they were to perceive their firm to be overvalued.

In this case, the pecking order needs to be reversed. Now, the manager of the acquiring firm would want to engage in market timing and purchase the target firm using overvalued equity in its own firm, rather than cash.[8]

Overconfident Acquirer and Overconfident Target

If the target firm's managers are overconfident, they will be prone to overvalue their firm relative to the market. In this case, they may require a premium above the mar-ket value before being willing to accept the acquiring firm's bid. As will be seen in the following examples, premiums are common and sometimes very large.

Asymmetric Information

In the preceding example, the managers of a firm worth $2 million consider acquiring a target firm whose market value is $1 million. Suppose that in confidential discussions, the managers of the potential acquirer learn that the target firm has developed a new technology whose value is not reflected in its current $1 million market capitalization. The acquirer also learns that the new technology would be the only basis for the value of the combined firms to exceed $3 million.

The managers of the target firm explain that they are trying to decide whether they should develop the new technology themselves or instead be acquired and let the acquiring firm develop the new technology. They have done a careful analysis to assess how much the new technology is worth, and they have shared some information with the managers of the acquiring firm, enough for the latter to estimate that the value of the new technology is $850,000.

Because the target managers have only engaged in partial disclosure, the acquiring firm's managers have established a value range centered on $850,000. The low end of the value range is $0, and the high end of the value range is $1.7 million. Moreover, the acquiring firm's managers believe that any value in this range is as likely as any other. They have concluded that were they to be fully informed, they would share the same value for the new technology as the managers of the target firm.

CONCEPT PREVIEW	The acquiring firm's managers typically make value-based decisions in a risk-neutral manner. Risk neutral means that they do not require a risk premium. Put yourself in the position of a manager in the acquiring firm. What is the maximum price you would pay to acquire the target firm?
Question 10.2	

The absolute maximum that a risk-neutral bidder answering Concept Preview Question 10.2 should consider paying for the target is $1.85 million, the sum of the market value and the expected value of the synergy. However, that does not mean that a risk-neutral bidder should be willing to pay that amount. Indeed, if the acquiring firm offered to pay $1.85 million and the target firm's board accepted the offer, the acquiring firm should be concerned. Why?

The target firm's managers and board know the true value of the new technology. Suppose that the value of the new technology were to be $500,000, less than the $850,000 estimate. In that case, the intrinsic value of their firm would be $1.5 million. The target firm's board would be only too happy to sell the firm for $350,000 more than its intrinsic value. In this situation, the acquiring firm would overpay, thereby experiencing the winner's curse.

Of course, the new technology might be worth more than $850,000. However, if this were the case, the target firm's managers would reject the $1.85 million offer. The target firm managers would rather develop the new technology themselves.

Because the target firm will only accept offers in which the acquiring firm overpays, the acquiring firm should offer no more than $1 million. That is the lesson of the example: Assume the worst when the other party is better informed.

10.5 AOL TIME WARNER:
THE DANGER OF TRUSTING MARKET PRICES

In January 2000, the Internet service provider America Online (AOL) announced its intention to acquire the media conglomerate Time Warner. The purchase price, $165 billion in AOL stock, set an acquisition record. The merger between AOL and Time Warner illustrates excessive optimism, overconfidence, inefficient prices, and the winner's curse on a grand scale.

Strategy and Synergy

The goal of merging AOL and Time Warner was to create a distribution channel whereby Time Warner's media products would be delivered to millions of consumers via Internet broadband. Time Warner brought media products and a television cable network to the combination. As the dominant Internet service provider (ISP) at the time, AOL brought an installed base of AOL subscribers to the combination.

Time Warner's products were known the world over: CNN, HBO, *Time* magazine, *Fortune* magazine, *People* magazine, *Sports Illustrated*, Warner Brothers, Warner Music Group, *Entertainment Weekly*, Looney Tunes, and Cartoon Network. In 2000, CNN was available to one billion television viewers. Time Warner magazines had 30 million subscribers.

AOL was an Internet service provider that packaged Internet access with e-mail and other services. By 2000, AOL had more than 20 million members, and its subscriber rolls were growing at the rate of 50 percent. However, most of these members accessed AOL using low-speed dial-up rather than high-speed cable. High speed is a necessary ingredient for broadband delivery. Notably, Time Warner operated the second largest cable television network in the United States, with 13 million subscribers.

Time Warner had the content to be delivered via the Internet, along with the required bandwidth. AOL had the Internet expertise along with a huge subscriber base. The potential synergy seemed obvious to Time Warner CEO Gerald Levin who had been frustrated in his attempts to bring an Internet focus to Time Warner. The potential synergy also seemed obvious to AOL's CEO Steve Case who felt that AOL had only one main asset, its subscribers, and was vulnerable to a competitive threat from Microsoft.

Valuation

The combination of AOL and Time Warner occurred at the height of the technology stock bubble. Notably, the market's judgment of the overall merger was favorable, with the shareholders of Time Warner benefiting at the expense of the shareholders of AOL. On the day of the announcement, the value of the combined companies rose by 11 percent, or $27.5 billion. However, Time Warner stock increased by 39 percent ($32 billion), while AOL stock declined by 2.7 percent ($4.5 billion).

In January 2000, the market capitalization of AOL was $185.3 billion, over twice as large as the $83.7 billion market capitalization of Time Warner. A similar statement applies to P/E, where earnings are measured before taxes, interest, depreciation and amortization (EBITDA). With the peak of the bubble not two months away, was AOL overvalued at the time?

An opinion piece in *Fortune* magazine suggests that AOL could not have been priced at intrinsic value in January 2000.[9] Why? The answer depends on residual income (the portion of earnings that remain after investors have been paid the cost of capital) because the present value of the residual income stream implied by its market valuation was far larger than any firm at any time had ever produced. Moreover, AOL's actual residual income at the time was close to zero.

AOL's CEO was Steve Case, and Time Warner's CEO was Gerald Levin. Did Steve Case knowingly purchase AOL with overvalued stock? And correspondingly, did Gerald Levin and Time Warner's shareholders trust market prices?

Steve Case

Steve Case did not trust market prices. AOL's internal memos indicate that Case judged that dot-com stocks, including the stock of AOL, were overpriced and that he sought to exploit the overpricing.[10] Moreover, he expected that Internet stocks would collapse in the not too distant future and sought to protect AOL shareholders by acquiring a more mature firm.[11] Case eventually offered 45 percent of a combined AOL Time Warner to Time Warner shareholders. Under the terms of the deal, Gerald Levin would be chief executive of AOL Time Warner, while Steve Case would be its chairman.

Gerald Levin

Gerald Levin trusted market prices. During a press conference to announce the merger Levin stated: "Something profound is taking place. I believe in the present valuations. Their future cash flow is so significant, that is how you justify it."[12]

Ted Turner

Ted Turner, the creator of CNN, was a major shareholder in Time Warner. He owned 100 million shares that he acquired through the sale of CNN to Time Warner three years before and held an operating role overseeing his former holdings. Turner was a very colorful figure. At first he apparently opposed the merger of AOL and Time Warner, asking: "Why should I give up stock in a $25 billion company for shares of this little company?"[13]

However, Turner's financial advisers apparently trusted market prices and persuaded him to back the deal, arguing that the merger would increase the value of his holdings. In his own colorful way, he announced his support at a news conference saying[14]:

> Shortly before nine o'clock last night, I had the honor and privilege of signing a piece of paper that irrevocably cast a vote of my 100 million shares for this merger. I did it with as much or more excitement and enthusiasm as I did on that night when I first made love some forty-two years ago.

For a brief time, the merger of AOL and Time Warner increased Ted Turner's wealth by $4 billion. However, he subsequently lost $7 billion in the next two years as the market value of the combined firm declined. In February 2003, Turner announced his resignation as vice chairman of AOL Time Warner.

Publicly, Turner expressed regret at having sold CNN and his Turner Broadcasting organization to Time Warner in 1996. It is rare for executives to admit to being overconfident, but Turner is uncharacteristic in many ways. He stated[15]:

> At the time, I owned nine percent of Time Warner, and I figured Jerry (Levin) thought that he bought me, but I thought I bought them. But nine percent is not fifty-one. I guess I got a little overconfident.

Asset Writedown

In April 2002, AOL Time Warner wrote down $54 billion in goodwill, a charge to its earnings that reflected the decline in the value of the combined firm. Among Time Warner's various businesses, which ones had generated disappointing cash flows?

AOL

Looking back 12 months from the end of the third quarter of 2002, the operating profit for most of AOL Time Warner businesses experienced positive growth. Publishing had grown by 26 percent, networks had grown by 16 percent, and the music business had grown by 10 percent. However, AOL's operating earnings fell by 30 percent.[16]

What had happened? In 2002, total revenue for America Online declined by approximately 6 percent, to about $8.9 billion. Its advertising revenue declined to $1.6 billion, from $2.6 billion in 2001. A chief factor was the collapse of many dot-com firms, who advertised and sold their products through AOL.

In addition, the rate at which new subscribers were signing up with AOL began to fall. Between 1995 and 2000, the subscription rolls had grown at a compound annual growth rate of 50 percent. However, the rate of growth slowed to 24 percent in the first half of 2002 and then to 8 percent in the second half of 2002, when AOL had 35.3 million members.

On September 18, 2003, AOL Time Warner dropped the "AOL" from its name. A press release announcing the name change stated: "We believe that our new name better reflects the portfolio of our valuable businesses and ends any confusion between our corporate name and the America Online brand name for our investors, partners and the public."

What's in a name? The change elicited an interesting reaction. At the time, Harris Funds owned 42 million shares of AOL Time Warner stock, primarily in its Oakmark funds. Henry Berghoef, director of research at Harris Associates, stated: "I'm not going out to buy more stock because of a change of name," but then added: "As silly as it sounds, it is healthy psychologically."[17] Psychologically? Might he be referring to salience, availability bias, and the affect heuristic?

Expectations and Accounting

Exhibit 10.1 depicts the market capitalization of AOL Time Warner from the time of its merger through December 2002. From its peak value, the firm had lost roughly 80 percent of its value. Part of the loss stemmed from false expectations.

EXHIBIT 10.1 AOL Time Warner, Market Capitalization, Jan. 2001–Dec. 2002

Source: Center for Research in Security Prices.

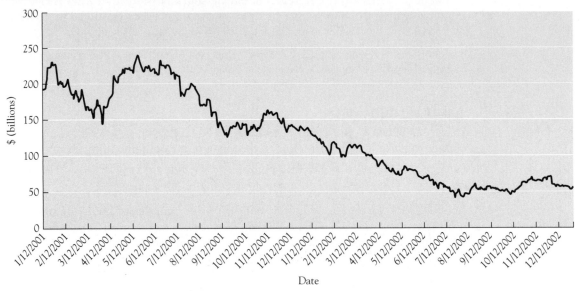

Date

In seeking support from analysts for the merger, AOL had forecast that earnings would grow by 30 percent. Apparently, those forecasts appeared unrealistic to the person in charge of investor relations at Time Warner. Her name was Joan Nicolais, and she seems to have voiced her concern, preferring instead to provide realistic guidance to Wall Street analysts. The financial press reported her saying that AOL was "basically an elaborate spin machine," whose numbers did not add up. Not surprisingly, Nicolais did not play the investor relations role for a combined AOL Time Warner. That post went to an AOL executive.[18]

In July 2002, *The Washington Post* ran an article alleging that in order to increase the earnings that it would report prior to the merger being completed, AOL had engaged in accounting improprieties. Shortly thereafter, both the SEC and the Department of Justice launched investigations.

Hubris

The hubris hypothesis states that overconfident executives exhibit hubris, overpay for acquisitions, and subsequently experience the winner's curse. Is hubris a characteristic anyone has applied to the principals in the case of AOL and Time Warner?

Steve Case

The adjective *hubris* has frequently been applied to Steve Case. Examples include article headings such as "Doomed Relationship Forged in Hubris," from the *New*

Zealand Herald,[19] and "Alec Klein Examines How Executive Hubris Destroyed the AOL-Time Warner Merger," from the *Star-Tribune*.[20] A *BusinessWeek* editorial stated:

> AOL's merger with Time Warner was, in retrospect, unreal. Distributing entertainment and news over many digital platforms—computers, cell phones, and handhelds—was Case's grand vision. Way too grand, it turned out. His hubris extended to the merger itself. The two corporations had vastly different cultures and didn't mesh.[21]

Gerald Levin

The New York Times did not paint a flattering picture of the executives at Time Warner, stating: "If Case was guilty of hubris, then the Time Warner management team was guilty of ignorance and credulity, industry analysts and academics say."[22] However, Gerald Levin did exhibit hubris, in that he felt no need to consult other executives before agreeing to the merger. Initially, Levin had insisted on a 50-50 split so that the combination would qualify as a merger of equals. However, on his own, without even consulting his board, he agreed to a 45-55 split, thereby leading to an AOL takeover of Time Warner.

In January 2003, Steve Case was pressured to resign as chair of AOL Time Warner. He did so and was replaced by Richard Parsons, Time Warner's chief executive.

10.6   HEWLETT-PACKARD AND COMPAQ COMPUTER: BOARD DECISIONS[23]

In 1999 Carleton (Carly) Fiorina became the chief executive of Hewlett-Packard (H-P). In May 2002, H-P acquired Compaq Computer in a takeover that featured considerable drama. The family foundations established by founders Hewlett and Packard both opposed the merger and actively fought it in a proxy battle. This acquisition offers important lessons about the psychological aspects of executive thinking.

In 1999, H-P was involved in three broad business segments: (1) enterprise computing and services for businesses, (2) personal computers (PCs), and (3) imaging and printing. Board members and executives concurred that that H-P's enterprise computing business was losing the ability to respond effectively to changing customer requirements and that regaining this ability would require significant new investment. They also concurred that H-P's operating margin on PCs was at best breakeven, compared to a 7 percent margin for industry leader Dell Computer.

As for imaging and printing, this was the H-P's most profitable business: Ink-jet and laser printers and the steady revenue stream from consumables, such as ink and toner cartridges, produced 93 percent of total imaging operating profits and 118 percent of overall operating profits. However, the board judged that remaining competitive in imaging and printing required continued investment for growth and tighter linkages with enterprise information technology.

The Merger Alternative

Although H-P's board began to consider a wide range of alternatives such as exiting the PC business and spinning out the image and printing division, its members focused on a major acquisition. One of the H-P board's primary goals was to acquire a firm that would enable it to confront industry leader IBM more effectively. In 2001 IBM was gaining strength, as was PC leader Dell Computer, whereas H-P was losing momentum. H-P had missed its earnings target for the fourth quarter of fiscal 2000 and subsequently provided guidance for lower future earnings. In this respect its managers were operating in the domain of losses, at least psychologically.

H-P's board discussed both Eastman Kodak and Apple Computer as possible acquisition candidates, but in the end rejected both. It also sought, unsuccessfully, to acquire the accounting firm PricewaterhouseCoopers (PWC).

In June 2001, Fiorina contacted Michael Cappellas, the CEO of Compaq Computer, in order to explore the possibility of licensing some Compaq technology. Those discussions evolved from a conversation about licensing to a dialogue about a possible merger. During July, H-P asked both McKinsey & Co. and Goldman-Sachs to evaluate such a merger.

Psychological Basis for the Decision to Acquire Compaq

On July 19, 2001, Fiorina raised the merger issue with the other eight members of H-P's board. Only three expressed interest. H-P director Sam Ginn raised doubts about becoming more deeply involved in the PC business. He pointed out that both H-P's computer business and Compaq's computer business were not especially profitable. The consultants at McKinsey responded to his concerns by saying that even a small profit in PCs would translate into a decent return on invested capital.

Outside director Patricia Dunn took an outside view. Dunn was vice chair of Barclay's Global Investors, H-P's third largest shareholder. She noted that history has produced many unsuccessful technology mergers and asked what would make the odds of this one any better? The consultants at McKinsey responded by citing $2.5 billion a year in cost savings, which led her to feel more positively about a possible combination.

Nevertheless Fiorina managed to induce H-P's board to support her proposal to acquire Compaq. She did so through her use of framing, handing each director a sheet of paper with the following three questions[24]:

1. Do you think the information-technology industry needs to consolidate, and, if so, is it better to be a consolidator or a consolidatee?

2. How important is it to our strategic goals to be Number 1 or Number 2 in our chief product categories?

3. Can we achieve our strategic goals without something drastic?

Consider whether Carly Fiorina's questions appealed to the directors' natural tendency to be overconfident? Did she frame the issue for them in a way that placed them in the domain of losses? In speaking about drastic action, did she induce them to be risk seeking?

The directors slept on Fiorina's questions. The next morning their positions began to change. Sam Ginn indicated that his main goal was to compete with IBM and that merging with Compaq would help. Phil Condit, the CEO of Boeing Co. at the time, stated that although mergers are difficult, focused acquirers are able to make them successful.

Valuation

In September 2001, H-P and Compaq signed a merger agreement. Their joint press release indicated that the deal would consist of a stock-for-stock merger whereby one share of Compaq stock would be equivalent to 0.6325 of an H-P share. The merged firm would have about $87 billion in sales and 145,000 employees.

Consider how H-P's executives and board assessed the value of the merger in order to arrive at the terms of exchange. The calculation began with net income. According to First Call, the firm known for tracking corporate earnings and earnings estimates, analysts were predicting that H-P's net income for calendar year 2003 would be $2.4 billion and that Compaq's net income would be $588 million.[25] They perceived the after-tax synergies to H-P shareholders for the year to be $1.6 billion,[26] an amount that would be offset by a loss of $364 million in after-tax revenues stemming from the merger.[27]

Taking these amounts together resulted in a net income projection of $4.2 billion for 2003. Given the terms of the merger whereby one share of Compaq stock would be equivalent to 0.6325 of an H-P share, H-P shareholders' portion of the $4.2 billion net income was $2.728 billion. This represented a 13 percent increase over the $2.4 billion net income forecast for H-P as a stand-alone firm.

H-P's goal was to achieve $2.5 billion in synergies per year in four key areas. The largest area was head-count reduction: $1.5 billion in synergy was expected to come by reducing head count by 10,000 by 2002 and 15,000 by 2003. The other three areas were procurement, the closing of manufacturing facilities, and the closing of administrative facilities.

Notably, in August 2002, H-P reported that it was exceeding the plan. It expected to hit its $2.5 billion target one year ahead of plan and to achieve a synergy gain of $3.0 billion in fiscal year 2004.

H-P placed a value of $21.2 billion on the expected synergy stream. Exhibit 10.2 illustrates how H-P arrived at this value, beginning with the $2.5 billion described in the preceding paragraph.

Implicit within Exhibit 10.2 is the assumption that the merger between H-P and Compaq would produce $1.5 billion in after-tax cost savings every year into perpetuity. McKinsey suggested that the cost savings stream be capitalized using a P/E ratio of 20, in that H-P had historically traded at about 20 times earnings. The resulting value of $29.4 billion was discounted back to the announcement date using a discount rate of about 15 percent, to arrive at a figure of $21.2 billion.

On September 4, 2001, when H-P and Compaq announced their merger, H-P offered to pay a premium of $2.1 billion over the average market value of Compaq

EXHIBIT 10.2

Note: Values given in $(billions).
Source: Company Media Relations, Hewlett-Packard.

Synergies	Impact of Revenue Loss	Net Synergies	After-Tax Net Synergies (26% tax rate)	Future Value of Net Synergies at 20 × P/E	Present Value of Net Synergies at 20 × P/E
2.5	0.5	2.0	1.5	29.4	21.2

stock during the preceding month. On September 4, the premium actually amounted to $1.2 billion, or 6.9 percent of the September 4 value of Compaq's stock. H-P's market capitalization was $35.3 billion on that day, and Compaq's market capitalization was $17.7 billion. Shares outstanding for H-P were 1.94 billion, and for Compaq 1.7 billion. In the view of H-P's board and executives, the share-exchange ratio of 64/36 implied Compaq's fair share of the synergy amounted to $7.6 billion, more than the premium H-P was paying.

H-P's Board Accepts Reality

Two years after the H-P–Compaq merger closed, the printing unit contributed 30 percent of H-P's revenue and 80 percent of its profit. Some analysts actually assessed H-P's printer business to be more valuable than the firm as a whole. Despite achieving the promised cost savings, the merger failed to improve the firm's competitive position in its other businesses.

EXHIBIT 10.3   **Cumulative Returns for H-P, IBM, Dell, S&P 500, May 2002–Jan. 2005**

Source: Telerate.

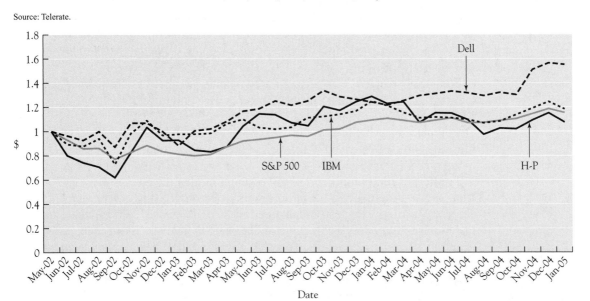

Date

From the time the merger went into effect in May 2002 until March 2004, H-P's stock performed about as well as competitors Dell and IBM. However, in April 2004, H-P began to miss key performance targets that CEO Fiorina had set during the firm's merger with Compaq. Between May 2002 and January 2005, the firm's stock returned 7 percent, less than the 15.8 percent returned by the S&P 500. In contrast, IBM returned 18.3 percent and Dell returned 55.5 percent during this period. See Exhibit 10.3.

In February 2005, *The Wall Street Journal* characterized H-P's business services group as second-tier, relative to industry leader IBM, and noted that its computer division was losing its battle against Dell.[28] That month, H-P's board dismissed Carly Fiorina as CEO of H-P and named independent director Patricia Dunn as nonexecutive chair.

Summary

As a general rule, the more optimistic and overconfident executives are, the more they engage in acquisitions and the more they leave their investors vulnerable to experiencing the winner's curse. In situations where the market value of a firm roughly measures its intrinsic value, excessively optimistic and overconfident executives overestimate the synergy from acquisitions but believe their own firms to be undervalued. As a result, these executives favor paying for target firms using cash instead of stock.

A longholder is an executive who holds his or her stock options until very near expiration. Executives who are excessively optimistic and overconfident according to press coverage and the longholder criterion are especially prone to engage in acquisitions and prefer to pay in cash instead of stock. Moreover, they tend to discount the negative market reaction to their acquisition announcements.

Acquirers who always trust prices leave themselves vulnerable to the winner's curse during times when investors are irrationally exuberant about target firms. WorldCom's acquisitions serve as an example. Targets who always trust prices and accept payment in the form of the acquirer's stock leave themselves vulnerable to seller's remorse, the flip side of the winner's curse. Time Warner provides such an example.

Managers who participate in acquisitions often do so when they perceive themselves to be operating in the domain of losses. H-P's acquisition of Compaq illustrates this phenomenon. The H-P–Compaq example also serves to illustrate the psychological phenomena that guide the thinking of executives and directors.

Additional Behavioral Readings

Anders, G., *Perfect Enough: Carly Fiorina and the Reinvention of Hewlett-Packard,* New York, Penguin, 2003.

Durfee, D., "A Question of Value," *CFO Magazine,* March 1, 2005.

Malmendier, U. and G. Tate, "Who Makes Acquisitions? CEO Overconfidence and the Market's Reaction," Working Paper, Stanford University, 2002.

Roll, R., "The Hubris Hypothesis of Corporate Takeovers." In R.H. Thaler (ed.), *Advances in Behavioral Finance,* New York: Russell Sage Foundation, 1993, pp. 437–458.

Key Terms

dilution cost, *166*   hubris hypothesis, *162*   winner's curse, *162*

Explore the Web

www.viacom.com
The Web site for Viacom.

www.timewarner.com/corp
The Web site for Time Warner.

www.sundayherald.com/42280
An article about H-P's acquisition of Compaq Computer.

Chapter Questions

1. Under the purchase accounting method, a firm that pays more than the fair value for an acquirer amortizes the difference over time on its income statement. In the 1990s, mergers between equally sized firms qualified for treatment as a pooling of interests, in which case no amortization was required. John McCormack, a senior vice president at the consulting firm Stern Stewart, is quoted as follows[29]:

   > The accounting model, in brief, says that the value of a company is its current earnings per share multiplied by a standard, industry-wide P/E ratio. . . . Take the case of Bernie Ebbers of WorldCom. I used to think he was brilliant until I heard him explain in a public forum why it was really important to have acquisitions created under the pooling-of-interests accounting method rather than the purchase method. These accounting effects have absolutely no effect on future cash flows, but they will definitely affect EPS. And if you had been persuaded by your investment bankers, as Bernie apparently was, that the value of MCI-WorldCom shares was your earnings per share multiplied by your industry P/E ratio, then you might have believed pooling accounting was important.

   Discuss John McCormack's statements in the context of heuristics and biases, and relate the discussion to the market valuations of AOL and Time Warner.

2. In the chapter discussion of the merger between H-P and Compaq, H-P director Sam Ginn initially voiced doubts about the deal. However, the McKinsey experts retorted that even a slim profit in PCs would mean a decent return on invested capital. Do you detect any agency conflicts in this exchange?

3. H-P director Patricia Dunn works in the banking industry, where consolidation mergers have worked out well in the long run but are vulnerable in the first two years. She responded positively to the McKinsey consultants' statements that a merger between H-P and Compaq would produce significant cost savings. Discuss her perspective.

4. H-P executives indicate that they use traditional discounted cash flow (DCF) analysis to evaluate investment projects and that the firm's cost of capital is about 12 percent. Consider Exhibit 10.2 which shows how McKinsey consultants proposed that H-P value the cost savings stream stemming from its merger with Compaq. On October 15, 2003, H-P's forward P/E ratio was 16.1, less than its historical value that stood around 20. H-P executives suggest that the lower P/E ratio reflected continued investor uncertainty about whether or not the merger would be successful. Discuss the manner in which H-P executives valued the expected cost savings stream when evaluating the merger. In particular address the following questions: Was the technique H-P executives used the same, or comparable, to traditional DCF analysis? Do you believe that H-P paid a reasonable premium for Compaq? Are there any valuation implications attached to H-P's P/E ratio being at 16 rather than 20?

5. A traditional counterargument to the behavioral position described in the chapter is that the chapter arguments only focus on problematic acquisitions. For example, consider consumer products firm Colgate-Palmolive. In 1984 Reuben Mark became CEO of Colgate-Palmolive, taking over from Keith Crane. Like Wayne Huizenga, articles appeared in *The Wall Street Journal* over the years describing Mark as *optimistic* or *confident*. Unlike Wayne Huizenga, no such attribution appears to have been made to Keith Crane, at least in the financial press. Moreover, according to the longholder criterion, Reuben Mark is excessively optimistic and overconfident, but Keith Crane was not. During 11 years at the helm of Colgate-Palmolive, Reuben Mark conducted several acquisitions, of which two were large. Mark also divested businesses where Colgate-Palmolive was not a leader. In contrast, Keith Crane did not conduct a single acquisition. Both Huizenga and Mark conducted acquisitions uniformly throughout their tenures. Neither concentrated acquisition activity in the final years of his option's duration. For example, Mark held an option that expired in 1992. Indeed, between 1990 and 1992 he conducted two acquisitions. However, between 1985 and 1988 he conducted three acquisitions. Colgate-Palmolive appears to have thrived under Mark's leadership. The March–April 2003 issue of the publication *Financial Executive* reports that Colgate-Palmolive's five-year return on equity (ROE) was 71.9 percent, much higher than the industry ROE of 46.5 percent and 12.2 percent for the S&P 500. Does the experience of Colgate-Palmolive not present evidence that contradicts the behavioral position?

Additional Resources and Materials for Chapter 10 Are available at www.mhhe.com/shefrin

Minicase

PSA Peugeot Citroen SA and DaimlerChrysler AG

In 1997 executives of the automobile firm PSA Peugeot Citroen SA observed that their competitors began to merge. Daimler acquired Chrysler to become Daimler-Chrysler AG. General Motors Corp. purchased a 20 percent stake of Fiat's auto division and held an option to purchase the remaining 80 percent. Ford Motor Co. purchased Jaguar, Land Rover, and Volvo.

PSA resisted the pressure to mimic the acquisition activity of its competitors. The firm had learned the hard way about the cost of making an acquisition. In 1974 the French automobile maker Peugeot acquired Citroen, and the result was disappointing. The firm's CEO Jean-Martin Folz had stated that managers cannot easily bring out new products when they are distracted by the challenge of integrating two firms. And PSA was intent on bringing out new products.

PSA's competitors faced disappointments of their own. One of the most dramatic examples involves Daimler-Chrysler AG. Prior to its takeover of Chrysler in 1998, Mercedes was the number one luxury brand in the world, known for top quality, and it sold more luxury automobiles in the United States than any other automobile firm. At the time of the takeover, Mercedes' CEO Jürgen Schrempp predicted that the combined firm would become the most profitable automobile manufacturer in the world.[30]

By the end of 2004, Mercedes had slipped from first position in the United States to fourth position. Beginning in 2002, the quality of its automobiles began to slide. Its engineers began to add features that they found intriguing but were not valued by its customers. As for Chrysler, it lost $2 billion in 2000, and $1 billion in the second quarter of 2003. In late 2003, Chrysler introduced a new successful model, the 300C. Although its profit improved, the overall profitability of DaimlerChrysler continued to disappoint investors. In July 2005, under pressure from shareholders, CEO Schrempp announced that he would retire at year-end, three years before the expiration of his contract.

As DaimlerChrysler slipped, PSA did well. Between 1998 and 2002, PSA's sales grew by 62 percent (to $61.8 billion). PSA became the world's sixth-largest automobile firm, surpassing Honda Motor Corp. and Hyundai Motor Co.

Case Analysis Question

1. Discuss the main lessons to be learned from the behavior of the executives at PSA and DaimlerChrysler. In your discussion, compare the behavior of executives at PSA and DaimlerChrysler with executives in the examples described in the chapter text.

Chapter **Eleven**

Application of Real-Option Techniques to Capital Budgeting and Capital Structure

The main objective of this chapter is for students to demonstrate that they can identify the manner in which psychological phenomena affect managers' use of real-option techniques.

After completing this chapter students will be able to:

1. Explain why opaque framing causes managers to refrain from using real-option techniques.
2. Explain how excessive optimism affects the investment policies of managers who use real-option techniques.
3. Explain how overconfidence affects the investment policies of managers who use real-option techniques.
4. Explain why excessive optimism and overconfidence mitigate the impact of agency conflicts associated with debt overhang and asset substitution.
5. Describe how real-option techniques can mitigate managers' tendencies to throw good money after bad.

This chapter is available at www.mhhe.com/shefrin

Glossary

acceptance   Group discussion tends to induce group members to accept a decision too readily.

accuracy   Groups outperform individuals when it comes to intellectual tasks, but do worse than individuals when it comes to judgmental tasks.

affect   Emotional feeling.

affect heuristic   Basing decisions primarily on intuition, instinct, and gut feeling.

anchoring and adjustment   People form an estimate by beginning with an initial number and adjusting to reflect new information or circumstances. However, they tend to make insufficient adjustments relative to that number, thereby leading to anchoring bias.

anomalies   Empirical phenomena that appear to be puzzles with respect to the efficient market hypothesis.

availability bias   People overweight information that is readily available and intuitive relative to information that is less salient and more abstract.

aversion to a sure loss   People choose to accept an actuarially unfair risk in an attempt to avoid a sure loss.

base rate information   Information pertaining to the general environment.

behavioral APV   The inclusion of behavioral elements in adjusted present value to reflect either mispricing or managerial biases.

behavioral life cycle hypothesis   Over the course of their lives, people use mental accounts to cope with potential self-control problems that cause inadequate savings.

bias   A predisposition toward error.

casino effect   Preference for the small probability of a large payoff.

catering   Choosing a dividend policy with the purpose of responding to investors' psychological needs, be those needs associated with preferences or with investor sentiment.

confirmation bias   People attach too much importance to information that supports their views relative to information that runs counter to their views.

conjunction fallacy   Miscalculating the probability of an event that is defined as the conjunction or simultaneous occurrence of a series of separate events.

debias   Reduce susceptibility to biases and framing effects.

desirability   One of the factors contributing to excessive optimism, commonly understood to be wishful thinking.

dilution cost   The value that acquirers believe that the target's shareholders receive because the acquiring firm's stock is undervalued in the market.

endowment effect   People attach a greater value to an object once they regard it as part of their endowment than before it becomes part of their endowment.

escalation of commitment   The tendency to throw good money after bad.

excessive optimism   People overestimate how frequently they will experience favorable outcomes and underestimate how frequently they will experience unfavorable outcomes.

extrapolation bias or hot-hand fallacy   Unwarranted extrapolation of past trends in forming forecasts.

familiarity   Essentially a form of availability bias, where available information is familiar information.

frame   Synonymous for description.

framing effect   A person's decision is influenced by the manner in which the setting for the decision is described.

gamblers' fallacy   The tendency to overweight the probability of an event because it has not recently occurred at a frequency that reflects its probability.

groupthink   The drive for achieving group consensus overrides the realistic appraisal of alternative courses of action.

hedonic editing   People prefer to experience gains separately rather than together, but integrate small losses into larger gains.

heuristic   A rule of thumb used to make judgment or a decision.

hindsight bias   The tendency to view events as obvious or almost certain in hindsight when they are neither obvious nor almost certain when viewed in foresight.

hot issue market   Demand for new issues is relatively high.

hubris hypothesis   Firms experience the winner's curse in mergers and acquisitions because of hubris.

illusion of control   People overestimate the extent to which they can control events.

illusion of effectiveness   Unwarranted confidence in the decision.

incentive compatibility constraint   The principal chooses the carrot-and-stick differential in terms of pay for performance so as to induce the agent to represent the interests of the principal.

initial underpricing   The offer price is too low, resulting in a large first-day price pop.

inside view   Taking a perspective on a project by focusing on the details specific to that particular project.

limits of arbitrage   Smart investors do not fully exploit mispricing because of the attendant risks that the mispricing will become larger before it becomes smaller.

longholders   Excessively optimistic, overconfident CEOs who hold their options into the final year.

long-term underperformance   New issues earn lower returns than stocks with comparable characteristics against which they have been matched.

loss aversion   Psychologically, people experience a loss more acutely than a gain of the same magnitude.

mental accounting   Mentally separating information into manageable pieces, by maintaining separate accounts.

momentum   Recent losers tend subsequently to underperform the market, and recent winners tend subsequently to outperform the market.

narrow framing   Treating a repeated risk as if it were a one-shot deal.

nonoverpayment constraint   The principal does not overpay the agent.

$1/n$ heuristic   A simple rule of thumb that assigns equal weight to all choices under consideration.

opaque framing   Describing a decision task in a manner that renders the consequences of the decision difficult to discern.

outside view   Taking a perspective on a project by comparing the characteristics of a specific project with a large population of projects which are similar in nature.

overconfidence   People make mistakes more frequently than they believe and view themselves as better than average.

overreaction   The percentage change in market price in response to an event is too large.

overweighting of small probabilities   People tend to overweight low probabilities attached to extreme events.

participation constraint   The principal offers attractive enough terms to the agent to induce the agent to participate.

P/E heuristic   An approach to valuation based on multiplying a P/E ratio and an earnings forecast.

PEG heuristic   An approach to valuation based on multiplying a PEG ratio, an earnings forecast, and a forecast of the growth rate.

polarization   Group processes tend to accentuate attitudes toward risk.

poor information sharing   Group members fail to share enough information with other group members.

post-earnings-announcement drift   The stocks of firms that announce positive earnings surprises experience positive drift after the announcement, while the stocks of firms that announce negative earnings surprises experience negative drift after the announcement.

preference reversal   Choosing low-value alternatives over high-value alternatives.

press coverage overconfidence indicator   The press uses the words *optimistic* and *confident* to describe an executive.

price-to-sales heuristic   An approach to valuation based on multiplying a price-to-sales ratio and a sales forecast.

prospect theory   A general psychological approach that describes the way people make choices among risky alternatives.

reference point   Benchmark used to measure gains and losses.

regret   An emotion that occurs when people imagine having taken a different decision than the one they actually took, one that would have turned out favorably rather than unfavorably.

representativeness   People make judgments based on stereotypic thinking, asking how representative an object or idea is to the class to which it belongs.

self-attribution error   The tendency for people to take credit for positive outcomes and to blame others or bad luck for negative outcomes.

self-control   The act of exercising control over one's impulses, usually to delay gratification.

sensitivity of investment to cash flow   Investment depends on how much cash a firm holds.

sentiment   Aggregate investor error, either excessive optimism or excessive pessimism.

singular information   Unique information directly related to a situation or object.

social loafing   Group members reduce their contributions, instead relying on others to exert the requisite effort.

sunk cost   An expenditure made in the past that is irrevocable.

transparent framing   Describing a decision task in a manner that renders the consequences of the decision easy to discern.

underreaction   The percentage change in market price in response to an event is too small.

visibility   How noticeable a project or activity is to others.

willingness to pay   How much a person or group is willing to pay to acquire something.

winner's curse   The winning bid in an auction results in the winner overpaying.

winner–loser effect   Extreme past losers tend subsequently to outperform the market, and extreme past winners tend subsequently to underperform the market.

Endnotes

Chapter 1

1. See Manju Puri and David Robinson, 2005. "Optimism and Economic Choice," Working Paper, Duke University.

2. See Jeremy Siegel, "Big Cap Tech Stocks Are a Sucker Bet," *The Wall Street Journal,* March 14, 2000; "Not-Quite-So-Big-Cap Tech Stocks Are Still a Bad Bet," *The Wall Street Journal,* March 19, 2001.

3. See Simon Gervais and Terrence Odean, "Learning to Be Overconfident," *Review of Financial Studie*s vol. 14, 2001, pp. 1–27.

4. See "Bank of America Roundtable On: The Real Options Approach to Creating Value in the New Economy," *Journal of Applied Corporate Finance,* vol. 13, no. 2, 2000, pp. 45–63.

5. See Anna Wilde Mathews and Barbara Martinez, "E-Mails Suggest Early Vioxx Worries—As Evidence of Heart Risk Rose, Merck Officials Played Hardball; One Internal Message: 'Dodge!'" *The Wall Street Journal,* November 2, 2004.

6. See Baruch Fischhoff, "Debiasing." In Daniel Kahneman, Paul Slovic, and Amos Tversky (eds.), *Judgment Under Uncertainty: Heuristics and Biases.* Cambridge, MA: Cambridge University Press, 1982.

Chapter 2

1. Brealey-Myers use present value of growth opportunities (PVGO), and Ross-Westerfield-Jaffe use net present value of growth opportunities (NPVGO).

2. See Frank C. Evans, "Valuation Essentials for CFOs," *Financial Executive,* March/April 2002.

3. See P. Asquith, M. Mikhail, and A. Au, "Information Content of Equity Analyst Reports," Working Paper, Sloan School of Management, Massachussetts Institute of Technology, 2004.

4. See Mary Anne Ostrom, "Net Stocks Enjoying a Revival," *San Jose Mercury News,* May 3, 2003.

5. This was a joint chapter meeting of the Santa Clara Valley chapter and the San Francisco chapter.

6. Mark Rubash was the vice president, finance and investor relations and the chief accounting officer for eBay Inc. He discussed these issues with an executive MBA class at Santa Clara University on May 9, 2003.

7. Meeker coauthored the report with her colleague Brian Pitz. The report is available at the McGraw-Hill Web site **www.mhhe.com/shefrin.**

8. Meeker's report states: "We calculate the Cost of Equity at 9.5% based on a risk-free rate of 3.9%, . . . a risk premium of 4.0%, and beta of 1.38." This results in a CAPM-based rate of 9.5 percent. She explained that she uses the higher 12 percent rate in order to account for company specific risks.

9. Meeker used 330,259,000 shares outstanding, and adjusted the present value of the free cash flows by debt and cash holdings.

10. The new equity item also includes a $1.7 million dollar adjustment for exchange rates.

11. The authors of the report are Mark Rowen, Aimee Landwehr, and Anne Wickland.

12. Wingfield reports that he also sought to interview Mary Meeker, but she did not respond to his request.

13. The authors of the report are Wayne Hood and Matthew Laing.

Chapter 3

1. See J. Graham and C. Harvey, "The Theory and Practice of Corporate Finance: Evidence from the Field," *Journal of Financial Economics,* vol. 60, nos. 2–3, 2001, pp. 187–243. Of 4,400 firms, CFOs from 392 responded. Question responses were on a scale from 0 (not important) to 4 (very important).

2. See L. Gitman and P. Vandenberg, "Cost of Capital Techniques Used by Major US Firms: 1997 vs. 1980," *Financial Practice and Education,* vol. 10, no. 2, 2000, pp. 53–68.

3. See also R. F. Bruner, K. M. Eades, R. S. Harris, and R. C. Higgins, "Best Practices in Estimating the Cost of Capital: Survey and Synthesis," *Financial Practice and Education,* vol. 8, no. 21, 1998, pp. 13–28.

4. Because 75 percent of CFOs report using IRR and 75 percent using NPV, some managers must use both NPV and IRR.

5. There is a modified version of the payback method that uses discounted cash flows. However, Graham and Harvey report that few use it.

6. See A. Tversky and R. H. Thaler, "Anomalies: Preference Reversals," *Journal of Economic Perspectives,* 4, 4, 1990, pp. 201–11.

7. See James Flynn, Paul Slovic, and C. K. Mertz, "Gender, Race, and the Perception of Environmental Health Risks," *Risk Analysis,* vol. 14, no. 6, 1994, pp. 1101–1198.

8. See "Protecting Value Study: Has the World of Risk Really Changed?" Factory Mutual Insurance Company and Financial Executives Research Foundation, 2003.

9. See H. Wolinsky, "Iridium Failure Brought Motorola Back Down to Earth," *Chicago Sun-Times,* September 25, 2003.

10. See A. Marshall and W. Meckling, "Predictability of the Costs, Time, and Success of Development," that appeared in the National Bureau of Economic Research *The Rate and Direction of Investive Activity: Economic and Social Factors,* Princeton, NJ: Princeton University Press, 1962.

11. See B. Flyvbjerg, M. Skamris Holm, and S. Buhl, "Underestimating costs in public works projects: Error or Lie?" *Journal of the American Planning Association,* Summer, 2002, pp. 279–295. The transportation infrastructure projects are as prone to cost underestimation as other types of large projects.

12. See D. Axson, "It Doesn't Have to Be Spend and Hope," *Financial Executive,* September/October, 1996, pp. 18–24.

13. For projects requiring small technological advances, the ratio was 1.82.

14. See chapter 5 of E. Mansfield, J. Rapoport, J. Schnee, S. Wagner, and M. Hamburger, *Research and Innovation in the Modern Corporation.* New York: Norton, 1985.

15. See B. W. MacKenzie, "Looking for the Improbable Needle in a Haystack: The Economics of Base Metal Exploration in Canada," *CIM Bulletin,* vol. 74, no. 829, pp. 115–123, 1981. See also W. E. Roscoe, "Probability of an Economic Discovery in Canada," *CIM Bulletin,* vol. 64, 1971, pp. 134–137.

16. See E. Mansfield and R. Brandenburg, "The Allocation, Characteristics, and Outcome of the Firm's Research and Development Portfolio: a Case Study," *Journal of Business,* 1966, pp. 447–464.

17. See D. S. Tull, "The Relationship of Actual and Predicted Sales and Profits in New-Product Introductions," *Journal of Business,* 1967, pp. 233–250. Tull studied 24 firms and found that actual sales fell short of predicted sales in 66 percent of new products.

18. See E. Mansfield, J. Rapoport, J. Schnee, S. Wagner, and M. Hamburger, *Research and Innovation in the Modern Corporation.* New York: Norton, 1985.

19. See P. Hall, *Great Planning Disasters.* Berkeley, California: University of California Press, 1980.

20. "Why Do So Many Projects Still Miss Deadlines and Bust Budgets?" *Computing,* October 13, 1988.

21. These data are described in the Standish Research Paper, Chaos Study. See **www.standishgroup.com.** The data are also discussed in a Web site article, January 5, 2003, by J. Suzuki entitled "Why Do Software Development Projects Fail So Often?" See **members.cox.net/johnsuzuki/softfail.htm.**

22. See A. Snow and M. Keil, "A Framework for Assessing the Reliability of Software Project Status Reports," *Engineering Management Journal,* vol. 14, no. 2, 2002, pp. 20–26.

23. These failures are documented in R. Glass, *Software Runaway: Lessons Learned from Massive Software Project Failures.* Upper Saddle, NJ: Prentice-Hall, 1998.

24. The partner is Tony Rocker, and they run lots of scenarios, quoted in the article "In Business—Lies, Damn Lies and Cost Estimates," *Building,* May 9, 2003.

25. See A. Tversky and D. Kahneman, "Judgment Under Uncertainty: Heuristics and Biases," *Science,* vol. 185, 1974, pp. 1124–1131.

26. Nevertheless, the 73 percent is a significant improvement over the 44 percent figure that prevailed in 1980.

27. See L. May, "Sunk Costs Are Not So Fully Drowned after All," *Australian Financial Review,* July 8, 1988; B. Staw, "Knee-Deep in the Big Muddy: A Study of Escalating Commitment toward a Chosen Course of Action," *Organizational Behavior and Human Performance,* vol. 20, 1976, pp. 27–44.

28. J. Nathan traces the history of Sony Corporation in his book *Sony: The Private Life.* Boston: Houghton Mifflin Company, 1999.

29. Quoted in "Has Syntex Run Out of Steam? Wall Street Is Impatient with Sluggish Sales and Few New Products," *Business Week,* July 12, 1993, pp. 144–146.

30. See David Yermack, "Flights of Fancy: Corporate Jets, CEO Perquisites, and Inferior Shareholder Returns," Working paper, New York University, 2005.

31. See D. Lovallo and D. Kahneman, "Delusions of Success," *Harvard Business Review,* July 2003, pp. 56–60.

32. See G. Reynolds, "Risk Management in a Resource Industry," MBA dissertation, Michael Smurfit Graduate School of Business, University College, Dublin, 2000. The survey used a Delphi technique.

33. This case is taken from Mark Keil, "Pulling the Plug: Software Project Management and the Problem of Project Escalation," *MIS Quarterly* vol. 19, no. 4, 1995, p. 421. Although the minicase pertains to a large computer firm called CompuSys and its associated project Config, these are not their real names. Some of the items in the box Debiasing for Better Decisions are taken from this article.

Chapter 4

1. See Richard Brealey, Stewart Myers, and Franklin Allen, *Principles of Corporate Finance,* 8th ed., New York, NY: McGraw-Hill/Irwin, 2006, p. 154.

2. See Ivo Welch, "Views of Financial Economists on the Equity Premium and on Professional Controversies," *Journal of Business,* vol. 73, no. 4, 2000, pp. 501–537.

3. See Hersh Shefrin and Meir Statman, "Making Sense of Beta, Size and Book-to-Market," *The Journal of Portfolio Management,* (Winter) vol. 21, no. 2, 1995, pp. 26–34.

4. Respondents used data that was current at the time, not the data in Exhibit 4.1, which pertains to April 2000. The survey run in April 2000 involved 10 money managers at a well-known hedge fund that was written up in *The Wall Street Journal* who completed the supplementary *Fortune* survey. Intel and Unisys were among the stocks included in the survey. Of the 10 money managers, only 2 provided return expectations that were positively correlated with their risk assessments. Only one hedge fund manager provided expected returns and risk assessments, for Unisys and Intel, such that a higher expected return was assigned to the riskier stock. In addition, there was a widespread of opinions among the managers. For Unisys, the hedge fund managers' expected returns ranged from −12 percent to 20 percent, and their risk assessments ranged from 4 to 9 on a scale of 0 to 10. For Intel, the managers' expected returns ranged from 11 percent to 65 percent, and their risk assessments ranged from 5 to 8. For what it is worth, Unisys outperformed Intel during the subsequent 12 months. The return to Unisys stock between April 2000 and March 2001 was −46 percent, whereas the return to Intel stock was −60 percent.

5. See Melissa Finucane, Ali Alhakami, Paul Slovic, and Stephen Johnson, "The Affect Heuristic in Judgments of Risks and Benefits," *Journal of Behavioral Decision Making,* vol. 13, 2000, pp. 1–17.

6. See Michael Cooper, Rolin Dimitrov, and P. Raghaveda Rau, "A Rose.com by Any Other Name," *Journal of Finance,* vol. LVI, no. 6, 2001, pp. 2371–2388.

7. See Alon Brav, Reuven Lehavy, and Roni Michaely, "Expected Return and Asset Pricing," Working paper, Duke University, 2002.

8. First Call sells this information to professional investors through an online system, providing their subscribers with almost instantaneous access to information generated by brokerage firms.

9. Published by the firm Value Line.

10. See Yoav Ganzach, "Judging Risk and Return of Financial Assets," *Organizational Behavior and Human Decision Processes,* vol. 83, 2000, pp. 353–370. Hersh Shefrin, 2001. "Do Investors Expect Higher Returns from Safer Stocks than from Riskier Stocks?" *Journal of Psychology and Financial Markets,* 2(4), 176–181. Gene Amromin and Steven A. Sharpe, 2005. "From the Horse's Mouth: Gauging Conditional Expected Stock Returns from Investor Surveys," Working paper, Federal Reserve Board.

11. See Campbell Harvey, "Implications for Asset Allocation, Portfolio Management, and Future Research II," *AIMR,* 2002, no. 1, pp. 97–99.

12. See Narasimhan Jegadeesh and Sheridan Titman, "Returns to Buying Winners and Selling Losers: Implications for Stock Market Efficiency," *Journal of Finance,* vol. 48, 1993, pp. 65–91.

13. See Dirk Jenter, Forthcoming. "Market Timing and Managerial Portfolio Decisions," *Journal of Finance.* See also Michael S. Rozeff, and Mir A. Zaman, "Overreaction and Insider Trading: Evidence from Growth and Value Portfolios," *Journal of Finance,* vol. 53, 1998, pp. 701–716.

14. See John Graham and Campbell Harvey, "The Theory and Practice of Corporate Finance: Evidence from the Field," *Journal of Financial Economics,* vol. 60, nos. 2–3, 2001, pp. 187–243.

15. Interview, February 9, 2001.

16. See Jonathan R. Laing, "The Bear That Roared: How Short-seller Jim Chanos Helped Expose Enron," *Barron's,* January 28, 2002, pp. 18–20.

17. See Brad Cornell, "Is the Response of Analysts to Information Consistent with Fundamental Valuation? The Case of Intel," *Financial Management,* Spring 2001, pp. 113–136.

Chapter 5

1. See Eugene Fama, "Random Walks in Stock Market Prices," *Financial Analysts Journal,* vol. 21, no. 5, September/October 1965, pp. 55–59.

2. See Eugene Fama, "Market-Efficiency, Long-Term Returns, and Behavioral Finance," *Journal of Financial Economics,* vol. 49, no. 3, 1998, pp. 283–306.

3. See Jon E. Hilsenrath, "One School of Thought on How Markets Act Gains Edge in Chicago—Mr. Thaler's Behavioral Theory Takes Lead over Mr. Fama's Efficiency Idea—Implications for Real-Life Problems," *The Wall Street Journal,* October 18, 2004.

4. See Eugene Fama, and Kenneth French, "Disagreement, Tastes and Asset Prices," Working Paper, University of Chicago, 2004.

5. See Justin Fox, "Learn to Play the Earnings Game (and Wall Street Will Love You)," *Fortune Magazine,* March 31, 1997, 76–80.

6. See John Graham, Campbell Harvey, and Shiva Rajgopal, "The Economic Implications of Corporate Financial Reporting," Working Paper, Duke University, 2004.

7. See Mary Bange and Werner De Bondt, "R&D Budgets and Corporate Earnings Targets," *Journal of Corporate Finance,* vol. 4, 1998, pp. 153–184.

8. See the article by G. Millman, "Capital Allocation: When the Right Thing Is Hard to Do," *Financial Executive,* September/October 2000, pp. 28–32, 34.

9. See Eugene Fama, Lawrence Fisher, Michael Jensen, and Richard Roll, "The Adjustment of Stock Prices to New Information," *International Economic Review,* 1969. These authors show that for the period 1926–1960, companies that split their stocks saw their market cap rise prior to the split.

10. See David Ikenberry, Graeme Rankine, and Earl Stice, "What Do Stock Splits Really Signal?" *Journal of Financial and Quantitative Analysis,* vol. 31, no. 3, 1996, pp. 1–21.

11. See David Ikenberry and Sundaresh Ramnath, "Underreaction to Self-Selected News: The Case of Stock Splits," *Review of Financial Studies,* vol. 15, no. 2, 2002, pp. 489–526.

12. See Mitchell Schnurman, "Radio Shack Parent Tandy Corp. to Split Stock 2-for-1," KRTBN Knight-Ridder Tribune Business News: Fort Worth Star-Telegram, May 26, 1999.

13. See Tim Loughran and Jay Ritter, "The New Issues Puzzle," *Journal of Finance,* vol. 50, 1995, pp. 23–51.

14. See Tim Loughran and Jay R. Ritter, "The Operating Performance of Firms Conducting Seasoned Equity Offerings," *Journal of Finance,* vol. LII, no. 5, December 1997, pp. 1823–50.

15. Exhibits 5.1 to 5.4 are based on data available at Jay Ritter's Web site (**bear.cba.ufl.edu/ritter**).

16. See Aydoğan Alti, "How Persistent Is the Impact of Market Timing on Capital Structure?" Working Paper, University of Texas, Austin, 2004.

17. See Tim Loughran and Jay Ritter, "Why Has IPO Underpricing Changed over Time?" *Financial Management,* vol. 33, no. 3, 2004, pp. 5–37.

18. See Tim Loughran and Jay Ritter, "Why Don't Issuers Get Upset About Leaving Money on the Table in IPOs?" *Review of Financial Studies,* vol. 15, 2002, pp. 413–443. Ljungqvist A. and W. Wilhelm, Jr., 2005. "Does Prospect Theory Explain IPO Behavior?" *Journal of Finance,* 60, 1759–1790.

19. See SEC litigation release 17327, January 22, 2002.

20. See Alon Brav and Paul Gompers, "Myth or Reality? The Long-Run Underperformance of Initial Public Offerings, Evidence from Venture and Non-Venture-Backed Companies," *Journal of Finance,* vol. 52, no. 5, 1997.

21. See Gregory Zuckerman, "CEOs Turn Mum About Projecting Earnings," *The Wall Street Journal,* March 1, 2005.

22. See Cintra Scott, "Smartmoney Daily Screen: Who's Right About 3Com?" September 15, 1999, *Dow Jones News Service.*

23. See "3Com Plans to Spin Off Palm Computing Unit to Focus on Networking," *Dow Jones Business News,* September 13, 1999.

24. See Owen Lamont and Richard Thaler, "Can the Market Add and Subtract? Mispricing in Tech Stock Carve-Outs," *Journal of Political Economy* 111, 227–268, 2003.

25. See P. Schultz and M. Zirman, "Do the Individuals Closest to Internet Firms Believe They Are Overvalued?" *Journal of Financial Economics,* vol. 59, 2001.

26. Guest lectures presented by former 3Com executives at Santa Clara University, April 29, 2005.

Chapter 6

1. See Paul Sweeney "Capital Structure: Credibility and Flexibility," *Financial Executive,* 2003, pp. 33–36.

2. See Malcolm Baker and Jeffrey Wurgler, "Market Timing and Capital Structure," *Journal of Finance,* vol. 57, no. 1, 2002, pp. 1–32.

3. See Dirk Jenter, forthcoming. "Market Timing and Managerial Portfolio Decisions," *Journal of Finance.*

4. See Baker and Wurgler, cited previously.

5. Interview with Eddie Le, Corporate and Investment Banking, Banc of America Securities, November 5, 2004.

6. See Susan Pulliam, "Mixed Blessing: How Hedge-Fund Trading Sent a Company's Stock on Wild Ride," *The Wall Street Journal,* December 28, 2004.

7. The top four are (1) earnings dilution, (2) amount of mispricing, (3) if the stock price has recently risen, and (4) providing stock in connection with employee stock ownership.

8. See Mark Flannery and Kasturi Rangan, "Partial Adjustment toward Target Capital Structures," Working Paper, University of Florida, 2004; and Mark Leary and Michael Roberts, "Do Firms Rebalance Their Capital Structures?" Working Paper, Duke University, 2004. See also Aydoğan Alti, "How Persistent Is the Impact of Market Timing on Capital Structure?" Working Paper, University of Texas, Austin, 2004.

9. See Rongbing Huang and Jay Ritter, "Testing the Market Timing Theory of Capital Structure," Working Paper, University of Florida, 2004.

10. See John Graham, "How Big Are the Tax Benefits of Debt?" *Journal of Finance,* vol. 55, 2000, pp. 1901–1941.

11. See Colin Mayer and Oren Sussman, "A New Test of Capital Structure," Working Paper, Saïd Business School, University of Oxford, 2004. Also see the Huang-Ritter paper.

12. Over 60 percent would reduce repurchases, but less than 30 percent would reduce dividends.

13. David Ikenberry, Josef Lakonishok, and Theo Vermaelen, "Market Underreaction to Open Market Share Repurchases," *Journal of Financial Economics,* vol. 39, 1995, pp. 181–208.

14. See Jeremy Stein, "Rational Capital Budgeting in an Irrational World," *Journal of Business,* vol. 69, 1996, pp. 429–455.

15. See Jeremy Stein, "Agency, Information, and Corporate Investment." In George Constantinides, Milton Harris, and René Stulz (eds.), *Handbook of the Economics of Finance,* forthcoming.

16. This section is based on a presentation that Adaptec's chief financial officer at the time, David Young, made on November 9, 2001, at Santa Clara University.

17. See O. J. Blanchard, F. Lopez-de-Silanes, and A. Shleifer, "What Do Firms Do with Cash Windfalls?" *Journal of Financial Economics,* vol. 36, 1994, pp. 337–360.

18. See Kenneth Froot, "The Market for Catastrophe Risk: A Clinical Examination," NBER Working Paper no. 8110, February 2001. Revised in *Journal of Financial Economics,* vol. 60, 2001, pp. 529–571.

19. There are several studies documenting this phenomenon. See Owen Lamont, "Cash Flow and Investment: Evidence from Internal Capital Markets," *Journal of Finance,* vol. 52, no. 1, 1997, pp. 83–109.

20. See Armen Hovakimian and Gayane Hovakimian, 2005. "Cash Flow Sensitivity of Investment: Firm-Level Analysis," Working paper Baruch College and Fordham University.

21. Ulrike Malmendier and Geoffrey Tate, "Who Makes Acquisitions? CEO Overconfidence and the Market's Reaction," Working Paper, Stanford University, 2002.

22. Inclusion in this sample is based on lists compiled by *Forbes* magazine during the period.

23. See Ulrike Malmendier and Geoffrey Tate, "CEO Overconfidence and Corporate Investment," in the *Journal of Finance,* forthcoming.

24. Boards with 12 or fewer members are considered stronger than boards that have more than 12 members. Growth opportunities are typically measured by Tobin's Q, the ratio of the market value of a firm divided by the replacement cost of its assets.

25. See Malcolm Baker, Richard Ruback, and Jeffrey Wurgler. "Behavioral Corporate Finance: A Survey." In *The Handbook of Corporate Finance: Empirical*

Corporate Finance, edited by Espen Eckbo. New York: Elsevier/North Holland, forthcoming.

26. See "Buyback Binge of U.S. Companies Is Getting Costly—Firms Reverse Strategy, Buy Shares When Prices Are High," *The Wall Street Journal,* by staff reporters Robert McGough, Suzanne McGee and Cassell Bryan-Low in New York, December 19, 2000.

Chapter 7

1. See Merton, Miller, and Franco Modigliani, "Dividend Policy, Growth, and the Valuation of Shares," *Journal of Business,* vol. 34, 1961, pp. 411–433.

2. See Karen Talley, "S&P 500 Companies Are Poised to Pay Record-Level Dividends," *The Wall Street Journal,* May 19, 2004.

3. See "Dividend Mania: New Corporate Contagion?" *Barron's Online,* July 17, 2003.

4. More undergraduate students indicate a willingness to sell stock in order to finance consumption than graduate students. However, even here between 50 and 60 percent typically say that they would cut consumption by the full amount of the omitted dividend.

5. This case is discussed in Hersh Shefrin and Meir Statman, "Explaining Investor Preference for Cash Dividends." *Journal of Financial Economics,* vol. 13, June 1984, pp. 253–282.

6. See James Moore and Olivia Mitchell, "Projected Retirement Wealth and Savings Adequacy in the Health and Retirement Study," National Bureau of Economic Research, Working Paper 6240, 1997.

7. This problem was first run as a survey in 1987 and peoples' responses have been consistent across all replications of the original study. See Hersh Shefrin and Richard Thaler, "The Behavioral Life Cycle Hypothesis," *Economic Inquiry,* vol. XXIV, 1988, pp. 609–643.

8. See John Graham and Alok Kumar, "Dividend Preference of Retail Investors: Do Dividend Clienteles Exist?" Working Paper, Duke University, 2003, for empirical evidence involving older investors with low incomes.

9. The Shefrin–Statman article cited earlier discusses the behavioral basis for why investors find cash dividends attractive.

10. From William Doyle, "Your Money: Well-Chosen Utility Stocks Can Be a Good Investment," *Atlanta Journal and Constitution,* May 30, 1991, p. G2.

11. From "Answers to Your Money Questions," *Kiplinger's Personal Finance,* June 1, 2003.

12. See John Graham and Alok Kumar, cited earlier.

13. See Elias Rantapuska, 2005. "Do Investors, Reinvest Dividends and Tender Offer Proceeds?" Working Paper, Helsinki School of Economics.

14. See Yaniv Grinstein and Roni Michaely, "Institutional Holdings and Payout Policy," *Journal of Finance,* forthcoming.

15. See Scott Thurm, "Companies: Cisco Systems' Shareholders Reject Proposal for Dividend," *The Wall Street Journal,* November 20, 2002.

16. See Franklin Allen and Roni Michaely, "Payout Policy." In George Constantinides, Milton Harris, and René Stulz (eds.), *North-Holland Handbooks of Economics,* North Holland Amsterdam, 2001.

17. See John Lintner, "Distribution of Incomes of Corporations among Dividends, Retained Earnings, and Taxes," *American Economic Review,* vol. 46, no. 2, 1956, pp. 97–113.

18. See Alon Brav, John Graham, Campbell Harvey, and Roni Michaely, "Payout Policy in the 21st Century." Working Paper, Duke University, 2004. Survey responses were obtained from 300 CFOs who filled out a questionnaire, and 23 CFOs or treasurers of prominent corporations who participated in a one-hour field survey. By way of contrast, Lintner's study involved 30 companies.

19. There was over 80 percent agreement with the first three statements, over 70 percent agreement with the fourth, and over 60 percent agreement with the fifth.

20. This quotation is taken from the version of the paper, dated November 14, 2002.

21. Discussed in Chapter 6.

22. See John Long, "The Market Valuation of Cash Dividends: A Case to Consider," *Journal of Financial Economics,* vol. 6, 1978, pp. 235–264.

23. See Malcolm Baker and Jeffrey Wurgler, "A Catering Theory of Dividends," *Journal of Finance,* vol. 59, 2004, pp. 271–288. These authors define catering more narrowly than in the chapter, essentially focusing on initiating dividends to exploit mispriced equity.

24. See Shlomo Benartzi, Roni Michaely and Richard Thaler, "Do Changes in Dividends Signal the Future or the Past?" *Journal of Finance,* vol. LII, no. 3, 1997, pp. 1007–34.

25. See Chapter 5 on inefficient markets.

26. See Roni Michaely, Richard Thaler, and Kent Womack, "Price Reactions to Dividend Initiations and Omissions: Overreaction or Drift?" *Journal of Finance,* vol. L, no. 2, 1995, pp. 573–608.

27. See the discussion in Chapter 6 about the De Bondt–Thaler winner–loser effect.

28. The author of the article is Amy Baldwin.

29. See "Unsafe Harbors: Folks Who Like to Buy a Stock and Forget It Face Rude Awakening" that appeared on the front page of the February 7, 2001, issue of the *Wall Street Journal.*

30. See Gregory Zuckerman and James Bandler, "Investors Seek to Rewind Kodak," *The Wall Street Journal,* October 21, 2003.

31. See E. S. Browning, "Dividend Stocks Haven't Caught Investors' Fancy," *The Wall Street Journal,* January 31, 2005.

32. See Kathleen Fuller and Michael Goldstein, 2004. "Do Dividends Matter More in Declining Markets?" Working paper, University of Georgia.

Chapter 8

1. See Eric Rasmussen, *Games and Information: An Introduction to Game Theory.* Blackwell, Malden, MA, 2001.

2. See Michael C. Jensen and Kevin, Murphy, "CEO Incentives—It's Not How Much You Pay, But How," *Harvard Business Review,* no. 3, May–June 1990, pp. 138–153. See also Michael C. Jensen and Kevin J. Murphy, "Performance Pay and Top Management Incentives," *Journal of Political Economy,* vol. 98, 1990, pp. 225–264.

3. See Simi Kedia and Abon Mozumdar, "Performance Impact of Employee Stock Options," Working Paper, Rutgers University, 2002.

4. See Paul A. Gompers, Joy L. Ishii, and Andrew Metrick, "Corporate Governance and Equity Prices," *Quarterly Journal of Economics,* vol. 118, no. 1, February 2003, pp. 107–155.

5. See Carol J. Loomis, "Executive Pay: 'This Stuff Is Wrong.' That's the Conclusion of Most of the Insiders Who Talked to *Fortune*—Candidly—about CEO Pay. And You Know What's Even Worse? They Don't See How the Overreaching Can Be Stopped," *Fortune,* June 11, 2001, vol. 143, iss. 14, p. 72. In the interest

of taste, some quotations from this article that appear in the text have been edited for colorful language.

6. These remarks provide support for the "managerial power approach" proposed by Lucian Arye Bebchuk and Jesse Fried, "Executive Compensation as an Agency Problem," *Economic Perspectives,* vol. 17, no. 1, 2003, pp. 71–92.

7. See Jeremy Stein, "Efficient Capital Markets, Inefficient Firms: A Model of Myopic Corporate Behavior," *Quarterly Journal of Economics,* vol. 104, 1989, pp. 655–669. Stein discusses a model of rational signal jamming, where managers take excessive risk to distinguish themselves relative to others, because they are rewarded in good times but are not penalized in bad times when many firms experience unfavorable outcomes.

8. See Nittai Bergman and Dirk Jenter, "Employee Sentiment and Stock Option Compensation," Working Paper, Massachussetts Institute of Technology, 2003.

9. See Michael Schroeder, "Under Gun from SEC, Bristol, Others Divulge Accounting Issues," *The Wall Street Journal,* August 15, 2002.

10. Kate Kelly, "Sealed, Delivered but Not Yet Signed by CEOs," *The Wall Street Journal,* July 25, 2003.

11. See David Denis, Paul Hanouna, and Atulya Sarin, 2005. "Is there a Dark Side to Incentive Compensation?" Working paper, Purdue University.

12. See "A Diagnosis of Fraud at HealthSouth," *Financial Times,* April 14, 2003.

13. See "Excerpts of Recorded Conversation Between Scrushy and Owens," *The Associated Press,* April 11, 2003.

14. Jeffrey Toobin, "A Bad Thing," *The New Yorker,* March 22, 2004, p. 60.

15. See Jonathan Weil and Mark Maremont, "SEC Bars PricewaterhouseCoopers Partner from Audits," *The Wall Street Journal,* August 14, 2003.

Chapter 9

1. See J. Edward Russo and Paul Schoemaker, *Decision Traps: The Ten Barriers to Brilliant Decision-Making and How to Overcome Them,* New York: Simon & Schuster, 1989.

2. This material is taken from the lecture notes of John Payne and Gerry DeSanctis, who in 2000 taught "Managerial Effectiveness" at the Fuqua School of Business, Duke University.

3. See Irving Janis, *Groupthink,* Houghton-Mifflin, Boston, MA, 1982.

4. See Garold Stasser and William Titus, "Pooling of Unshared Information in Group Decision Making: Biased Information Sampling During Discussion," *Journal of Personality and Social Psychology,* vol. 48, no. 6, 1985, pp. 1467–1478.

5. See Carol J. Loomis, "Executive Pay: 'This Stuff Is Wrong.' That's the Conclusion of Most of the Insiders Who Talked to *Fortune*—candidly—about CEO Pay. And You Know What's Even Worse? They Don't See How the Overreaching Can be Stopped." *Fortune,* June 11, 2001, vol. 143, iss. 14, p. 72.

6. See Kurt Eichenwald, "Enron's Collapse: Audacious Climb to Success Ended in a Dizzying Plunge," *The New York Times,* January 31, 2002, p. ND1.

7. Information in this section about Enron's board has been documented in Bethany McLean and Peter Elkind, *The Smartest Guys in the Room: The Amazing Rise and Scandalous Fall of Enron,* New York: Portfolio, The Penguin Group, 2003.

8. See Rebecca Smith and John R. Emshwiller, "'24' Days: Behind Enron's Demise," *The Wall Street Journal,* vol. 24, no. 3, 1997, pp. 275–300.

9. See "The Enron and Tyco Cleanups," *The Wall Street Journal,* August 23, 2002.

10. "Evidence on EVA? ®", *Journal of Applied Corporate Finance,* Summer 1999, 8–18.

11. See Chris Hogan and Craig Lewis, 2004. "The Long-Run Performance of Firms Adopting Compensation Plans on Economic Profits," Working Paper, Owen Graduate School of Management, Vanderbilt University.

12. See James Surowiecki, "Board Stiffs," *The New Yorker,* March 8, 2004, p. 30.

13. See Steven Perlstein, "Who'll Direct Corporate Directors?" *Washington Post,* June 18, 2003.

14. See Carol Hymowitz, "Corporate Governance (A Special Report)—How to Fix a Broken System—A Rush of New Plans Promise to Make Corporate Boards More Accountable; Will They Work?" *The Wall Street Journal,* February 28, 2003.

15. See Susan Pulliam, Deborah Solomon, and Carrick Mollenkamp, "Ex-WorldCom Chief Built Personal Empire on Borrowing Binge—Some of the Same Banks with Ties to Telecom Made Loans to Ebbers—Soybeans, Yachts and Timber," *The Wall Street Journal,* January 3, 2003.

16. The article also included a discussion on the views of PSINet's CEO about investors. It included the following quotation concerning its CEO William Schrader: "I don't care what Wall Street thinks. We run our company for our customers, not Wall Street. They know it, and they don't like it."

17. See Ram Charan, and Geoffrey Colvin. "Why CEOs Fail," *Fortune,* June 1999, pp. 68–79.

18. See G. Whyte, "Escalating Commitment in Individuals and Group Decision Making: A Prospect Theory Approach," *Organizational Behavior and Human Decision Processes,* vol. 54, 1993, pp. 430–455.

19. See Jack Stack with Bo Burlingham, *The Great Game of Business,* New York: Currency Doubleday, 1992.

20. See p. 158, Stack and Burlingham.

21. See p. 158, Stack and Burlingham.

22. See Mary Bange and Michael Mazzeo, "Board Composition, Board Effectiveness, and the Observed Form of Takeover Bids," *Review of Financial Studies,* forthcoming.

23. Christine Russell, "Problems in Ending a Project: Theory and Case Study." Student Paper, Santa Clara University, 1983, written for Professor Meir Statman. At the time these events took place, Christine Russell was an MBA student at Santa Clara University, where she wrote a case study on project termination at her firm. All the quotations involving Shugart are taken from her paper.

Chapter 10

1. See Richard Roll, "The Hubris Hypothesis of Corporate Takeovers." In Richard H. Thaler (ed.), *Advances in Behavioral Finance,* New York: Russell Sage Foundation, 1993, pp. 437–458.

2. See E. C. Capen, R. V. Clapp, and W. M. Campbell, "Competitive Bidding in High-Risk Situations," *Journal of Petroleum Technology,* vol. 23, 1971, pp. 641–53.

3. See Sara Moeller, Frederik Schlingemann, and René Stulz, "Wealth Destruction on a Massive Scale? A Study of Acquiring-Firm Returns in the Recent Merger Wave," *Journal of Finance,* vol. LX, no. 2, 2005, pp. 757–782.

4. See Ulrike Malmendier and Geoffrey Tate, "Who Makes Acquisitions? CEO Overconfidence and the

Market's Reaction," Working Paper, Stanford University, 2003.

5. See Thomas Lys and Linda Vincent, 1995. "An Analysis of Value Destruction in AT&T's Acquisition of NCR," *Journal of Financial Economics,* 39, 353–378, p. 27.

6. See "The McKinsey Quarterly Chart Focus Newsletter," March 2005, **www.mckinseyquarterly.com/ newsletters/chartfocus/2005_03.htm,** "Where Mergers Go Wrong," May 5, 2005; The McKinsey Quarterly, **www.mckinseyquarterly.com/article_ abstract .aspx?ar=1402&L2=5&L3=4&srid=63&gp =0;** and Kris Frieswick, "Fool's Gold," *CFO Magazine,* February 1, 2005.

7. See Don Durfee, "A Question of Value," *CFO Magazine,* March 1, 2005.

8. See Andrei Shleifer and Robert Vishny, 2003. "Stock Market Driven Acquisitions," *Journal of Financial Economics* 70, 295–311.

9. See Geoffrey Colvin, "Time Warner, Don't Blame Steve Case," *Fortune,* February 3, 2003.

10. See Alec Klein, *Stealing Time: Steve Case, Jerry Levin and the Collapse of Time Warner,* Simon & Schuster, July 2003. Klein is a Washington Post reporter who covered AOL for that paper. His book draws on extensive reporting and sources within AOL, including confidential internal memos. New York, NY.

11. For a general treatment of acquirers exploiting mispricing, see Andrei Shleifer, and Robert Vishny, cited above.

12. See David Usborne, "A Megamerger That Will Change Our Lives," *The San Diego Union-Tribune,* January 16, 2000. In the interest of taste, this quotation has been edited.

13. See David Ignatius, "AOL Grows Up," *The Washington Post,* January 11, 2000.

14. See Aaron Patrick, "Ted's Deal as Sweet as Love," *Australian Financial Review,* January 12, 2000.

15. See Kathryn Harris, "Turner Quits—But Will He Leave Quietly?" *Dominion Post,* February 1, 2003.

16. See Martin Peers and Ken Brown, "AOL's Winners and Losers," *The Wall Street Journal,* January 14, 2003.

17. See "Time Warner drops AOL name: Board of No. 1 Media Company Votes to Drop AOL from Front of Name; Stock Symbol Changing," **www.cnn.com**, September 18, 2003.

18. See "Levin, Case Incompatible from the Start," *Newsweek,* 12/9/02, vol. 140, iss. 24, p. 53.

19. January 11, 2003.

20. The article was written by Eric Wieffering and appeared on July 13, 2003.

21. See "A Scapegoat Named Steve Case," *BusinessWeek,* 1/27/03, p. 124.

22. See Steve Lohr, "AOL Failed to Perform as a Growth Engine for Time Warner," *The New York Times,* January 16, 2003.

23. I thank Jeff Clarke and Chris Robell from Hewlett-Packard for their assistance in preparing material for this section, and Brigida Bergkamp for her assistance in coordinating the interviews.

24. George Anders, *Perfect Enough: Carly Fiorina and the Reinvention of Hewlett-Packard.* Portfolio, 2003.

25. Additional information comes from Bank of America Research. These estimates were dated October 11, 2001.

26. This figure was based on management's estimated pretax synergies of $2.17 billion in calendar year 2003 and earnings before interest and taxes (EBIT) impact from revenue loss of ($493 million) in calendar year 2003. The calculation assumes a 26 percent effective tax rate.

27. This calculation assumes that H-P shareholders would own 64.4 percent of the combined company at 0.6325 times the share-exchange ratio.

28. See Jesse Eisinger, "H-P's Next Step Is to Unlock Value," *The Wall Street Journal,* February 10, 2004.

29. See "University of Maryland Roundtable on Real Options and Corporate Finance," *Journal of Applied Corporate Finance,* vol. 15, no. 2, 2003, pp. 8–23.

30. See "Auto Reverse: Slide in Mercedes's Performance Dents Chrysler's Recent Revival," *The Wall Street Journal,* February 9, 2005.

Index

A

Ability, overconfidence about, 6
Accenture, 135
Accuracy, in group process, 146
Acquisition premium, 167
Acquisitions. *See* Mergers and acquisitions
    (M&A)
Adaptec, 99–102, 104–105, 107, 108
Adjusted present value (APV), 96–98
Affect, defined, 10
Affect heuristic, 2
    acquisitions and, 10, 164
    in capital budgeting, 40–42
    choice and, 41–42
    defined, 10
    risk and return and, 60–61, 69
    value and, 41–42
Agency conflicts, 127–144
    of analysts, 34, 86–87
    auditing and, 133–140, 143–144
    in capital budgeting, 46–47, 50–52
    compensation and, 104, 128–133,
        136–140, 156–157
    at Enron, 134–136, 140, 148–151
    excessive optimism and, 34, 46–47
    in initial public offerings (IPOs), 86–87
    loss aversion and, 50
    nature of, 2
    overconfidence among directors and
        executives, 130–132
    paying for performance in practice,
        128–130
    of security analysis, 34, 86–87
    stock options and, 132–133, 136–140
    traditional approach to, 127–128
    in valuation, 34
Alhakami, Ali, 71, 188
Allen, Franklin, 57, 119, 124, 188, 191
Allen, Robert, 163
Alti, Aydoğan, 189, 190
America Online (AOL), 159, 169–173
Amgen, 84, 96–97, 143
Analysts. *See* Security analysts
Anchoring and adjustment, 2
    defined, 9

excessive optimism and, 46
    to growth, 9
Anders, George, 177, 194
Andersen Consulting, 135
Anomalies
    defined, 76
    market efficiency and, 75–78
AOL Time Warner, 159, 169–173
Apple Computer, 174
Applied Materials, 40
Arbitrage
    defined, 78
    limits of, 78–80
    market efficiency and, 75, 78–80
Arthur Andersen, 134–135, 140
Ashland Inc., 125
Asquith, P., 186
AT&T, 108–109, 112, 116, 125, 159, 162, 163
Au, A., 186
Auditing, 133–140, 143–144
Augustin, Larry M., 86
AutoNation, 97–99, 107–108, 164
Availability bias, 2
    defined, 9
    Motorola/Iridium and, 42–43
    out of sight, out of mind, 9
Aversion to sure loss, 2, 13–15
    defined, 14
    hoping to beat the odds, 14–15
    reluctance to terminate losing projects
        and, 48–49
Axson, D., 187

B

Baker, Malcolm, 107, 124, 189, 191
Baldwin, Amy, 191
Baldwin-United, 72
Baltimore Ravens, 109
Bandler, James, 191
Bange, Mary, 189, 193
Bank of America, 152
Bankruptcy, costs of, 92
Barclay's Global Investors, 174
Barnako, Frank, 24

Barrett, Craig, 72–73, 163
Base rate information, 65–66
Baumer, William, 109
Bebchuk, Lucian Arye, 192
Behavioral APV, 96–98
Behavioral corporate finance
    biases in, 2, 3–8
    debiasing and. *See* Debiasing
    framing effects in, 2, 10–15
    heuristics in, 2, 8–10
    importance of, 2–3
    pitfalls and. *See* Behavioral pitfalls
    traditional corporate finance versus, 1–2
Behavioral life cycle hypothesis, 114–115
Behavioral pitfalls, 2–3
    of Adaptec, 100
    of Arthur Andersen, 135
    of AutoNation, 97
    CEO compensation and, 131
    of Cisco Systems, 118
    of dividend policy, 116, 118
    of eBay, 23
    of HealthSouth, 137
    of Herman-Miller, 81
    of Internet bubble, 24
    of Merck & Co., 11
    of mergers and acquisitions, 163, 164
    of Motorola/Iridium, 41
    of PSINet, 153
    of Sony, 49
    of Sun Microsystems, 4, 104
    of Syntex Inc., 51
Belsky, Gary, 16
Benartzi, Shlomo, 191
Berghoef, Henry, 171
Bergkamp, Brigida, 194
Bergman, Nittai, 192
Berkshire Hathaway, 108–109
Bernstein, Peter, 16
Beta
    expected return versus, 60–63
    market risk premium and, 56–57
Better-than-average effect, 131–132
Biases, 3–8. *See also* Debiasing
    confirmation bias, 2, 7, 50–52, 146
    defined, 3

Biases *(continued)*
    in estimating growth, 31–32
    in estimating market risk premium, 64–68
    excessive optimism, 2, 3–6, 44–47
    extrapolation bias, 65–66
    framing effects and, 27–31
    illusion of control, 2, 8
    overconfidence, 2, 6–7, 42–43
    in risk and return, 58–59, 61–62, 66–68
    valuation heuristics and, 27–34
"Big Dig," Boston, excessive optimism
    and, 44
Blanchard, O. J., 190
Blockbuster Entertainment Group, 164
Board of directors
    of Enron, 150–151
    of Hewlett-Packard, 174, 176–177
    independent directors on, 136, 150,
        174, 177
    overconfidence of, 130–132
Boeing Co., 91, 175
Book-to-market equity, 61–63
Boston Market, 135
Boudoukh, Jacob, 119
Brandenburg, R., 187
Brav, Alon, 188, 189, 191
Brealey, Richard, 57, 186, 188
Brown, Ken, 135, 194
Browning, E. S., 24, 191
Bruner, R. F., 186
Bryan-Low, Cassell, 190
Bryant, Andy, 163
Buechner, Maryanne Murray, 24
Buffett, Warren, 108–109, 129
Buhl, Soren, 46–47, 187
Burlingham, Bo, 158, 193
BusinessWeek, 4, 6–8, 16, 104, 109, 173
Byrne, Harlan S., 164

C

California Public Employees' Retirement
    System (CalPERS), 130
Campbell, W. M., 193
CAP (competitive advantage period), 37
Capen, E. C., 193
Capital asset pricing model (CAPM), 23,
    56–57, 60, 75
Capital budgeting, 38–55
    affect heuristic in, 40–42
    agency conflicts in, 46–47, 50–52
    confirmation bias and, 50–52
    excessive optimism in, 44–47

    internal rate of return (IRR) and, 38–40
    losing projects, reluctance to terminate,
        48–50
    Motorola/Iridium and, 41–43, 46, 53–54
    net present value (NPV) and, 38, 39–40
    overconfidence in, 42–43
    payback rule and, 39–41
    Sony and, 49–50
    survey evidence for use of, 39–52
    Syntex Inc. and, 50–52
    traditional treatment of, 38–39
Capital structure, 92–109
    behavioral adjusted present value (APV)
        and, 96–98
    excessive optimism and, 101–105
    financial executive approach in practice,
        93–96
    financial flexibility and, 94–95, 98–99
    overconfidence and, 101–105
    project hurdle rates and, 98–99
    return on equity (ROE) and, 12–13
    sensitivity of investment to cash flow,
        99–101
    short-term versus long-term horizons
        and, 105–106
    traditional approach to, 92–95
Cappellas, Michael, 174
Case, Steve, 159, 170, 172–173, 194
Cash flow, capital structure and, 99–101
Casino effect, 132–133
Catering
    defined, 111
    to investor tastes for dividends, 122–124
Celati, Luca, 71
Cendant, 135–136
Cerent Corp., 163
CFO Magazine, 11, 164
Channel Tunnel, excessive optimism and,
    45, 47
Chanos, James, 72, 159, 188
Charan, Ram, 193
Chase, Marilyn, 51
Chellgren, Paul, 125
ChevronTexaco, 116
Chicago Sun-Times, 142
Chief executive officers (CEOs). *See also*
    Financial executives
    compensation of, 103, 104, 128–133
    excessively optimistic, 102–104, 164
    groupthink and, 153–154
    in mergers and acquisitions, 162–164
    overconfident, 102–104, 130–132, 164
    Sarbanes-Oxley Act (2002) and,
        135–136

Chief financial officers (CFOs). *See* Finan-
    cial executives
Choice
    affect heuristic and, 41–42
    of auditor, as signal, 134
Chrysler, 179, 180
Cisco Systems, 4, 7, 118, 163
Citigroup, 111
Citizens Communications, 125
Citizens Utility Company, 123, 125
Clapp, R. V., 193
Clark, Don, 163
Clarke, Jeff, 194
Cleveland Clinic, 14
Cline, Isaac, 18
CNN, 170, 171
Cobalt, 4, 6, 10
Coca-Cola, 111, 135–136
Cockiness, 6–7
Colgate-Palmolive, 179
Colvin, Geoffrey, 193
Compaq Computer, 87, 159,
    173–177, 178
Compensation
    agency conflicts and, 104, 128–133,
        136–140, 156–157
    group process and, 156–157
Computing, 45
Condit, Phil, 175
Confirmation bias, 2
    defined, 7
    in groupthink, 146
    Syntex Inc. and, 50–52
    turning a blind eye, 7
Conflict of interest. *See* Agency conflicts
Conjunction fallacy, 46
Consolidated Edison, 113–114, 125
Constantinides, George, 124, 190, 191
Control. *See* Illusion of control
Convertible debt, 94–95
Cook Data Services, 164
Cooper, Michael, 188
Cornell, Brad, 188
Corporate financial decisions.
    See Behavioral corporate
    finance; Traditional corporate
    finance
Craig, Susanne, 24
Crane, Keith, 179
Credit Suisse First Boston (CSFB),
    87, 89
Cross selling, 164
Curfman, Gregory, 17
Cypress Semiconductor Corp., 108

D

DaimlerChrysler AG, 179–180
Davis Langdon & Everest, 47
Debiasing
    for agency conflicts, 140
    for aversion to sure loss, 15
    for capital budgeting decisions, 47, 52
    for capital structure decisions, 106
    defined, 15
    for dividend policy, 124
    for group process, 154, 155–157
    for market efficiency, 88
    for risk and return assumptions, 63, 69
    for valuation decisions, 34
De Bondt, Werner, 189
De Bondt-Thaler winner-loser effect, 76, 77
Debt policy. *See also* Capital structure
    loss aversion and, 12–13
Debt-to-equity ratios, 94, 95, 100
Dell Computer, 9, 159, 173, 174, 176, 177
Denis, David, 192
Denny, Wayne, 125
Denver airport, excessive optimism and, 44
Deogun, Nikhil, 163
DeSanctis, Gerry, 192
Desirability, excessive optimism and, 46
Dilution, 94, 98
Dilution cost, 166–167
Dimensional Fund Advisors (DFA), 89
Dimitrov, Rolin, 188
Discounted cash flow (DCF) analysis, 1
    acquisitions and, 10
    capital structure and, 105
    eBay and, 24–34
    PEG heuristic and, 32–33
Disney, 91
Dividend payout ratio, 20
Dividend policy, 110–126
    behavioral pitfalls and, 116, 118
    catering to investor tastes for dividends, 122–124
    financial columnists and, 116
    financial executives and, 118–122
    individual investors and, 112–117, 122–124
    price effects of, 123
    professional investors and, 117
    tax policy and, 111–112
    traditional approach to, 56–57, 110–111
Donnelley (R.R.) & Sons, 155
Doyle, William, 116, 191
Dugan, Ianthe Jeanne, 135

Duke University, 71, 93–96, 107
Dunn, Patricia, 174, 177, 178
Durfee, Don, 177, 193
Dutta, Rajiv, 23, 73

E

Eades, K. M., 186
Earnings announcements, post-earnings announcement drift and, 77–78
Earnings dilution. *See* Dilution
Earnings per share (EPS)
    capital structure and, 94
    EBITDA analysis, 28–31, 33–34, 169–170
    in valuation process, 20–21
Eastman Kodak, 125–126, 174
eBay, 22–34, 35, 36, 72–73, 89
Ebbers, Bernard, 152
EBITDA analysis, 28–31, 33–34, 169–170
Edison International, 125
Efficiency. *See* Market efficiency
Eichenwald, Kurt, 192
Eisinger, Jesse, 194
Elkind, Peter, 192
Emerson Electric, 116
Employee stock ownership, group process and, 157
Emshwiller, John R., 192
Enprostil, 51
Enron, 134–136, 140, 147–151, 158, 159
Ernst & Young LLP, 47, 137–139, 141
Escalation of commitment, 49–50
Eureka problem, in group process, 146
Eurotunnel, excessive optimism and, 45
Evans, Frank C., 186
Excessive optimism, 3–6
    agency conflict determinants of, 34, 46–47
    of analysts, 24, 33–34, 63–64
    capital budgeting and, 44–47
    capital structure and, 101–105
    defined, 3
    of financial executives, 4–5, 33–34
    Internet and, 24
    in mergers and acquisitions, 162–164, 166–167
    in private-sector projects, 44–45
    psychological determinants of, 45–46
    in public-sector projects, 44
    for risk and return, 63–64
    of stockholders, 5–6

    stock options and, 136–137
    in valuation process, 33–34
Extrapolation bias, 65–66
ExxonMobil, 111, 116

F

Fama, Eugene, 75, 78, 80, 188, 189
Fama-French three-factor framework, 61–62, 76–78
Familiarity, excessive optimism and, 46
Fastow, Andrew, 148–150, 159
Federation of Women's Shareholders in American Business, 113
Fiat, 179
Financial Executive, 21, 93, 94, 179
Financial executives. *See also* Chief executive officers (CEOs)
    capital budgeting analysis and, 38–40
    capital structure and, 93–96
    dividend policy and, 118–122
    earnings guidance and, 80
    excessive optimism of, 4–5, 33–34
    extrapolation bias and, 65–66
    gambler's fallacy and, 68–69
    initial public offerings (IPOs) and, 87–88
    insider trading and, 68–69, 137
    limits of arbitrage and, 80
    market risk premium and, 64–66
    overconfidence of, 6–7, 130–132
    project discount rates and, 70
    reliance on valuation heuristics, 22–23
    risk and return and, 59–61, 64–66, 68–69
    Sarbanes-Oxley Act (2002) and, 135–136
Financial Executives International (FEI), 21, 23, 39–52, 66, 70, 93–101, 105, 107
Financial Executives Research Foundation, 39, 43
Financial Times, 78–79
Finucane, Melissa, 53, 71, 188
Fiorina, Carleton (Carly), 173–177
First Call Corporation, 62–64, 82, 175, 188
Fischhoff, Baruch, 186
Fisher, Lawrence, 189
Flannery, Mark, 190
Flynn, James, 53, 187
Flyvbjerg, Bent, 46–47, 187
FM Global, 39, 43
Folz, Jean-Martin, 179
Footstar Inc., 136
Forbes magazine, 109, 153

Ford Motor Co., 179
Fortune magazine, 11, 23, 59–61, 90, 130, 142, 148, 153–154, 170
Fox, Justin, 89, 189
Frame, defined, 10
Framing effects, 10–15
    aversion to sure loss, 2, 13–15
    biases and, 27–31
    defined, 10
    loss aversion, 2, 11–13
    narrow framing, 12
    prospect theory and, 10–15
Fraud
    agency conflict and, 135–136
    HealthSouth and, 137–140
    Sarbanes-Oxley Act (2002) and, 135–136
    stock options and, 136–140
Freiman, Paul, 51–52
French, Kenneth, 188
Fried, Jesse, 192
Fried, John, 50–52
Frieswick, Kris, 137, 193
Froot, Kenneth, 190
Fuller & Thaler, 89

G

Gallup, 66
Galveston, Texas, weather patterns in, 17, 18
Galvin, Robert, 41, 43, 54
Gambler's fallacy
    defined, 67
    financial executives and, 68–69
    professional investors and, 66–68
Ganzach, Yoav, 188
Garay, Gabriel, 51
Gasparino, Charles, 24
Gates, Bill, 9
Gemstar-TV Guide, 136
Genentech, 143
General Electric, 111
General Motors Corp., 22, 154, 179
Gervais, Simon, 186
Gilmartin, Ray, 14
Gilovich, Thomas, 16, 53
Ginn, Sam, 174, 175, 178
Gitman, L., 39, 186
Glass, R., 187
Gleghorn, George, 125
Goldman Sachs, 91, 174
Gompers, Paul A., 141, 189, 191–192
Gompers-Ishii-Merck index, 129–130
Google, 90

Graham, John, 53, 107, 124, 186–191
Great Game of Business, The, 158
Griffin, Dale, 16, 53
Grinstein, Yaniv, 191
Group process, 145–160
    debiasing and, 154, 155–157
    at Enron, 147–151, 158
    examples of, 147–154, 155–157
    polarization and, 146, 154–155
    process loss and, 145–146
    reasons for group errors, 146–154
    reluctance to terminate losing projects, 154–155
    traditional approach to, 145
    at WorldCom, 147–148, 151, 152, 158
Groupthink, 146–154
    at Enron, 150–151
    SRC and, 156
    at WorldCom, 152
Growth
    anchoring to, 9
    in valuation process, 20–21, 31–32
Guidance, 80

H

Hall, P., 187
Hamburger, M., 187
Handspring, 37
Hanouna, Paul, 192
Harley-Davidson, 111
Harris, Kathryn, 193
Harris, Milton, 124, 190, 191
Harris, R. S., 186
Harris Associates, 171
Harris Funds, 171
Harvard Business Review, 11
Harvard University, 14
Harvey, Campbell, 53, 186–189, 191
HealthSouth, 135–141
Hedonic editing, 115, 122–123
Herman-Miller North America, 81, 90
Heuristics, 8–10
    affect. *See* Affect heuristic
    anchoring and adjustment, 2, 9, 46
    availability bias, 2, 9, 42–43
    biases and, 28
    defined, 8
    dividend, 120
    $1/n$ heuristic, 33
    PEG heuristic, 21–23, 25, 27, 32–33
    P/E heuristic, 21, 25, 27, 32–33
    price-to-sales heuristic, 22, 25

representativeness, 2, 8–9
    valuation, 21–26, 27
Hewlett, Walter, 159
Hewlett, William, 159
Hewlett-Packard, 108–109, 159, 173–177, 178
Hietala, Pekka, 163, 164
Higgins, R. C., 186
Hill, Chuck, 82
Hilsenrath, Jon E., 188
Hindsight bias, 104
Hogan, Chris, 192
Holm, Mette Skamris, 46–47, 187
Hood, Wayne, 186
Hot-hand fallacy
    financial executives and, 65–66
    individual investors and, 66
Hot issue market
    defined, 82
    initial public offerings (IPOs) and, 82, 83–84
Hovakimian, Armen, 190
Hovakimian, Gayane, 190
Huang, Rongbing, 190
Hubris hypothesis, 162, 172–173
Huizenga, Wayne, 164, 179
Hurdle rates, 98–99
Hymowitz, Carol, 192–193

I

IBM, 135–136, 159, 174–177
Ibuka, Masaru, 49, 50
Ignatius, David, 193
Ikenberry, David, 189, 190
Illusion of control, 2
    defined, 8
    excessive optimism and, 46
    not made here, 8
Illusion of effectiveness, in group process, 146
ImClone Systems Inc., 142–143
Incentive compatibility constraint, 128
Individual investors
    dividend policy and, 112–117, 122–124
    excessive optimism of, 5–6
    hot-hand fallacy and, 66
    shareholder rights and, 129–130
Inefficiency. *See* Market efficiency
Information asymmetry, 149, 165, 168
Information sharing
    group process and, 146–147, 157
    problems of, 146–147

Initial public offerings (IPOs), 82–88
   dilemma concerning, 87–88
   Google, 90
   hot issues markets and, 82, 83–84
   initial underpricing of, 82, 84–87
   long-term underperformance of, 82,
      87–88
   Palm, 90–91
   VA Linux, 85–88
Initial underpricing
   defined, 82
   initial public offerings (IPOs) and, 82,
      84–87
Insider trading, 68–69, 137
Inside view, 47
Institutional Investor, 86–87
Institutional investors. *See* Professional
      investors
Intel, 8, 9, 57–60, 72–73, 108–109, 163
Internal rate of return (IRR), in capital bud-
      geting, 38–40
Internet
   behavioral pitfalls of, 24
   as representing overall economy, 8–9
Intuition, in capital budgeting, 40, 41–42
Investors. *See* Individual investors;
      Professional investors
Iraq, war in, 44
Iridium, 41, 42–43, 46, 53–54
Ishii, Joy L., 141, 191–192

J

Jaedicke, Robert, 150
Jaguar, 179
Janis, Irving, 192
J.C. Penney Co., 125
Jegadeesh, Narasimhan, 188
Jensen, Michael C., 141, 189, 191
Jenter, Dirk, 188, 189, 192
Johnson, Stephen, 71, 188
*Journal of the American Medical
     Association,* 17

K

Kahneman, Daniel, 2–3, 10–15, 16, 53, 133,
     186–188
Kaplan, Steve, 163, 164
Kaufman, Arnie, 125
Kedia, Simi, 191

Keil, Mark, 187, 188
Kellett, Stiles, 152
Kelly, Kate, 192
Klein, Alec, 172–173, 193
Knowledge, overconfidence about, 6–7
Kodak, 125–126, 174
Kopper, Michael, 149–150
Kozlowski, Dennis, 143–144
KPMG International, 46, 162
Kumar, Alok, 124, 191
Kynikos Associates Ltd., 159

L

Laing, Jonathan R., 188
Laing, Matthew, 186
Lakonishok, Josef, 190
Lamont, Owen, 89, 189, 190
Lancet, The, 14
Land Rover, 179
Landwehr, Aimee, 33, 186
Le, Eddie, 189
Leary, Mark, 190
Lee, Dan, 104
Lehavy, Reuven, 188
Lehman, Michael, 10
Lernout & Hauspie, 135–136
Levin, Gerald, 159, 170–171, 173, 194
Levitt, Arthur, 134–135
Lewent, Judy, 11, 17
Lewis, Craig, 192
Limits of arbitrage, 78–80
Lintner, John, 119–122, 191
Lipin, Steven, 163
LJM2, 148–150
Lohr, Steve, 194
Long, John, 191
Longholders, 103, 104, 179
Long-term underperformance
   defined, 82
   of initial public offerings (IPOs), 82,
      87–88
Loomis, Carol J., 131, 192
Lopez-de-Silanes, F., 190
Loss aversion, 11–15
   aversion to sure loss, 2, 13–15, 48–49
   capital budgeting and, 48–50
   debt aversion and, 12–13
   defined, 12
   escalation of commitment and, 49–50
   group process and, 154–155
Loughran, Tim, 89, 189
Lovallo, D., 53, 188

Luce, Charles, 113
Lys, Thomas, 193

M

MacGregor, Donald, 53
MacKenzie, B. W., 187
Malmendier, Ulrike, 107, 177, 190, 193
Mansfield, E., 187
Maremont, Mark, 192
Mark, Reuben, 179
Market capitalization
   in mergers and acquisitions, 171–172
   risk and return and, 61–62
Market efficiency, 74–91
   anomalies and, 75–78
   arbitrage and, 75, 78–80
   earnings guidance and, 80
   initial public offerings (IPOs) and,
      82–88
   mergers and acquisitions and, 161,
      165–168
   net present value (NPV) and, 80
   stock splits and, 81–82
   traditional approach to, 74–75
Market risk premium, 64–68
   financial executives and, 64–66
   nature of, 56–57
Market timing, capital structure and,
     93–94, 100
Market-to-book ratio, 94
Marriott, J. Willard, 164
Marriott International, 164
Marshall, A., 187
Martell, Duncan, 104
Martha Stewart Living Omnimedia,
     142–143
Martin, John, 35
Martinez, Barbara, 11, 186
Mathews, Anna Wilde, 11, 186
Mauboussin, Michael, 35
May, L., 187
Mayer, Colin, 190
Mazzeo, Michael, 193
McCormack, John, 178
McCready, John, 47
McDonald's, 22
McGee, Suzanne, 190
McGough, Robert, 190
MCI, 152
McKinsey & Co., 163–164, 174, 175,
     178, 193
McLean, Bethany, 192

McNealy, Scott, 3–10, 16, 103–104
Meckling, W., 187
Meeker, Mary, 23–34, 36, 186
Mental accounting, 114
Mercedes, 179–180
Merck & Co., 10–15, 17
    behavioral pitfalls of, 11
    loss aversion and, 11–15
Mergers and acquisitions (M&A), 161–180
    acquisition premium and, 167
    affect heuristic and, 10, 164
    AOL/Time Warner, 159, 169–173
    asymmetric information and, 168
    behavioral pitfalls of, 163, 164
    efficient prices and, 161, 165–167
    excessive optimism and, 162–164,
        166–167
    Hewlett-Packard/Compaq Computer,
        159, 173–177, 178
    inefficient prices and, 167
    overconfidence and, 162–164, 166–167
    traditional approach to, 161
    winner's curse and, 162, 163
Merrill Lynch, 149
Mertz, C. K., 53, 187
Metamor, 153
Metrick, Andrew, 141, 191–192
Michaely, Roni, 119, 124, 188, 191
Microsoft, 4, 9, 85, 108–109, 112
Mikhail, M., 186
Miller, Merton, 92–95, 110–111, 190
Millman, G., 81, 189
Mitchell, John, 41
Mitchell, Olivia, 190
Modigliani, Franco, 92–95, 110–111, 190
Modigliani-Miller (MM) tradeoff theory,
    92–95, 110–111, 114
Moeller, Sara, 193
Mollenkamp, Carrick, 193
Momentum, 76–77
Monaghan, Craig, 97
Montier, James, 35
Moore, James, 190
Moore, Willis L., 18
Morgan Stanley, 23–34, 35, 89, 91
Morita, Akio, 49, 50
Morrell, Paul, 47
Motorola, 4, 41–43, 46, 53–54
Mozumdar, Abon, 191
Murphy, Kevin, 141, 191
Myers, Stewart, 57, 186, 188
Myers-Majluf pecking-order theory, 92–95,
    96, 100

N

Naprosyn, 51
Narrow framing, 12
Nathan, John, 49, 187
National Association of Corporate Treasur-
    ers, 39, 43
National Association of Securities Dealers
    (NASD), 87, 152
National Bureau of Economic Research
    (NBER), 4–5
National City, 116
NCR, 162, 163
Neale, Gary L., 126
Net present value (NPV)
    acquisitions and, 10
    in capital budgeting, 38, 39–40
    capital structure and, 98–99
    growth opportunities and, 20–21,
        31–32
    role of, 80
New England Journal of Medicine, The, 17
New issues. *See also* Initial public offerings
        (IPOs)
    of debt, 94–95
    of equity, 93–94, 96
New Yorker, The, 150
New York Times, The, 173
Nickels, Elizabeth, 81
Nicolais, Joan, 172
Nipsco Industries Inc., 125, 126
Nobel Prize in Economics, 2–3, 10–15
Nonoverpayment constraint, 128

O

Odean, Terrence, 186
$1/n$ heuristic, 33
One-size-fits-all heuristic, 70
Optimism. *See* Excessive optimism
Ostrom, Mary Anne, 186
O'Sullivan, Kate, 11
Outside view, 47
Overconfidence, 2
    about ability, 6
    in capital budgeting, 42–43
    capital structure and, 101–105
    defined, 6
    among directors and officers, 6–7,
        130–132
    in group process, 146
    about knowledge, 6–7

in mergers and acquisitions, 162–164,
        166–167
    Motorola/Iridium and, 41, 42–43
    press coverage overconfidence indicator,
        102–104
    psychological determinants of, 42–43
    stock options and, 136–137
    Sun Microsystems and, 6–7, 103–104
Overreaction, 78
Overweighting of small probabilities, 133
Owens, William, 192

P

Pacific Gas & Electric, 125
Palm Inc., 35, 37, 72, 90–91
PalmOne, 35, 37
PalmSource, 35, 37
Paramount, 163, 164
Parmalat, 135–136
Parsons, Richard, 173
Participation constraint, 128
Patrick, Aaron, 193
Payback rule
    in capital budgeting, 39–41
    intuition and, 40, 41–42
Payne, John, 192
PDA Palm, 90–91
Pecking-order theory, 92–95, 96, 100
Peers, Martin, 194
PEG heuristic, 21–23
    defined, 22
    discounted cash flow (DCF) analysis
        and, 32–33
    eBay and, 23, 25, 27, 32–33
P/E heuristic, 32–33
    defined, 21
    eBay and, 25, 27
Penney (J.C.) Co., 125
Perlstein, Steven, 192
Peters, Ellen, 53
Petty, J. William, 35
Physicians Sales & Service, 155
Pick-a-number game, 78–80
Piotrowski, Julie, 137
Pitz, Brian, 25, 26, 186
Planning, group process and, 156
Polarization, in group process, 146,
    154–155
Poor information sharing, 146–147, 157
Post-earnings announcement drift, 77–78
Preference reversal, 42

Press coverage overconfidence indicator, 102–104
Price effects, of dividend policy, 123
Price-to-earnings (P/E) ratio
    of AOL, 169–170
    of eBay, 32–33
    of Sun Microsystems, 6
Price-to-sales heuristic
    defined, 22
    eBay and, 25
PricewaterhouseCoopers LLP, 143–144
PricewaterhouseCoopers (PWC), 174
Private-sector projects, excessive optimism in, 44–45
Producers, The (musical), 127–128
Professional investors
    dividend policy and, 117
    excessive optimism of, 5–6
    gambler's fallacy and, 66–68
    shareholder rights and, 129–130
Project discount rates, survey evidence on, 70
Prospect theory, 10–15
    auditing and, 133–134
    defined, 10
    market efficiency and, 77
    overweighting of small probabilities and, 133
Prudential, 33, 36, 89
PSA Peugeot Citroen SA, 179–180
PSINet, 147–148, 153–154, 158
PSINet Europe, 107, 109
Public-sector projects, excessive optimism in, 44
Pulliam, Susan, 189, 193
Puri, Manju, 186
PVGO. *See* Net present value (NPV)

Q

Quattrone, Frank, 87
Qwest Communications, 136

R

Radio Shack, 81–82
Rajgopal, Shiva, 189
Ramnath, Sundaresh, 189
Rangan, Kasturi, 190
Rankine, Graeme, 189
Rantapuska, Elias, 191

Rapoport, J., 187
Rappoport, Alfred, 35
Rashtchy, Safa, 33, 34, 36
Rasmussen, Eric, 191
Rathman, George, 84
Rau, P. Raghaveda, 188
Recessions
    of 2001, 4–5
    GDP growth rates during, 7
Red Hat Inc., 85–86
Redstone, Sumner, 163, 164
Reference point, 14
Regret, in escalation of commitment, 50
Reifman, Alan, 71
Representativeness, 2
    defined, 8
    of Internet for overall economy, 8–9
    of risk and return, 58–59, 65, 67, 69
Republic Industries, 164
Repurchases
    behavioral APV and, 96–98
    dividend policy versus, 118–119
    financial flexibility and, 98–99
    stock price declines following, 108–109
Research and development (R&D), earnings and, 80
Return. *See* Risk and return
Return on equity (ROE)
    capital structure and, 12–13
    in valuation process, 20, 32, 37
Return on invested capital (ROIC), 40
Return on net assets before interest and tax (RONABIT), 40
Return on operating assets (ROOPA), 40
Reynolds, G., 188
Richardson, Matthew, 119
Risk and return, 56–73. *See also entries beginning with* "Return"
    affect heuristic and, 60–61, 69
    bias and, 58–59, 61–62, 66–68
    dividend policy and, 111–112, 115
    financial executives and, 59–61, 64–66, 68–70
    individual stocks and, 57–64
    initial public offerings and, 84
    market risk premium and, 56–57, 64–68
    project discount rates and, 70
    relationship between, 59–60
    representativeness and, 58–59, 65, 67, 69
    security analyst return expectations for, 62–64
    traditional approach to, 56–57
Ritter, Jay R., 82–84, 86, 89, 189, 190

Robell, Chris, 194
Roberts, Leonard, 81–82
Roberts, Michael, 119, 190
Robinson, David, 163, 164, 186
Roche Holding Ltd., 51
Rocker, Tony, 187
ROIC (return on invested capital), 40
Roll, Richard, 177, 189, 193
RONABIT (return on net assets before interest and tax), 40
ROOPA (return on operating assets), 40
Roscoe, W. E., 187
Rowen, Mark, 33, 186
Rozeff, Michael S., 188
R.R. Donnelley & Sons, 155
Rubash, Mark, 23, 186
Russell, Christine, 193
Russo, J. Edward, 158, 192

S

Sagawa, Paul, 91
SAIC, 155, 158
S&P 500
    Adaptec versus, 105
    Cypress Semiconductor Corp. versus, 108
    Dell Computer versus, 176
    die-rolling and, 64–65
    dividends and, 111
    eBay versus, 22
    HealthSouth versus, 137, 138–139
    Hewlett-Packard versus, 176, 177
    IBM versus, 176
    Intel versus, 73
    Nipsco versus, 126
    professional investors and, 66–68
    Republic Industries versus, 164
    risk and return and, 64–67
    Sun Microsystems versus, 5–6
    Wal-Mart versus, 90
San Jose Mercury News, 87
Sarbanes-Oxley Act (2002), 135–136
Sarin, Atulya, 192
Scalzo, Richard, 143–144
Schlingemann, Frederik, 193
Schnee, J., 187
Schnurman, Mitchell, 189
Schoemaker, Paul, 158, 192
Schrader, William, 109, 153, 193
Schrempp, Jürgen, 179–180
Schroeder, Michael, 192

Schultz, P., 189
Scott, Cintra, 189
Scrushy, Richard, 137, 139–140, 192
Security analysts
    agency conflicts of, 34, 86–87
    excessive optimism of, 24, 33–34, 63–64
    gambler's fallacy and, 68
    return expectations of, 62–64
    underpricing of IPOs and, 86–87
    valuation by, 23–34
Security market line, 56, 60–63
Self-attribution error, 130–131
Self-control, 115
Semistrong-form efficiency, 74–75
Sensitivity of investment to cash flow, 99–101
Shareholder rights, 129–130
Sharp, Ian, 153
Shefrin, Hersh, 71, 124, 188, 190–191
Shleifer, Andrei, 190, 193
Shugart, 160, 193
Siegel, Jeremy, 186
Signaling theory
    auditor choice and, 134
    dividends and, 121–122, 123
Singular information, 65–66
Sloan, Alfred P., 154
Slovic, Paul, 53, 71, 186–188
Smith, Rebecca, 192
Smith, Roger, 154
Smith, Vernon, 2–3
Smurfit, Michael, 188
Snow, A., 187
Social loafing, 147
Solaris (software), 4
Solomon, Deborah, 193
Sony, 49, 50
Soss, Wilma, 113
Southern Co., 116
Spinning, 87
Spitzer, Eliot, 87
Springfield Remanufacturing Corporation (SRC), 155–157
Stack, Jack, 155–156, 158, 193
Standards, group process and, 155–156
Standish Group, 39, 53
Stanford Business School, 150
Stanford University, 14
Stasser, Garold, 192
Statman, Meir, 124, 188, 190, 193
Stein, Jeremy, 107, 190, 192
Stempel, Robert, 154
Stern-Stewart, 158, 178

Stevens, Lionel, 118
Stewart, James, 73
Stewart, Martha, 142–143
Stice, Earl, 189
Stockholders. *See* Individual investors; Professional investors
Stock options, 104, 129, 132–133
    casino effect and, 132–133
    fraud and, 136–140
    overvaluing, 132
Stock ownership, group process and, 157
Stock splits, 81–82
Strauss, Gary, 104
Strong-form efficiency, 74–75
Stulz, René, 124, 190, 191, 193
Sunbeam, 135–136
Sunk costs, 48
Sun Microsystems, 3–10, 16, 17, 40, 103–104, 109
Surowiecki, James, 150, 158, 192
Sussman, Oren, 190
Suzuki, J., 187
Swartz, Mark, 143–144
Sweeney, Paul, 97, 189
Syntex Inc., 50–52

T

Talley, Karen, 190
Tandy Corporation, 81–82
Tate, Geoffrey, 107, 177, 190, 193
Tax policy, dividend policy and, 111–112
Thaler, Richard H., 89, 187, 189–191, 193
Thornburgh, Richard, 151
3Com, 37, 90–91
Thurm, Scott, 118n, 163, 191
Time magazine, 24
Time Warner, 159, 169–173, 178
Titman, Sheridan, 188
Titus, William, 192
Toobin, Jeffrey, 142, 192
Traditional corporate finance.
        See also Market efficiency;
        Net present value (NPV)
    agency conflicts and, 127–128
    auditing and, 134–135
    capital asset pricing model (CAPM) and, 23, 56–57, 60, 75
    capital budgeting in, 38–39
    capital structure in, 92–95
    discounted cash flow (DCF) analysis in, 1, 10, 20–21, 24–34, 105

dividend policy in, 56–57, 110–111
EBITDA analysis in, 28–31, 33–34, 169–170
group process and, 145
mergers and acquisitions in, 161
risk and return in, 56–57
Tufts University, Center for the Study of Drug Development, 50–51, 53
Tull, D. S., 187
Turley, Jim, 141
Turner, Ted, 170–171
Turner Broadcasting, 171
Tversky, Amos, 2–3, 10–15, 133, 186, 187
Tyco, International, 143–144

U

UBS/Gallup polls, 66
Underreaction, 78, 97–98
Unisys, 57–60
U.S. Bancorp Piper Jaffray, 33
U.S. Department of Justice, 172
U.S. Food and Drug Administration (FDA), 11, 14–15, 51, 142–143
U.S. Securities and Exchange Commission (SEC), 13, 24, 85, 91, 104, 134–136, 137, 143–144, 172
U.S. Weather Service, 18
Unwarranted acceptance, in group process, 146
Ursus Partners, 72
Usborne, David, 193
UUNet Technologies, 152

V

VA Linux Systems, 85–88
Valuation, 20–37
    agency conflicts in, 34
    biases in, 27–34
    capital structure and, 104–105
    discounted cash flow (DCF) approach to, 1, 10, 20–21, 24–34
    of eBay, 22–34
    growth opportunities approach to, 20–21, 31–32
    heuristics for, 21–26, 27
    in mergers and acquisitions, 168–171, 175–176
    undervalued equity, 96–99
Value Line Investment Survey, 62–64

Value-maximizing approach, 1
Vandenberg, P., 39, 186
Variances, 157
VA Software, 85–88
Vaughan-Adams, Liz, 137
Vermaelen, Theo, 190
Viacom, 163, 164, 178
Vincent, Linda, 193
Vioxx, 11, 13–15, 17
Vishny, Robert, 193
Visibility, in escalation of commitment, 49
Volvo, 179

W

Wagner, S., 187
Waksal, Samuel, 142–143
Walker, Brian, 81, 90
Wall Street Journal, The, 17, 24, 33, 36, 44,
        72, 73, 78, 84, 91, 111, 112, 118,
        136, 143, 149, 152, 163, 164, 177,
        179
Wal-Mart, 23, 24, 36, 90, 111
Walton, Sam, 90

Washington Post, The, 151, 172
Waste Management Inc., 135
Weak-form efficiency, 74–75, 77
Weil, Jonathan, 137, 192
Weisz, William, 41
Welch, Ivo, 188
Wetzel, Steve, 125
Whitman, Meg, 34, 73
Whyte, G., 158, 193
Wickland, Anne, 33, 186
Widows-and-orphans stocks, 112, 116
Wieffering, Eric, 194
William and Flora Hewlett
        Foundation, 159
Willingness to pay (WTP), 42
Wills, Harold (Pete), 153
Wilmington Trust, 116
Wingfield, Nick, 33, 35, 186
Winn-Dixie Stores, 111
Winner-loser effect, 76, 77
Winner's curse
        defined, 162
        examples of, 163
        hubris hypothesis, 172–173
        in mergers and acquisitions, 162, 163

Wolinsky, H., 41, 187
Wollenberg, Skip, 163, 164
Womack, Kent, 191
Woolley, Scott, 153
WorldCom, 135–136, 140, 147–148, 151,
        152, 158, 163
Wurgler, Jeffrey, 107, 124, 189, 191

X

Xerox, 135–136
Xilinx, 40

Y

Yermack, David, 188
Young, David, 99–101, 190

Z

Zaman, Mir A., 188
Zirman, M., 189
Zuckerman, Gregory, 189, 191